TALENT IDENTIFICATION AND DEVELOPMENT IN SPORT

Identifying talent in athletes and developing that ability to its fullest potential is a central concern of sport scientists, sports coaches and sports policy makers. This book offers a comprehensive synthesis of current knowledge in talent identification and development in sport, from the biological basis of ability to the systems and processes within sport through which that ability is nurtured.

Written by a team of leading international experts, the book explores key factors and issues in contemporary sport, including:

- genetics;
- secondary factors such as birth date, cultural context and population size;
- perceptual motor skill acquisition and expertise;
- sports development policy;
- in-depth case studies, including European soccer, East African running and US gymnastics.

With an emphasis throughout on practical implications and processes for those working in sport, the book offers an authoritative evaluation of the strengths and weaknesses of contemporary systems for identifying and developing talent in sport. This is important reading for any student, researcher or practitioner with an interest in skill acquisition, youth sport, elite sport, sports coaching or sports development.

Joseph Baker is with the Lifespan Health and Performance Laboratory in the School of Kinesiology and Health Science, York University, Canada and a visiting research fellow at Leeds Metropolitan University, UK. His research focuses on optimal human development, particularly issues affecting the acquisition of sport expertise.

Steve Cobley is a senior lecturer in skill acquisition and sport psychology within the Carnegie Faculty at Leeds Metropolitan University, UK. His specific research interests focus upon developmental factors that constrain learning, attainment and performance.

Jörg Schorer is a research associate at the Institute of Sport Science at the Westfälische Wilhelms-University Münster, Germany. His research interests are not only within the field of talent identification and development, but also in expertise in sport, perceptual-motor skills and sport psychology.

TALENT IDENTIFICATION AND DEVELOPMENT IN SPORT

International perspectives

Edited by Joseph Baker,
Steve Cobley and Jörg Schorer

Routledge
Taylor & Francis Group

LONDON AND NEW YORK

First published 2012
by Routledge
2 Park Square, Milton Park, Abingdon, Oxon OX14 4RN

Simultaneously published in the USA and Canada
by Routledge
711 Third Avenue, New York, NY 10017

Routledge is an imprint of the Taylor & Francis Group, an informa business

British Library Cataloguing in Publication Data
A catalogue record for this book is available from the British Library

Library of Congress Cataloging in Publication Data
Talent identification and development in sport : international perspectives /
edited by Joseph Baker, Jörg Schorer and Steve Cobley.
    p. cm.
  1. Sports. 2. Sports administration. 3. Sports and state. 4. Sports—Social
aspects. 5. Sports—Physiological aspects. 6. Athletic ability. I. Baker,
Joseph. II. Schorer, Jörg. III. Cobley, Steve.
GV706.8.T35 2011
796—dc22   2011000892

ISBN: 978–0–415–58160–8 (hbk)
ISBN: 978–0–415–58161–5 (pbk)
ISBN: 978–0–203–85031–2 (ebk)

Typeset in Bembo
by Keystroke, Station Road, Codsall, Wolverhapton

Printed and bound in Great Britain by
CPI Antony Rowe, Chippenham, Wiltshire

DEDICATION

Joseph Baker
For dad – David William Baker (1943–2010)

Steve Cobley
To my grandparents (lives passed) and Natalie (a life begun)

Jörg Schorer
For my parents

CONTENTS

LIST OF ILLUSTRATIONS

Figures

Tables

CONTRIBUTORS

Joseph Baker, PhD, is with the Lifespan Health and Performance Laboratory in the School of Kinesiology and Health Science, York University, Canada and a visiting research fellow in the Carnegie Research Institute at Leeds Metropolitan University in the United Kingdom. His research focuses on optimal human development, particularly issues affecting the acquisition of sport expertise. He is past president of the Canadian Society for Psychomotor Learning and Sport Psychology and the author/editor of four books and more than 100 peer-reviewed articles and book chapters.

Dirk Büsch, PhD, is Vice-Director of the Institute for Applied Training Science and Head of the Department of Game and Combat Sports as well as Youth Elite Sport in Leipzig, Germany. His research focuses on movement and training science in youth and elite sports, with a preference for game sports as well as methodological aspects of research.

Chris Chapman is a National Player Development Manager for the Rugby Football League (RFL). Chris joined the RFL in 2005 as the Performance Youth Coach overseeing the Player Performance Pathway and coaching within the England youth structure, before moving to the national player development role in 2009. During this time, Chris has combined research and player development models to create, develop and evolve the RFL player development system.

Steve Cobley, PhD, is a senior lecturer in skill acquisition and sport psychology within the Carnegie Faculty at Leeds Metropolitan University, UK. Here he teaches across both undergraduate and post-graduate provision associated with sports science and physical education. His specific research interests focus upon developmental factors that constrain learning, attainment and performance. An interest shared with local and international colleagues.

Dave Collins, PhD, is Professor and Director for the Institute of Coaching and Performance at UCLan. He also runs a performance psychology consultancy, 'Grey Matters', providing support and management services across a variety of domains.

Carlton Cooke, PhD, is the Carnegie Professor of Sport and Exercise Science, head of the Carnegie Research Centre for Sports Performance and Director of Research for Leeds Metropolitan University. Carlton gained all his HE qualifications from the University of Birmingham, the last of which was his PhD in 1990. Carlton joined Leeds Metropolitan University in 1990 and has specialized in Exercise Physiology and Biomechanics. Carlton has researched, presented and published extensively on aspects of sports performance and physical activity, exercise and health, as well as providing sports science support to high performance athletes, teams and national governing bodies throughout the UK.

Keith Davids, PhD, is Professor and Head of Human Movement Studies at Queensland University of Technology, Australia. His research interests include the theoretical frameworks of ecological psychology and dynamical systems theory applied to the study of neurobiological cognition and action. A particular interest concerns the role of constraints in motor learning and the implications for the acquisition of movement coordination.

Marije T. Elferink-Gemser, PhD, is assistant professor at the Center for Human Movement Sciences, University Medical Center Groningen, University of Groningen in the Netherlands. Her main interest lies in the field of performance development towards expertise in children. Her studies are characterized by their longitudinal design, focusing on multidimensional performance characteristics of both the youth athletes and their environment.

Damian Farrow, PhD, holds a joint appointment as a Professor of Sports Science within the School of Sport and Exercise Science/ISEAL at Victoria University and the Australian Institute of Sport (AIS). Damian was appointed the inaugural Skill Acquisition Specialist at the AIS in 2002 where he has been responsible for the provision of evidence-based support to Australian coaches seeking to measure and improve the design of the skill-learning environment. He has worked with a wide range of sub/elite sports programmes at the AIS as well as professional sports teams. His research interests centre on understanding the factors critical to sport expertise and talent/skill development, with a particular interest in the role of perceptual–cognitive skill and practice methodology.

Lennart Fischer is a student at the Institute for Sport Science (University of Münster, Germany). In addition to his studies he works as a research assistant at the

Department of Sport Psychology and supports the GHF in realising its talent selection. His main research interests are talent development, perceptual expertise, attention and motor learning.

Jason Gulbin, PhD, is the General Manager for the Australian Sports Commission's National Talent Identification and Development (NTID) program. He holds a BEd in Post Primary Physical Education (1990) and was awarded his PhD in the field of exercise physiology at Griffith University (Gold Coast) in 1999. His research interests focuses on multidisciplinary, applied talent identification and development themes with a particular interest in maximising the efficiency of the talent development pathway for athletes, coaches and sports.

Sean Horton, PhD, is an assistant professor in the Department of Kinesiology at the University of Windsor. His research interests lie primarily in the area of skill acquisition and expert performance, both in young athletes and as individuals age. Recent projects have focused on various environmental factors that influence talent development.

Hugo Kerhervé is a PhD Scholar in Talent Transfer at the Australian Institute of Sport and is currently enrolled as a PhD candidate at the Queensland University of Technology in Brisbane. His main research interests include Talent Development and Sports Performance. Hugo previously completed a Masters degree at Université Jean Monnet, Saint-Etienne, France focusing on Exercise and Handicap Physiology.

Áine MacNamara, PhD, is a Senior Lecturer in Elite Performance in the Institute of Coaching and Performance at the University of Central Lancashire. The Institute for Coaching and Performance is focused on developing providers of, and the systems employed in, the enhancement of performance. Áine is currently researching talent development processes across different performance domain, with a particular interest in the role that psychological characteristics play in the realization of potential.

John O'Hara, PhD, has worked at Leeds Metropolitan University since June 2000. He is currently a Senior Lecturer in Sport and Exercise Science, within the Carnegie Faculty. John is a British Association of Sport and Exercise Sciences accredited Sport and Exercise Physiologist. He has a vast amount of experience working with amateur and high performance athletes and teams across a range of sporting disciplines throughout the UK. John gained his PhD in 2009, which focused on carbohydrate metabolism and endurance performance. John's research also focuses on different aspects of elite sports performance.

Jan Pabst, PhD, is currently employed as the Head of the Research Group Handball at the Institute for Applied Training Science in Leipzig, Germany. He supports the German handball national teams with its work scientifically.

Elissa Phillips is a Cricket Australia PhD Scholar in Biomechanics and Performance Analysis at the Australian Institute of Sport and is currently enrolled as a PhD candidate at the Queensland University of Technology in Brisbane. Alongside her PhD studies Elissa contributes to the Cricket Australia Fast Bowling Programme. Her main research interests include talent development and coordination dynamics in fast bowling.

Yannis Pitsiladis, PhD, is a Reader in Exercise Physiology at the Institute of Cardiovascular and Medical Sciences in the College of Medicine, Veterinary and Life Sciences at the University of Glasgow, and founding member of the International Centre for East African Running Science (ICEARS), set up to investigate the determinants of the phenomenal success of east African distance runners in international athletics. Recent projects also include the study of elite sprinters from Jamaica and the US, and the study of world class swimmers. He is a Visiting Professor in Medical Physiology at Moi University (Eldoret, Kenya) and Addis Ababa University (Addis Ababa, Ethiopia). He is a member of the Scientific Commission of the International Sports Medicine Federation (FIMS), and a member of the List Committee of the World Anti-Doping Agency (WADA). He is also a Fellow of the American College of Sports Medicine (ACSM).

Ian Renshaw, PhD, is a Senior Lecturer in the School of Human Movement Studies at Queensland University of Technology, Australia. His research interests include an ecological dynamics approach to perception and action in sport, sports coaching and the development of a nonlinear pedagogy for talent development, teaching and coaching of sport. Ian currently acts an advisor on skill acquisition for the Cricket Australia/AIS Centre of Excellence.

Rebecca Rienhoff, MEd, is a PhD Student at the Department of Sportpsychology of the Institute for Sport Science (University of Münster, Germany). During her studies she worked as a research assistant in different talent selection and development projects in cooperation with the GHF. Her specific research interests during the PhD focus on the field of expertise, especially perceptual expertise, attention and motor learning.

William (Bill) Sands, PhD, is the Director of the Monfort Family Human Performance Research Laboratory at Mesa State College. He is the former Recovery Center Leader, Head of Sport Biomechanics and Engineering and Senior Physiologist for the US Olympic Committee in Colorado Springs, Colorado. He has over 35 years of experience in Olympic sports. Dr Sands has served as an associate professor at the University of Utah, Co-Director of the Motor Behavior Research Laboratory with adjunct appointments in Bioengineering and Physical Therapy, Director of Research and Development for USA Gymnastics, and the Scientific Commission of the International Gymnastics Federation.

Jörg Schorer, PhD, is a research associate at the Institute of Sport Science at the Westfälische Wilhelms-University Münster. After being 'unfairly' not selected as a youth handball player and preparing other real talents as a regional coach, he is now working as a researcher in this field. His other research interests include sensory-motor expertise, maintenance of skills with age, and focus of attention in motor control situations.

Peter Sichelschmidt is the Sports Director at the German Handball Federation and worked prior as University Lecturer for Handball and Training Sciences at the German Sports University in Cologne. He acted many years as a coach in first and second German Men's Handball League as well as a National Coach for Men's Youth and Junior teams. He holds the German A-License and the European Master Coach Diploma, is Lecturer and Delegate of the International and European Handball Federations, Member of the IHF-Commission of Organizing and Competition for more than ten years and participated in three Olympic Games, six European Championships and 16 World Championships.

Bernd Strauß, PhD, is full professor in Sport Psychology and dean of the faculty of Psychology and Sport Sciences at the Westfälische Wilhelms-University Münster. He is former president of the German Society of Sport Sciences (2003–09). Currently he is Associate editor of Psychology of Sport and Exercise (Elsevier) as well as of the German Journal of Sport Science (Springer). Here he teaches across both undergraduate and post-graduate provision associated with sports science and physical education. His specific research interests focus upon Expertise in Sports, social processes as well as methodological issues such as multivariate analyses of tests.

Kevin Till is currently a centenary PhD student within the Carnegie Faculty at Leeds Metropolitan University (UK). Kevin's research interests focus upon talent identification, selection and development within UK junior Rugby League. Throughout his studies, Kevin has worked with the UK Rugby League's national governing body the Rugby Football League (RFL). Kevin is also a strength and conditioning coach working with the Super League club, Castleford Tigers RLFC.

Chris Visscher, PhD, is professor of youth sports and head of the Center for Human Movement Sciences at the University of Groningen and the University Medical Center Groningen in the Netherlands. His current interests include motor development, cognition and performance in sports.

PREFACE

The practice of identifying and nurturing talented youth so that they can excel in the future has long been evident in varying domains and in various guises. Perhaps no domain has embraced the potential of talent identification and development to the extent of sport. Success in sport has become increasingly valuable politically, socially and economically, and in parallel with this occurrence, there has been increased funding and resources (e.g., human capital) devoted to this effort. This book is in recognition of these broad events, and the emerging scientific field of research examining talent identification and development.

The overarching purpose of this book is to provide a 'state of the science' overview of empirical and practical information for sport administrators, coaches, parents, athletes, applied sport scientists and students about current issues in the identification and development of sport talent. To achieve this purpose, we have divided the book into two main sections bookended between introductory and concluding chapters. In the first section, leading researchers from the field of athlete development explain their research and how this work informs our understanding of the process of sport skill acquisition. A general framework we have used to organize this section is Baker and Horton's (2004) notion of primary and secondary influences on sport development (see Cobley *et al.*, Chapter 1). The chapters by Baker (Chapter 2) as well as MacNamara and Collins (Chapter 3) focus on the primary influences of genetics and psychological factors on athlete development. Then, Horton (Chapter 4) focuses largely on secondary environmental influences such as culture, birthplace and birthdate. The chapters by Farrow (Chapter 5), Renshaw, Davids, Phillips and Kerhervé (Chapter 6) examine and explain athlete development more globally, from the perspectives of cognitive psychology and dynamical systems theory respectively.

Our intent is that Section 1 provides the necessary theoretical background for readers to understand the various processes at work in Section 2, which provides a series of case studies examining international success stories from the 'trenches' of talent identification and development. Here, specialist contributors working with a range of individual (e.g., gymnastics, Chapter 7 by Sands; running, Chapter 11 by Pitsiladis) and team sports (e.g., soccer, Chapter 8 by Elferink-Gemser & Visscher; rugby league, Chapter 9 by Till *et al.*; and handball, Chapter 10 by Schorer *et al.*) describe the unique constraints inherent with their sport contexts. Further, and more specifically, they highlight how athletic talent is being identified and developed, as well as how systems themselves are presently evolving. The culmination of Section 2 is Chapter 12 by Gulbin, which overviews and reflects upon Australia's national approach to talent identification and development programme.

To guide chapter content in Section 2, authors were asked to consider the following questions (where possible):

- How does your sport context go about identifying talent or selecting athletes for further development?
- How does your sport context nurture talent across stages/phases of development?
- What are the key issues that presently affect talent identification and development in your sport?
- What further research and understanding is required in this area?
- What advice can you provide to administrators, coaches, parents, or athletes involved in talent identification practices in your sport context?

Our hope is that these particular questions are relevant to readers interested in sport talent identification and development, regardless of whether it's through personal involvement as an athlete, coach, trainer, sport administrator or as a parent hoping to help their child navigate sport's sometimes daunting talent systems. Whether through their role as researcher, practitioner or both, contributors to this text have ensured that readers will be well informed of good practices as well as areas where improvements are necessary to address current limitations. To aid in achieving these outcomes, the concluding chapter of the book draws upon the information presented in Sections 1 and 2. Optimistically, we hope that this final chapter (a) underscores the similarities between work being conducted by researchers and put into action by practitioners, (b) highlights 'best practices' in talent identification and development, and (c) identifies the limits of our knowledge, while providing ways they can be resolved. Collectively, this discussion will inform the next generation of research in this emerging field.

While we have tried to organize chapters sequentially when it was appropriate to do so, it is not necessary that readers approach the book in this way. Readers can dip in and out of sections as necessary. The sections and chapters stand alone in their focus and content, yet remain closely aligned to our overarching purpose of informing a 'better' system for talent identification and development in sport. Perhaps the most significant opportunity from this book is the potential for cross-fertilization of ideas between researchers and practitioners from different domains.

The text includes contributors from sport psychology, motor learning and skill acquisition, exercise physiology, and coaching. Through incorporating multi-disciplinary perspectives it is our hope that together we can find answers to questions that have thus far been elusive, such as: how do elite athletes develop? When is the most appropriate time for talent identification and development interventions? And, why do certain athletes succeed while others fail?

Joe Baker, Steve Cobley and Jörg Schorer
December 2010

Reference

Baker, J. & Horton, S. (2004). A review of primary and secondary influences on sport expertise. *High Ability Studies*, *15*, 211–28.

1

IDENTIFICATION AND DEVELOPMENT OF SPORT TALENT

A brief introduction to a growing field of research and practice

Steve Cobley, Jörg Schorer and Joseph Baker

Understanding the nuances of athlete development is a cornerstone of the sports sciences, allowing us to explain the exceptional performances of the sporting elite. Increasingly, evidence indicates that the process of athlete development is not as elusive as once assumed and that through scientific study we can develop a more comprehensive understanding of the constraints and facilitators of sport expertise.

The process of identifying and developing athletic talent has occurred ever since the spirit of competition and sport acquired a central position in Ancient Greece. Even prior to the ancient Olympics (776 BCE approximately), archaeological evidence suggests that state-dictated *gymnasia* within Greek cities acted as the first formalised schools where city youth were provided opportunities to develop their athletic skills for contests under the tutelage of physical trainers, philosophers and musicians (Ghristopoulos, 2003). In preparing for particular events (e.g., wrestling) at local or national festivals (e.g., Panathenaia) as well as religious events (e.g., Olympia), talented youth trained for admiration and the honour of victory.

In the more recent past, specialist training facilities have served to expose athletic talent to highly experienced coaches in the most technologically advanced training environments. Perhaps the best example of a more focused, national talent identification and development system was employed by the former German Democratic Republic, and the Soviet bloc countries. More recently, countries such as Australia, China, the United Kingdom and the United States have invested considerable resources into the identification and development of the next wave of sporting champions.

The Australian Institute of Sport (AIS; see Chapter 12) for instance (created in 1981 after a poor performance at the 1976 Games), has been a model for many nations. Figure 1.1 illustrates the improvement in Olympic performance for Australia since the creation of the AIS. If we assume that all other factors have remained constant (e.g., genetic predisposition would not have changed in such a short period) then

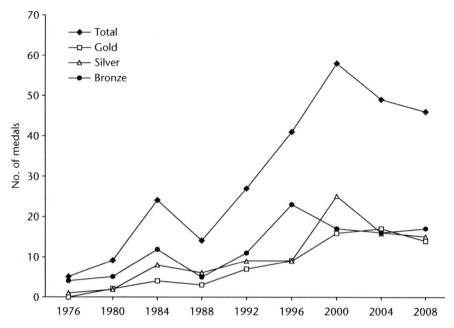

FIGURE 1.1 Australia performance at the Olympic Games after poor performance in 1976 and the creation of the Australian Institute of Sport in 1981.

this improvement reflects the importance of exposure to critical resources (financial and other) on the international competitive stage. Similarly, progressive and substantial financial investment has underpinned UK Olympic sports since the mid-1990s. In Sydney 2000, 11 gold medals (28 in total) were attained, for Athens 2004 there were 9 golds (amongst 30 medals) returned, while in the four years leading up to the 2008 Beijing Olympics, £235 million (mostly derived from national lottery funding; Harris, 2010) supported Team Great Britain's 19 gold medals (at a cost of £12.36 million per gold) and 47 medals overall (£5 million per medal; Syed, 2008; see Green & Houlihan 2005 for an overview of national policies). Such examples emphasise that the process of identifying and developing athletic talent can be seen as a valuable business to many governments worldwide.

Clarifying terminology

At this point, it is valuable to clarify precisely what we mean by *'talent'* and to distinguish between the processes of talent identification and development. Some (e.g., Gagné, 2003; 2004) have argued for a difference between talent and giftedness – specifically that outstanding natural abilities develop into specific expert skills – and while this distinction has a certain theoretical relevance, it does little to inform the process of identifying athletes with the greatest potential (i.e., regardless of whether this refers to 'talent' or 'giftedness') so that they can be provided with the resources essential for them to capitalise on it.

Over the past century, discussions of talent have been generally embedded within the broader nature vs. nurture debate. This debate, which has framed discussions of performance, intelligence and most other topics in human development, is devoted to determining whether development results from biological raw material (i.e., genes) or environmental influences (e.g., experiences). Using this framework to explain sporting achievement, talent becomes an important issue; being able to identify the athlete with the greatest potential for exceptional achievement is critical to the nature position of this debate.

Even today within popular media and layperson discussions, descriptions of talent are often prefixed with words such as 'natural', inferring an inherited predisposition to do a particular task without effort or training. The history of sport science is rich with diversions into the role of 'natural' ability. For instance, prior to the 1960s, many researchers (e.g., McCloy & Young, 1954) supported the existence of a general motor ability. However, although the notion that some athletes have a general ability to perform motor tasks and/or a general ability to learn motor tasks (Brace, 1927; McCloy, 1937) is intuitively appealing, there is little empirical support for this position (Gire & Expenschade, 1942; Gross, Griessel, & Stull, 1956). On the contrary, there is considerable support for the opposing position, that skilled performance is highly specific to the task being performed and that there is little association between skills even in similar tasks (e.g., Drawatzky & Zuccato, 1967).

What is talent?

Despite the fact that the nature vs. nurture debate still enthrals lay discussion and students in introductory courses in psychology, few researchers argue for the singular role of either genes or environment in determining achievement. As Davids and Baker (2007) emphasise, both environment and genetics promote or limit adaptability in a dynamic interplay of genetic raw material, personal experience and chance occurrence. Moreover, while the scientific community has largely moved away from the nature vs. nurture debate as an explanatory framework for human achievement in favour of models of gene-environment interaction, the role of talent (i.e., potential) remains important. At its most basic level, talent refers to the quality (or qualities) identified at an earlier time that promotes (or predicts) exceptionality at a future time. Talent may, therefore, refer to the presence or absence of specific genetic markers that are important for success (e.g., see Chapter 2) or to acquired psychological skills that facilitate an athlete's navigation through the complex pathway of athlete development (e.g., see Chapter 3). However, while the qualities distinguishing the talented from the un-talented may vary (e.g., different sport contexts), here talent plainly refers to an individual's *potential* for success in a domain.

While most people believe they know talent when they see it, establishing a valid and reliable measure of this concept with clear defining characteristics is much harder (cf. Hohmann, 2009). What people normally describe as talent is superior performance in a given sport task; exemplified by using the case of the 100m sprint. The person running faster at a given age or point in their development is usually considered as being the most talented. Beyond this narrow definition however, anthropometric (e.g., height, weight), motor (e.g., speed, coordination) and psychological (e.g., motivation, stress resistance) characteristics play an important role, underpinning the athlete's performance. Most models of athlete development highlight the complex interplay among the characteristics underpinning immediate performance and long-term development. For instance, Baker and Horton (2004; Figure 1.2) proposed that the influences on athlete development could be categorised as primary or secondary. *Primary* factors are direct influences on the acquisition of skills or performance and include elements that an athlete contributes either intentionally or unintentionally to their own performance (i.e., genes, training and psychological characteristics). Primary factors are often constrained by *secondary* influences that buffer their effect on skills and/or performance (i.e., secondary factors have no direct effect). Baker and Horton highlighted the role of socio-cultural factors (among others); for example, high levels of cultural support can facilitate access to resources that encourage involvement (e.g., more facilities, greater sport funding) thereby promoting higher levels of skill by making training easier. In this example, cultural support (the secondary factor) influences performance through its impact on training (the primary factor).

As noted in these models and in several of the subsequent chapters, talent is not merely a performance outcome, a set of particular characteristics or a straightforward linear process. Multiple factors (e.g., individual, social, environmental) determine whether someone demonstrates the potential for success.

What is talent identification?

In sport, talent identification (or talent selection) describes the process of recognising and selecting players who show potential to excel at a more advanced level of competition. For instance, in Canada it is common practice to identify (through 'try

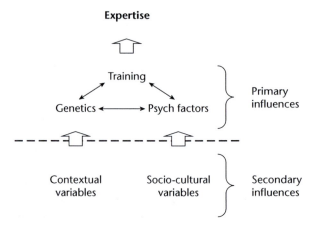

FIGURE 1.2 Baker and Horton's (2004) model of the interaction between primary and secondary influences on athlete development.

outs' or 'trials') talented ice hockey players from the general population of players so that they can play at a more elite 'representative' level of competition. Based on the qualities presumed to be important for success at a future higher level, 'scouts' (coaches, trainers, applied sport scientists) attempt to identify players meeting their prescribed criteria (i.e., the talented players). On this basis, 'talented' individuals are selected for programmes dedicated to more focused investment by national (e.g., Australia, see Chapter 12) and localised sport governing bodies (e.g., UK Rugby League, see Chapter 9).

What is talent development?

Talent development refers to the provision of the most appropriate (i.e., facilitative) environments for athletes to accelerate their learning and performance (Abbott & Collins, 2004). This may involve systematic instruction, counselling, sport science support (e.g., nutritional advice, strength and conditioning) as well as high quality training and practice. Inherent within typical developmental programmes are high quality and intensive training programmes (e.g., progressively higher volumes, intensities, durations) that aim to adapt and prepare the athlete, accelerating their path (i.e., reducing the time required for performance adaptations) to becoming an elite adult performer. Settings that provide essentially more time for participation and which do not invoke physical, psychological and performance adaptation and acceleration should not be considered as talent development environments.

To summarise, *talent identification* refers to early recognition (relative to being an adult) of potential for excelling in a particular task. This is done in the hope of further nurturing this potential, through attention to the provision of appropriate training and resources (i.e., the process of *talent development*).

How does talent identification and development typically occur?

Cobley and Cooke (2009; see Figure 1.3) provide a model summarising how typical talent identification and development systems operate. The model does not reflect any specific developmental system, but rather attempts to outline generic trends relevant across team sport contexts. Working from left to right, identification procedures are often applied during child or youth stages of development. Identification may include a series of testing and subjective assessment procedures. Typically, whether single or repeated measurements on (an) identified variables(s), and/or subjective assessment criteria (e.g., coach observations), these practices identify a sample of athletes, who generally represent either the current 'best' or those deemed to show the most potential for future success, compared to a normative participating population. Once selected through identification processes, a comparatively smaller percentage of players begin to access the next developmental stage within a system.

The model acknowledges that the factors determining whether someone is indeed talented are not fixed across sports. For instance, the unique task demands

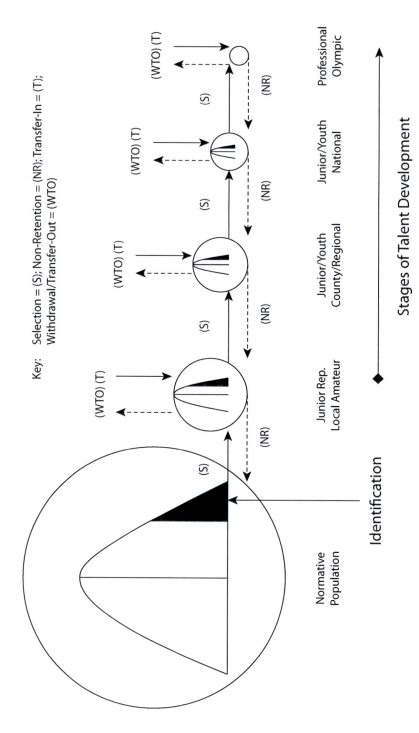

FIGURE 1.3 Cobley and Cooke's (2009) conceptual diagram of common stages in talent identification and development, from normative to elite populations, with particular relevance to field based team sports.

and requirements of respective sports (e.g., soccer vs. field-hockey) mean that factors subjectively assessed and/or measured to determine talent will change. Moreover, the model recognises that variables which may predict talent at a given stage (e.g., speed, height) will not remain the same across a single system. To exemplify, the factor(s) that may predict performance at the first selection stage (e.g., junior representative) may not necessarily predict performance at a higher skill level (e.g., junior regional or adult national; e.g., Mohammed *et al.*, 2009).

When identification and selection has occurred to create a talented group, the group then become more homogenous, at least on the variables used to identify and select them originally (e.g., anthropometrics, physical performance). These predicting variables now have less (or no) power in predicting further levels of selection. For subsequent levels of development, where there is a reduced pool of athletes, other factors (e.g., technical skill, tactical awareness) become predictive, discriminating those deemed more suitable for a higher level of development and competition. At these points, athletes not selected for further development may either remain at the skill/performance level while they are still able (e.g., stay with a regional Under 14s soccer team until the age limit is reached). They may decide to transfer to another level of competition (e.g., from competitive to recreational involvement), transfer to another sport (e.g., club representative soccer to cricket) or withdraw from the sport altogether.

Perhaps because the pool of potential is reduced with each successive stage of selection, talent identification and development systems increasingly encourage highly trained athletes who are not suitable for the highest levels of competition in a given sport, to transfer to a sport context that shares similar performance qualities (e.g., physical – Bullock *et al.*, 2009). Likewise, individuals may enter, or transfer, into later stages of a sport developmental system – having not initially been identified as part of a sport-specific identification or development strategy – if they show potential in one or several key performance indicators. However, transfer is increasingly less likely as one progresses (i.e., to the right of Figure 1.3) across the development system. If an athlete is able to transfer into the sub-elite or elite level, it is likely they experienced similar stages of training and development in a parallel system (e.g., national level rowing – cycling).

At the national and international levels, those selected show a more 'rounded profile' of physical, cognitive, psychological and technical attributes and skills for their sport context. In a small sample of highly skilled homogenous athletes, the unique combination of attributes leading to performance success becomes a prominent feature distinguishing performers at the highest level of performance.

Assumptions of talent identification and development programmes

Based on the definitions above and as highlighted in the following chapters, there are two general assumptions that underpin empirical research and applied practices in sport talent identification and development. These generally highlight the challenges for the field, show why it is so difficult to find optimal solutions, but also illustrate why working with talented athletes is so compelling.

Assumption 1: Talent is identifiable: The basic assumption underpinning all talent identification programmes is that talent (i.e., potential) is identifiable and therefore measurable. Existing research suggests that we have limited understanding of the qualities associated with talent identification, and what we do know is fraught with bias and subjectivity. For instance, common indicators of athletic talent such as speed, power and body size are confounded by maturation (see Pearson, Naughton & Torode, 2006). This may refer generally to normal growth and development throughout childhood and youth, or more specifically to the timing and tempo of puberty. The impact of maturation on physical performance in youth is perhaps best described by 'relative age' (see Horton, Chapter 4) – defined as the age of an individual relative to peers in their social comparison group (e.g., Under 13 annual age-group in soccer). Relatively older athletes, generally appear larger, stronger and faster than their age-matched peers simply because they are chronologically older and more likely to be at a more advanced state of maturation. Whether coaches have utilised standardised measurements or tests (e.g., 30 metre sprint), or a pre-determined subjective schema (e.g., perceptions of technical skills), the relatively older (or more mature) are disproportionately more likely to be identified as 'talented'. Unfortunately, although this assumption lies at the foundation of talent identification and development, the evidence supporting its validity has been largely equivocal.

Assumption 2: Adult performance can be predicted by earlier performance: In some sports (e.g., rowing; Bourgois *et al.*, 2000, 2001; Ingham *et al.*, 2002) anthropometric and physical test batteries have successfully predicted a significant proportion of elite adult performance. These tests can have high value and relevance in specific sports (i.e., in closed, isolated and repetitive tasks). However, many studies and practitioners assume that the same variables can be extrapolated backward from adults and be applied to youth. Similarly, researchers have identified many behavioural (e.g., training types), perceptual (e.g., pattern recognition) and cognitive skills (e.g., decision-making, event anticipation) that delineate the adult expert athlete from the near or non-expert. These same testing protocols are also used by progressive talent programmes to identify and determine potentially talented youth (e.g., German handball, Chapter 10).

In team sport contexts (e.g., field-hockey), which have both player interaction and object manipulation (i.e., representing more 'open' tasks), anthropometric and physical test batteries have a much reduced (if any) predictive power of elite adult level performance (refer to Vaeyens *et al.*, 2008). Unfortunately this has not prevented sport governing bodies from conducting 'fishing expeditions' into youth populations that have typically included one-off cross-sectional testing of youngsters, often during early adolescence, on specific anthropometric (e.g., height, body mass) and physical variables (e.g., VO^2 max). These can – and may reinforce – particular suppositions, namely that tomorrow's sporting champions are closely (if not exclusively) associated with the early emergence of physical propensities, biases that can detrimentally impact assessment and selection of youthful talent.

Neither of the above assumptions is easily remedied. However let us be clear, just because something is difficult to measure does not mean it doesn't exist. Hypothetically, it seems reasonable to expect that *if* we knew what qualities to look for at an early age or stage of development *then* it would be beneficial to identify athletes with these qualities. That said, very little empirical research has focused on measurement issues and how such information applies across contexts (i.e., adults – youth; closed – open contexts). While these general assumptions remain in the background, researchers and practitioners need to acknowledge how these assumptions limit our understanding. As emphasised in forthcoming chapters, they can inform and guide future work, helping talent identification and development become a viable science with practices based on solid evidence.

Most important though, we should not refrain from working with athletic talent simply because we are aware of our limitations. It is the responsibility of those working in the field, whether researching or practising, to improve present understanding. This can only be achieved via cooperation between all stakeholders involved in the sport system. The chapters that follow synthesise current theoretical understanding in the initial chapters, while later chapters showcase applied collaborative research within talent identification and development systems across the globe. While significant momentum has been gained in recent years, there is considerable work ahead. This book aims to lay the foundations and generate initial momentum for such work.

References

Abbott, A., & Collins, D. (2004). Eliminating the dichotomy between theory and practice in talent identification and development: Considering the role of psychology. *Journal of Sports Sciences, 22*, 395–408.

Baker, J. & Horton, S. (2004). A review of primary and secondary influences on sport expertise. *High Ability Studies, 15*, 211–28.

Bourgois, J., Claessens, A. L., Janssens, M., Van Renterghem, B., Loos, R., Thomis, M., Philippaerts, R., Lefevre, J., & Vrijens, J. (2001). Anthropometric characteristics of elite female junior rowers. *Journal of Sports Sciences, 19*, 195–202.

Bourgois, J., Claessens, A. L., Vrijens, J. M., Philippaerts, R., Van Renterghem, B., Thomis, M., Janssens, M., Loos, R., & Lefevre, J. (2000). Anthropometric characteristics of elite male junior rowers. *British Journal of Sports Medicine, 34*, 213–16.

Brace, D. K. (1927). *Measuring motor ability*. New York: A. S. Barnes.

Bullock, N., Gulbin, J. P., Martin, D. T., Ross, A., Holland, T., Marino, F. (2009). Talent identification and deliberate programming in skeleton: Ice novice to Winter Olympian in 14 months. *Journal of Sports Sciences, 27*, 397–404.

Cobley, S., & Cooke, C. (2009). Talent identification and development: An overview of research and practice. Paper presented in the Carnegie Seminar Series, Carnegie Faculty, Leeds Metropolitan University, Leeds, December.

Davids, K. & Baker, J. (2007). Genes, environment and sport performance: Why the Nature-Nurture dualism is no longer relevant. *Sports Medicine, 37*, 961–80.

Drawatzky, J. N. & Zuccato, F. C. (1967). Interrelationships between selected measures of static and dynamic balance. *Research Quarterly, 38*, 509–10.

Gagné, F. (2003). Transforming gifts into talents: The DMGT as a developmental theory. In N. Colangelo & G. A. Davis (Eds), *Handbook of gifted education* (pp. 60–74). Boston: Allyn and Bacon.

—— (2004). Transforming gifts into talents: The DMGT as a developmental theory. *High Ability Studies, 15,* 119–47.

Ghristopoulos, G. A. (2003). *The Olympic games in ancient Greece.* Athens, Greece. Ekdotike Athenon S.A.

Gire, E. & Espenschade, A. (1942). The relationship between measures of motor educability and learning specific motor skills. *Research Quarterly, 13,* 43–56.

Green, M. & Houlihan, B. (2005). *Elite sport development: Policy learning and political priorities.* Abingdon: Routledge.

Gross, E., Griessel, D. C., & Stull, G. A. (1956). Relationship between two motor educability tests, a strength test, and wrestling ability after eight weeks of instruction. *Research Quarterly, 27,* 395–402.

Harris, N. (2010) The big question: What lessons do the Vancouver Games offer for London 2012? *The Independent.* 2 March, http://www.independent.co.uk/extras/big-question/the-big-question-what-lessons-do-the-vancouver-games-offer-for-london-2012-1914 324.html (accessed on 23 October 2010).

Hohmann, A. (2009). *Entwicklung sportlicher Talente an sportbetonte Schulen.* Petersberg: Michael Imhof.

Ingham, S. A., Whyte, G. P., Jones, K., & Nevill, A. M. (2002). Determinants of 2,000m rowing ergometer performance in elite rowers. *European Journal of Applied Physiology, 88,* 243–46.

McCloy, C. H. (1937). An analytic study of the stunt type tests as a measure of motor educability. *Research Quarterly, 8,* 46–55.

McCloy, C. H. & Young, N. D. (1954). *Tests and measurements in health and physical education* (3rd edn). New York: Appleton-Century-Crofts.

Mohammed, H., Vaeyens, R., Matthys, S., Multael, M., Lefevre, J., Lenoir, M., Philppaerts, R. (2009). Anthropometric and performance measures for the development of a talent detection and identification model in youth handball. *Journal of Sports Sciences, 27,* 257–66.

Pearson, D. T., Naughton, G. A., & Torode, M. (2006). Predictability of physiological testing and the role of maturation in talent identification for adolescent team sports. *Journal of Science & Medicine in Sport, 9,* 277–87.

Syed, M. (2008). Unacceptable cost of heroes' Olympic success. *The Times.* 16 October, http://www.timesonline.co.uk/tol/sport/olympics/article4951145.ece (accessed 23 October 2010).

Vaeyens, R., Lenoir, M., Williams, M. A., & Philippaerts, R. M. (2008). Talent identification and development in sport: Current models and future directions. *Sports Medicine, 38,* 703–14.

SECTION ONE

Theoretical and conceptual models for understanding talent identification and development

2

DO GENES PREDICT POTENTIAL?

Genetic factors and athletic success

Joseph Baker

Rick Macci, coach of Venus and Serena Williams, Andy Roddick and Jennifer Capriati, has a new charge in his stable, four-year-old Australia tennis 'prodigy' Macy Lines. As attention to all things tennis grew before the US Open tournament in 2009, Macy was front and centre on news programmes across North America. According to her coach, 'I've never seen anybody that's bringing this genetically to the table' (Macci, quoted in Canning & Yeo, 2009). While Macy's trajectory in tennis is impossible to predict, the notion that athletic potential is constrained by genes is widespread among those working the frontlines of athlete development. This chapter will explore this notion and is intended as a primer for sports scientists working in talent identification and athlete development; that is, people who have a vested interest in genetic research as it relates to predicting a person's potential, but who may not have the necessary background to completely understand the methods used and the subtleties of existing evidence. It is not intended to be a 'cutting edge' review of research in this area; for that see Collins (2009).

The basics

Although discussions of the relative contributions of 'nature' and 'nurture' to exceptional performance can be traced to ancient Greece, scientific investigations began in the mid-nineteenth century largely resulting from the work by Charles Darwin and his cousin Francis Galton. Galton's *Hereditary Genius* provided the stimulus for much subsequent work and was heavily influenced by Darwinian theory. Generally, much of this early work focused on the overall contribution of genes to human variability measured by a statistic called *heritability* (the proportion of variance in a population that is attributed to genetic factors). Although heritability remains an important factor in understanding biological influences on human performance, genetic research was irrevocably changed in February 2001 with the publication of the human genome (Lander *et al.*, 2001; Venter *et al.*, 2001). However, to understand the importance of this contribution, we need to review some basic biology and genetics (Figure 2.1).

Each of us is the product of a unique *DNA* (Deoxyribonucleic acid) sequence, half of which we receive from our mother the other half from our father in the form of *chromosomes*. DNA is made up of a combination of four chemical bases – adenine, thymine, guanine and cytosine (abbreviated A, T, G and C), which group together into base pairs (A with T and G with C). Base pairs link together to form discrete sequences of DNA (e.g., AATCAGTT) called *genes*. Each gene corresponds to a specific biological outcome; for example, humans and other animals have a gene for limiting muscle growth through the regulation of a protein called myostatin. If the myostatin gene is missing or doesn't function properly, muscle growth is con-siderably greater – as in the case of the young child described in Schuelke *et al.* (2004) or the 'bully whippet' in dog breeding, which changes the normal whisper thin whippet into the canine equivalent of Mr Olympia (Mosher *et al.*, 2007). Unlike the myostatin example, which results from a mutation (i.e., normally, every person has the active myostatin gene), if the gene sequence produces normal variability in a population (e.g., human hair colour may be blonde, black, brown or red), this

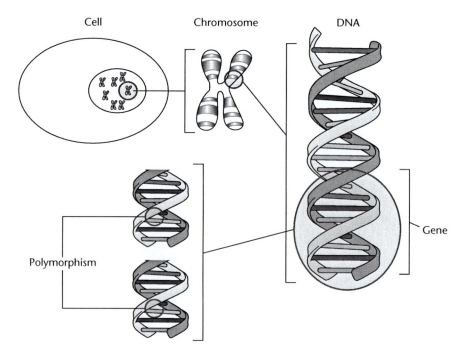

FIGURE 2.1 Building blocks of genetic influences on performance. The nucleus of cells contains 23 pairs of chromosomes, each containing an individual's unique genetic makeup contained in their DNA. Alterations in the genetic sequences (e.g., differences in the sequences highlighted in the small circles) between individuals are known as polymorphisms.

variability results from different *alleles* (a variant in the gene sequence) and is known as a *polymorphism* (the occurrence of many forms of a given gene). One of the sections below summarises a polymorphism related to the gene for Angiotensin Converting Enzyme (ACE), which may relate to performance in endurance and power sports.

The *genome* is the total of all genes present in an individual. Currents estimates are that the human genome has between 20,000 and 25,000 genes containing about 3 billion base pairs. An individual's collection of genes is referred to as their *genotype*. A person's genotype (i.e., their genetic 'raw material') and the host of influences from their environment result in their *phenotype* – the physical manifestation of a characteristic (e.g., how tall they are, the colour of their hair, how they respond to stress, etc.). Since publication of the human genome map, researchers can systematically explore the influence of specific genes on health and fitness-related outcomes using either scans for one or more candidate genes or scans of the entire genome for unique combinations of genetic markers. These endeavours have been very successful; the most recent update to the Human Gene Map for Performance and Health-Related Fitness Phenotypes (Bray *et al.*, 2009) notes over 200 genes related to health and/or performance. The sections below consider how this research informs us about the role of genetics in talent identification and development.

Genes and their role in promoting athletic excellence

Genes are the currency of natural selection, the mechanism of continued species evolution, and variations in the presence/absence of a given gene result in the enormous diversity we see between individuals. Data from the Human Genome Project indicate that humans share greater than 99 per cent of their DNA (maybe as much as 99.9 per cent), which means the variability we see within our population is due to a relatively small amount of different DNA and how it interacts with a variety of other factors, which we'll get to later. The sections below consider some of the landmark studies in this area and how they relate to our understanding of the development of exceptional performers.

The Minnesota Study of Twins Reared Apart

The study of monzygotic and dizygotic twins has long been the method of choice for genetic researchers. Monozygotic twins are especially appealing because they have the same genes (i.e., 100 per cent of their DNA is shared), while dizygotic twins share approximately 50 per cent of their genes. For over three decades, researchers at the University of Minnesota – Twin Cities have used a variety of methods to examine the role of genetic factors in personality and related psychological variables. The Minnesota Twin Family Study is an umbrella term for several projects including the Minnesota Twin Registry, the Sibling Interaction and Behavior Study, and, perhaps most relevant for our discussion, the Minnesota Study of Twins Reared Apart (MISTRA). A major obstacle for researchers examining genetic influences using twins is separating the effects of their shared environment from the effects of their shared DNA. MISTRA attempts to avoid this limitation by examining twins that were separated in infancy and reared apart. The assumption is that these twins will have the same DNA but will have been reared in entirely different environments. More than 100 sets of twins or triplets reared apart have completed the weeklong battery of tests at the University of Minnesota, which includes approximately 50 hours of medical and psychological assessment.

Much has been written about MISTRA and it has quickly become a classic in the field of psychology (although not without its critics; see Joseph, 2003). Most popular accounts of this research emphasise the amazing similarities between twins that have spent decades of the earliest parts of their development apart (see Segal, 2007). For instance, consider the 'Jim Twins'. They were adopted at the age of four weeks and both named 'Jim' by their adoptive parents. When they were reunited nearly 40 years later, they shared the following attributes:

- Both were married to women named Betty and divorced from women named Linda.
- One named his first son James Alan and the other named his first son James Allan.
- Both had an adopted brother whose name is Larry.
- Both named their pet dog 'Toy.'
- Both had some law-enforcement training and had been a part-time deputy sheriff in Ohio.
- Each did poorly in spelling and well in math.
- Each did carpentry, mechanical drawing and block lettering.
- Each vacationed in Florida in the same three-block-long beach area.
- Both twins began suffering from tension headaches at 18, gained ten pounds at the same time, and at the time of data collection were six feet tall and 180 pounds.

Not all of the MISTRA results are this notable (or sensational), but generally, the data indicate that genes account for a significant portion of the inter-individual variation in several psychological outcomes. For instance, MISTRA has shown high heritability for psychological outcomes such as general intelligence (Johnson et al., 2007), work values (e.g., altruism and autonomy; Keller, Bouchard, Arvey, Segal, & Dawis, 1992), job satisfaction (Arvey, Bouchard, Segal, & Abraham, 1989), and several measures of personality (e.g., DiLalla, Carey, Gottesman, & Bouchard, 1996; Tellegen et al., 1988). In sports, where most of these psychological characteristics are essential to the acquisition and demonstration of high levels of performance, genetic factors seem to play an important role. What is more, being able to identify who had the best work ethic, or the most appropriate personality for a given sport, may have important implications for talent identification.

Angiotensin converting enzyme

While psychology has focused on general concepts such as the ones discussed above, biologists and physiologists have examined specific genes. Since the mid-1990s, a significant amount of research has focused on a polymorphism in the gene for ACE, an enzyme involved in converting angiotensin I to angiotensin II, which controls blood pressure and fluid-electrolyte balance. The gene for ACE has two alleles which can vary according to whether they have (I for insertion) or do not have (D for deletion) a specific sequence of DNA 287 base-pairs long. As we would expect from a simple Punnett square (Figure 2.2), the percentage of people in a population with the genotypes for II (two insertion alleles), ID (an insertion and a deletion allele) and DD (two deletion alleles) is roughly 25 per cent, 50 per cent and 25 per cent respectively, although this varies by population (Woods, 2009).

Given that ACE seems to have an important role in the regulation of cardio-vascular function, it is not surprising that researchers have considered its relationship with athletic performance. Researchers proposed that since the I allele is associated with lower ACE activity it may be related to endurance performance. Initial examinations of endurance athletes ranging from Olympic rowers (Gayagay *et al.*, 1998) and Ironman triathletes (Collins *et al.*, 2004) to high altitude mountain climbers (Montgomery *et al.*, 1998) suggested that as aerobic endurance require-ments increase the proportion of the sample with the I-allele increased.

Despite early promise of research in this area, replication and, more importantly, prediction, proved difficult in subsequent studies. Although there are several reasonable explanations for this lack of consistency (e.g., between study hetero-geneity, inconsistent definitions of elite athlete), a recent review of research on ACE by Williams and Wackerhage (2009) summarised: 'Our considered view is that the ACE I/D polymorphism is probably associated with some aspects of physical performance . . . in some populations . . . but that the influence of this single polymorphism is probably modest' (p. 180). Opinions regarding ACE as a potential gene for sport performance are now considerably more muted than when it first emerged.

	D	I
D	DD	DI
I	DI	II

FIGURE 2.2 Punnett square demonstrating the frequency of ACE alleles in a population.

Gene–environment interaction: the HERITAGE family study

Although researchers continue to search for single genes that relate to successful performance, more fruitful investigations have begun delineating the inter-relationship between performance-related genetic factors and the developmental environment. For instance, consider the hypothetical relationships illustrated in Figure 2.3.

It shows a very simplistic interaction between a polymorphism (an individual could have one of three types of genes) and an environmental factor, in this case the amount of training an individual performs during their development. The individual with the greatest potential for the highest level of performance is the one with the most beneficial genetic makeup *and* performs the most training. While this example is completely theoretical, evidence continues to amass reflecting the accuracy of this model for explaining gene–environment interactions.

An excellent example comes from the HERITAGE (*HE*alth, *RI*sk factors, exercise *T*raining, *A*nd *GE*netics) family study (Bouchard *et al.*, 1995), a multi-site study conducted in the United States to examine (among other things) the influence of genetic factors on predictors of health and disease risk. The aim of the HERITAGE study was 'to study the role of the genotype in cardiovascular,

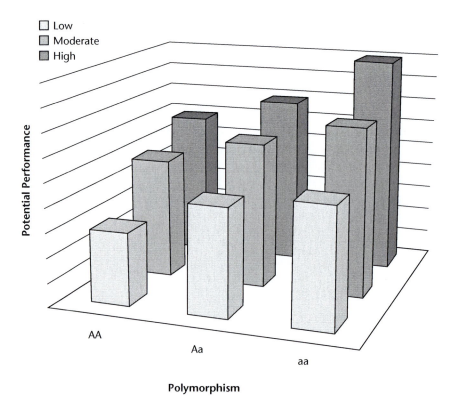

FIGURE 2.3 Hypothetical interaction between a polymorphism for exceptional performance (AA, Aa or aa) and amount of training (low, moderate or high).

metabolic, and hormonal responses to aerobic exercise training and the contribution of regular exercise to changes in several cardiovascular disease and diabetes risk factors' (p. 722, Bouchard et al., 1995). Families participating in the study included both biological parents and at least three biological children. Further, participants were healthy but essentially untrained, met body mass index and blood pressure requirements and had an absence of medical conditions or diseases. Participants in the HERITAGE study completed a battery of tests including questionnaires related to health and physical activity, anthropometric measurements, and blood tests. In addition, the participants completed six maximal exercise tests; three prior to a 20-week standardised aerobic training programme and three at the conclusion of the training programme.

Results from the HERITAGE study have been impressive and indicate that several variables related to physical performance are genetically constrained, for instance heart rate at rest (An et al., 1999) and the capacity to transport and use oxygen during exercise (e.g., maximal aerobic capacity, Bouchard et al., 1998; submaximal aerobic capacity, Pérusse et al., 2001); however, and more importantly, HERITAGE data indicate that an individual's response to exercise training is influenced by their genetic makeup (e.g., Bouchard et al., 1999; Rice et al., 2002). HERITAGE established that about half of the variability between an individual's maximal aerobic capacity is attributable to genetic factors. A recent re-examination of HERITAGE data (Timmons et al., 2010) found that roughly half of this variability (23 per cent) can be explained by the differences in 11 nucleotides, a C instead of a T, for example (known as a single nucleotide polymorphism). These findings indicate that significant amounts of inter-individual variation in cardiorespiratory function can be attributed to the presence or absence of specific genes. They also suggest that the level of attainment in activities where these factors are important (e.g., marathon running) will be affected by having an advantageous genotype (see Chapter 11 for more on this issue as it relates to African runners).

Collectively, these studies emphasise the subtlety and nuance associated with genetic influence on athlete development. Research in this area is progressing rapidly and in the section below three emerging issues are discussed.

Issue 1: Can we predict genetic potential in talent identification and development?

In principle, it should be possible to use genetic criteria to predict an individual's potential to become an elite athlete (or anything for that matter). Some have begun to explore this technology in an effort to maximise the likelihood of sporting success. For instance, a company in the United States performs scans for performance-related genes in newborn children for $149US. However, the validity of this exercise is highly questionable, largely because, at present, there is no clear evidence of what to look for. The company mentioned earlier searches for a gene called Alpha-actinin-3 (ACTN3), which produces a skeletal muscle protein thought to be a marker for two types of athletic ability – explosive power if you have the allele with the RR variant and endurance if you have the allele with the XX variant. While time (and replication) will ultimately determine whether ACTN3 is a robust indicator of genetic potential in sports, previous attempts (see ACE discussed earlier) to identify genetic markers have had limited degrees of success and, more importantly, our understanding of the relationships between these markers and their biological consequences is largely non-existent. Even if it were possible to perform a genetic scan to identify performance related markers we do not know how the presence or absence of these genes affects an individual's response to a given training stimulus. Consider the gene responsible for producing the protein for Collagen, Type 5, Alpha 1 (COL5A1), which seems to affect an individual's predisposition to Achilles' tendon (Mokone, Schwellnus, Noakes, & Collins, 2006) or anterior cruciate ligament injury (Poshumus et al., 2009). This gene, which encodes for a specific collagen protein relevant to flexibility of ligaments and tendons, could affect the amount and intensity of training individuals in certain sports can perform throughout their development – factors that are highly influential in predicting athlete development (see Chapters by Farrow, Horton, and Renshaw et al.); however, our understanding of this gene and its interaction with athlete training stimuli is in its infancy.

To sum up, if genetic markers can be identified that affect an individual's training response and there is sufficient understanding of the relationship between this marker and its training consequences then there may be some value for coaches, trainers and athletes for prescribing appropriate training based on genetic profile. However, there is no conclusive evidence on which to base this genetic search as of this writing. It is possible in principle but far from reality.

Issue 2: One gene or several . . . What is the likelihood of having the perfect genetic profile?

Although researchers continue to search for a single gene that would explain elite performance, the 'single gene as magic bullet' scenario (cf. Davids & Baker, 2007) is not likely to reflect the complexity of genetic influences on athlete outcomes. As an example, let's consider the genes associated with endurance performance. So far in this chapter we considered ACE and ACTN3 but these are just the current front runners. Williams and Folland (2008) noted 23 different genetic variants identified in previous research that relate to superior performance in endurance sports. On the one hand, this supports the conclusion that genes have a considerable influence on performance in this domain. On the other, Williams and Folland calculated that the odds of one individual having all of the preferential variants of these 23 genes were approximately one in 20 million. A recent examination of 46 world-class endurance athletes considered just seven of the 23 endurance polymorphisms noted by Williams and Folland and found that none of them had all of the favourable genes (Ruiz et al., 2009). It is possible, even probable, that very elite endurance athletes have several of the 23 variants (subsequent studies of multiple candidate genes will confirm this); however, given the small proportion of the population who will have grown up in the optimal environment for training in their specific sport and are lucky enough to be selected as part of a talent development programme (if one exists in their sport) it is highly unlikely that anyone – not seven-time Tour de France champion Lance Armstrong, marathon world record holder Paula Radcliffe, nor six-time Ironman World Champion legend Mark Allen – will have all of the 'best' genes for endurance performance.

It is also worth re-emphasising that genes do not operate independently of the environment. Although we know significantly more about the relationships between training stimuli and performance outcomes than we do about the role of specific genes on performance, we still have much to learn about the most effective training methods at different stages of development and how development may be positively or negatively influenced by the presence or absence of individual genes.

Issue 3: And to make the situation more challenging . . . epigenetics

Most models of genetic transference are based on the notion that DNA is transferred immutably from parent to child and that it carries the only information transmitted across the generations. Recently, genetics researchers have begun distinguishing from what they term 'hard inheritance', which is the transference of information via DNA, and 'soft inheritance', which affects DNA by preventing expression of certain genes but does not alter DNA sequence. The latter influence is known as *epigenetics*.

Some of the most convincing evidence for epigenetic influence comes from the Dutch Famine Study. During the last two years of the Second World War, Dutch citizens were placed under enormous dietary restriction. From November 1944 to May 1945, caloric intake was as low as 400 calories a day. Data from this study have shown that women pregnant during this time gave birth to babies who were of lower than average birth weight (a precursor to health problems like diabetes, cardiovascular disease and obesity; Roseboom *et al.*, 2006); however, most relevant to our discussion, the grandchildren of mothers pregnant during the famine were also smaller than average, suggesting that experiences that we have today may leave a lasting trace on subsequent generations. This mechanism might explain, at least partially, the obvious phenotypic differences between identical twins. Epigenetic influence does not readily fit into our current models of genetic influence on human behaviour and forces a re-examination of the possible links between biology and environment. Only then will we be able to understand epigenetic effects on talent identification and development.

Conclusions

As succinctly described by Kimble (1993), determining whether human variation is attributable to genes or environment is much like determining whether the area of a rectangle is attributable to height or width – both are inexorably bound together and performers are the product of their biological raw material and their developmental experiences. The field of sport genetics is advancing with great speed and 'breakthroughs' appear in the popular press on a fairly regular basis. Although there is some legitimacy to the notion that predicting performance potential based on genetic factors should one day be possible (given the heritability of most performance-related characteristics), we are far from having the necessary understanding and tools to put this notion into adequate practice. Most alarming, without this knowledge it is possible, even likely, that athletes found to possess undesirable genetic profiles may be marginalised and/or not provided the same training opportunities as their 'more gifted' peers. As in many areas of science and medicine, genetic technology is advancing more rapidly than our understanding of its limitations and consequences. The dynamic relationship between the excitement of new developments and the temperance needed for objective examination of their meaning highlights the complexity inherent in this rapidly developing field of research.

Despite the risks involved, it is clear that the future of research in talent identification requires an approach emphasising the interaction between genes and environment; continued focus on specific genetic or environmental factors in isolation will never adequately explain this complex issue. Multidisciplinary examinations of athlete development along with twin and family studies remain important steps forward. Moreover, the complexity of the relationships between genetic and environmental factors requires a long-term approach. Cronbach (1991) stated, 'serious interaction research ought to be a program of several years' duration, although there are few examples in behavioral science' (p. 87). Twenty years on, this remains a noticeable weakness of research in this area and a significant limitation to our understanding of genetic effects on talent identification and development.

References

An, P., Rice, T., Gagnon, J., Borecki, I. B., Pérusse, L., Leon, A. S. et al. (1999). Familial aggregation of resting blood pressure and heart rate in a sedentary population: The HERITAGE Family Study. American Journal of Hypertension, 12, 264–70.

Arvey, R. D., Bouchard, Jr. T. J., Segal, N. L., & Abraham, L. M. (1989). Job satisfaction: Environmental and genetic components. Journal of Applied Psychology, 74, 187–92.

Bouchard, C., An, P., Rice, T., Skinner, J. S, Wilmore, J. H. et al. (1999). Familial aggregation of VO2max response to exercise training: Results from the HERITAGE Family Study. Journal of Applied Physiology, 87, 1003–8.

Bouchard, C., Daw, W., Rice, T., Pérusse, L., Gagnon, J. et al. (1998). Familial resemblance for VO2max in the sedentary state: The HERITAGE Family Study. Medicine & Science in Sports and Exercise, 30, 252–58.

Bouchard, C., Leon, A. S., Rao, D. C., Skinner, J. S., Wilmore, J. H., & Gagnon, J. (1995). Aims, design, and measurement protocol. Medicine & Science in Sports and Exercise, 27, 721–29.

Bray, M. S., Hagberg, J. M., Pérusse, L., Rankinen, T., Roth, S. M., et al. (2009). The human gene map for performance and health-related fitness phenotypes: the 2006–7 update. Medicine & Science in Sports & Exercise, 41, 35–73.

Canning, A. & Yeo, S. (2009). 4-year-old tennis phenom has makings of a champ. http://abcnews.go.com/US/story?id=8449967 (accessed 7 July 2010).

Collins, M. (2009). *Genetics and sports*. Basel: Karger.

Collins, M., Xenophontos, S. L., Cariolou, M. A., Mokone, G. G., Hudson, D. E. *et al.* (2004). The ACE gene and endurance performance during the South African Ironman Triathlons. *Medicine and Science in Sports and Exercise, 36,* 1314–20.

Cronbach, L. J. (1991) Emerging views on methodology. In T. D. Wachs & R. Plomin (Eds) *Conceptualization and measurement of organism-environment interaction* (pp. 87–104). Washington, DC: American Psychological Association.

Davids, K. & Baker, J. (2007). Genes, environment and sport performance: Why the Nature-Nurture dualism is no longer relevant. *Sports Medicine, 37,* 961–80.

DiLalla, D. L., Carey, G., Gottesman, I. I., & Bouchard, Jr. T. J. (1996). Heritability of MMPI personality indicators of psychopathology in twins reared apart. *Journal of Abnormal Psychology, 105,* 491–99.

Doblhammer, G. (2004). *The late life legacy of very early life.* Springer: Berlin.

Gayagay, G., Yu, B., Hambly, B., Boston, T., Hahn, A. *et al.* (1998). Elite endurance athletes and the ACE I allele – the role of genes in athletic performance. *Human Genetics 103,* 48–50.

Johnson, W., Bouchard, T. J., McGue, M., Segal, N. L., Tellegen, A., Keyes, M., & Gottesman, I. I. (2007). Genetic and environmental influences on the Verbal-Perceptual-Image Rotation (VPR) model of the structure of mental abilities in the Minnesota study of twins reared apart. *Intelligence, 35,* 542–62.

Joseph, J. (2003). *The gene illusion: Genetic research in psychiatry and psychology under the microscope.* Ross-on-Wye: PCCS Books.

Keller, L. M. Bouchard, T. J., Arvey, R. D., Segal, N. L., & Dawis, R. V. (1992). Work values: Genetic and environmental influences. *Journal of Applied Psychology, 77,* 79–88.

Kimble, G. A. (1993). Evolution of the nature-nurture issue in the history of psychology. In R. Plomin & G. E. McClearn (Eds) *Nature, nurture and psychology* (pp. 3–25). Washington, DC: APA.

Lander, E. S. *et al.* (2001). Initial sequencing and analysis of the human genome. *Nature, 409,* 860–921.

Mokone, G. G., Schwellnus, M. P., Noakes, T. D., & Collins, M. (2006). The COL5A1 gene and Achilles tendon pathology. *Scandinavian Journal of Medicine and Science in Sport, 16,* 19–26.

Montgomery, H. E., Marshall, R. Hemingway, H., Myerson, S., Clarkson, P. *et al.* (1998). Human gene for physical performance. *Nature, 393,* 221–22.

Mosher, D. S., Quignon, P., Bustamante, C. D., Sutter, N. B., Mellersh, C. S., Parker, H. G. & Ostrander, E. A. (2007). A mutation in the myostatin gene increases muscle mass and enhances racing performance in heterozygote dogs. *PLoS Genetics, 3,* 779–86.

Pérusse, L., Gagnon, J., Province, M. A., Rao, D. C., Wilmore, J. H., Leon, A. S. *et al.* (2001). Familial aggregation of submaximal aerobic performance in the HERITAGE Family Study. *Medicine & Science in Sports and Exercise, 33,* 597–604.

Posthumus, M., September, A. V., Keegan, M., O'Cuinneagain, D., Van der Merwe, W., Schwellnus, M. P., & Collins, M. (2009). Genetic risk factors for anterior cruciate ligament ruptures: COL1A1 gene variant. *British Journal of Sports Medicine, 43,* 352–56.

Rice, T., Despres, J. P., Pérusse, L., Hong, Y., Province, M. A., Bergeron, J. *et al.* (2002). Fimilial aggregation of blood lipid response to exercise training in the health, risk factors, exercise training and genetics (HERITAGE) Family Study. *Circulation, 105,* 1904–8.

Roseboom, T., de Rooij, S. & Painter, R. (2006). The Dutch famine and its long-term consequences for adult health. *Early Human Development, 82,* 485–91.

Ruiz, J. R., Gómez-Gallego, F., Santiago, C., González-Freire, M., Verde, Z. *et al.* (2009). Is there an optimal endurance polygenic profile? *Journal of Physiology, 587,* 1527–34.

Schuelke, M., Wagner, K. R., Stolz, L. E., Hübner, C., Riebel, T. *et al.* (2004). Myostatin mutation associated with gross muscle hypertrophy in a child. *New England Journal of Medicine, 350,* 2682–88.

Segal, N. (2007). *Indivisible by two: Lives of extraordinary twins.* Boston, MA: Harvard University Press.

Tellegen, A., Lykken, D. T., Bouchard, Jr. T. J., Wilcox, K. J., Segal, N. L., & Rich, S. (1988). Personality similarities in twins reared apart and together. *Journal of Personality and Social Psychology, 54,* 1031–39.

Timmons, J. A., Knudsen, S., Rankinen, T., Koch, L. G., Sarzynski, M. *et al.* (2010). Using molecular classification to predict gains in maximal aerobic capacity following endurance exercise training in humans. *Journal of Applied Physiology, 108,* 1487–96.

Venter, J. C., Adams, M. D., Myers, E. W., Li, P. W., Mural, R. J. *et al.* (2001). The sequence of the human genome. *Science, 291,* 1304–51.

Wattie, N., Ardern, C. I., & Baker, J. (2008). Season of birth and the prevalence of overweight and obesity in Canada. *Early Human Development, 84,* 539–47.

Williams, A. G. & Folland, J. P. (2008). Similarity of polygenic profiles limits the potential for elite human physical performance. *Journal of Physiology, 586,* 113–21.

Williams, A. G. & Wackerhage, H. (2009). Genetic testing of athletes. In M. Collins (Ed.). *Genetics and sports* (pp. 176–86). Basel: Karger.

Woods, D. (2009). Angiotensin-converting enzyme, renin-angiotensin system and human performance. In M. Collins (Ed.). *Genetics and sports* (pp. 72–87). Basel: Karger.

3

BUILDING TALENT DEVELOPMENT SYSTEMS ON MECHANISTIC PRINCIPLES

Making them better at what makes them good

Áine MacNamara and Dave Collins

Given the low predictive value of talent identification models (Abbott & Collins, 2002; Martindale, Collins, & Daubney, 2005), it seems more sensible to consider the range of factors that underpin the capacity of a young athlete to realize their potential, rather than focus on those 'snapshot' characteristics hinting at unrealized capacity. Unfortunately, talent identification and development (TID) programs often ignore those very factors that may form the mechanisms for achieving success. The dearth in understanding and employment of key psychological characteristics is in stark contrast to the large body of literature examining the physical and anthropometric factors that contribute to elite performance (e.g., Nieuwenhuis, Spamer, & van Rossum, 2002; Pitsiladis & Scott, 2005; Yang *et al.*, 2003), a bias driven perhaps by inbuilt preference for 'harder', more (apparently) objective measures and the universal attraction of an objective measure based predictive test – the 'Holy Grail' of TID. Consequently, in order to optimize TID initiatives in sport, empirical research must be undertaken that provides evidence of the mechanisms that underpin progression and transfer in and between sporting activities, rather than performance when the snapshot is taken. Accordingly, this chapter is concerned with ensuring that aspiring elites have the best chance of becoming successful by equipping them with the psychological skills identified as prerequisites for learning and development, as well as eventual performance at the top level. This focus on empirical evidence and mechanistic approaches to talent development should increase the effectiveness of TID models, since crucial variables that contribute towards the fulfillment of potential are not ignored and scarce financial resources are not (mis)invested in a select few who may not develop into mature, elite performers.

Identifying mental skills and behaviors

For those already at the top, there is an abundance of literature highlighting the central role that psycho-behavioral factors play in elite performance (e.g., Ericsson & Charness, 1994, Durand-Bush & Salmela, 2002; Lens & Rand, 2000; Moore, Collins, Burwitz, & Jess, 1998). For instance, an array of psychological precursors (e.g., high level of commitment, long- and short-term goals, effective and appropriate imagery usage, focus, pre- and in-competition planning) have been found to distinguish successful performers from their less successful counterparts (Orlick & Partington, 1998). Supporting these findings, Gould and his colleagues (Gould, Damarjian, & Medbery, 1999) observed that successful Olympic athletes were more committed and focused, and engaged in more extensive mental preparation than less successful performers. Less successful athletes were not as effective in their planning and experienced problems related to focus and commitment. Further support for the role of psychological factors as key features of performance comes from Durand-Bush and Salmela's work (2002) with Olympic and world champions, which identified self-confidence and motivation as salient personal characteristics of elite athletes. Not only were these athletes confident about their ability to succeed, they were also motivated to invest considerable time and effort into training in order to be the best they could be. In addition, these elite athletes employed imagery and self-talk to both prepare for competition and to remain focused during high-level performances. Reflecting this literature, Kane stated that:

> The ultimate factors accounting for achievement are likely to be the unique personal and behavioral dispositions, which the individual brings to the actual performance.
>
> *(1986, p. 191)*

Recognizing the importance of psycho-behavioral characteristics should logically lead to a greater emphasis on the factors that propel development, and less emphasis (certainly during the early years) on physique and performance, a view supported by an increasing body of literature (e.g., Abbott & Collins, 2004). Reflecting the importance of psychological factors at elite levels of performance, the following section considers the literature that suggests psycho-behavioral factors facilitate the learning and development process in sport.

Negotiating the pathway to excellence

Various models of talent development are available in the literature (e.g., Bloom, 1985; Côté & Hay, 2002) that describe the various stages of development an athlete may progress through in order to reach an elite level. Recent research, however, has questioned the linear processes described by Côté and Bloom by suggesting that progression through these stages is both idiosyncratic and culturally mediated (Bailey *et al.*, 2010). In a similar finding to that of Ollis, MacPherson, and Collins (2006), and MacNamara *et al.* (2010a; 2010b), Toms (2005) demonstrated that the 'real world' experiences of young athletes did not follow a linear trajectory. Toms' (2005) study of young cricketers' socialization into their sport found that initial involvement in their sports club was contingent on positive socially mediated episodes, psycho-logical support, and motivation, as well as physical ability. This understanding is especially important as the pathway to excellence is usually complex, and the aspiring elite must optimize development opportunities (e.g., first-time appearances at a new level of competition), adapt to set backs (e.g., injury) and effectively negotiate transitions (e.g., selection onto teams) if they are to realize their potential. Without the psycho-behavioral characteristics to successfully deal with these developments, talent may well end up as unfulfilled potential.

Psychological characteristics of developing excellence

Lohman (1999) argues that the 'real crime of our educational system is not that it bores bright children, but that it does not teach them to cope with challenges' (p. 13). A similar case could be made in regard to talent development processes in sport. For example, Freeman (2001) suggests that those who achieve the greatest success in sport consistently employ psychological behaviours that optimize learning and focus. In contrast, underachievers often have unrealistic expectations, lower aspiration, and less persistence. Abbott and Collins (2004) suggest that these factors could be improved by employing a combination of effective psychological strategies such as goal setting, planning, and performance evaluation. In light of this, talent development processes must encourage young athletes to develop the skills and volitional control to maintain their involvement in the face of challenge and negative affect (Lohman, 1999). This contention is an important one, and is entirely consistent with other research that has established the effectiveness of employing psychological skills (e.g., goal setting and imagery) when learning a sports skill (e.g., Waskiewicz & Zajac, 2001), dealing with difficult times (e.g., overcoming an injury; Rose & Jevne, 1993), and competing at major events (Gould, Finch, & Jackson, 1993).

Fortunately, the need to consider the multiple components that facilitate the effective evolution of potential into achievement is gaining momentum in the literature (Abbott & Collins, 2004; Abbott, Collins, Sowerby, & Martindale, 2007; Bailey & Morley, 2006; MacNamara *et al.*, 2010a, 2010b). Interestingly, given the comparatively recent recognition of these ideas, they are hardly new. Abbott and colleagues' initial exposition (e.g., Abbott & Collins, 2002) drew directly on ideas expressed in 1971 (Kunst & Florescu, 1971; see also Tebbenham, Moore, Collins, Burwitz, Abbott, & Arnold, 1999). In a similar vein, Noble and colleagues (Noble, Subnotnik, & Arnold, 1996) suggested that these individual traits and characteristics, along with natural abilities, affect the manner in which aspiring elites interact with their environment, the talent domain, and the opportunities that are presented to them. An individual's reaction to these critical episodes – the manner in which individuals interpreted distinct incidents or more chronic experiences as facilitators and debilitators – will ultimately influence the trajectory of their developmental pathway (Ollis *et al.*, 2006). In short, these ideas are well founded both historically and across the literature.

In operationalizing these approaches, MacNamara *et al.*'s (2010a; 2010b) retrospective studies of elite sport performers identified a range of psychological factors that aided the realization of potential. They found that learning strategies, and particularly the employment of specific psychological behaviors (e.g., goal setting, planning, and realistic performance evaluation), helped athletes benefit maximally from practice and development opportunities. MacNamara *et al.* (2010a) termed these psycho-behavioral characteristics *Psychological Characteristics of Developing Excellence* (PCDEs), a term encompassing both the trait characteristics (the tendency to . . .) and the state-deployed skills (the ability to . . . when . . .) shown to play a crucial role in the realization of potential. Interestingly, PCDEs were not just mental skills such as imagery or goal setting but also included attitudes, emotions, and desires such as commitment and motivation. Accordingly, possession and systematic development of PCDEs seems a logical step, allowing young athletes to interact effectively with the developmental opportunities they are afforded (Côté & Hay, 2002; Simonton, 1999; van Yperen, 2009). Of course, equipping young athletes with these developmental skills will not necessarily guarantee high-level perfor-mance since a wide range of other variables influence the likelihood of reaching the top. However, it will provide aspiring elites with the capacity and competencies to strive to reach their potential; to 'be all that they can be' as the adverts put it! Notably, this 'striving' approach will also make a significant contribution to achievement in other domains, thereby providing sport with a genuinely educational agenda (see comments later in this chapter).

Of course, given the demonstrable need to invest considerable time into one's activity (cf. Dweck, 2008), it is not surprising that attitudes and behaviours facili-tative of deliberate practice are associated with effective development (Bailey & Morley, 2006). Determination and persistence (Bloom, 1985; Renzulli, 1986), self-efficacy (Johnson *et al.*, 2005), and autonomy (Schoon, 2000) have all been highlighted as necessary characteristics for the attainment of excellence. This claim is further supported by van Yperen's (2009) prospective study that identified psychological factors as a significant predictor of career success among male soccer players. Jones and Lavallee (2008) also propose that a range of life skills, defined as the transferable skills needed for everyday life, help people thrive in their chosen domain. This study found that adolescent athletes needed interpersonal (e.g., social skills, leadership, communication skills) and personal skills (e.g., self-organization, discipline, goal-setting) to maximize their potential in achievement domains. Research also suggests that a similar set of psychological characteristics act as transition mechanisms to guide athletes into effective and stable levels of performance (Abbott & Collins, 2004; Rose & Jevne, 1993).

The clear message here is that psychological factors play a central role in the effective evolution of potential into achievement. In fact, Abbott and colleagues (Abbott, Collins, Martindale, & Sowerby, 2002) posit that the relationship between psychological characteristics and performance might even be causative. Of course, the extent to which psychological factors are truly causal of success is difficult to determine, though their role in facilitating development is supported by a range of prospective (van Yperen, 2009), retrospective (Abbott & Collins, 2004; MacNamara et al., 2010a, 2010b), and longitudinal (MacNamara & Collins, 2010; Perleth & Heller, 1994) studies.

This burgeoning body of research suggests that PCDEs equip aspiring elites with the necessary skills to cope with the inevitable challenges of the development pathway (e.g. increased deliberate practice), as well as underpinning their capacity to make the most of their innate abilities and opportunities. For example, Abbott et al. (2007) offer the example of a lack of mental focus (Gould, Dieffenbach, & Moffett, 2002) as a factor that might hinder the development of a young, but otherwise 'talented' athlete. In fact, Abbott et al. question whether, in the absence of such a key characteristic as a positive work ethic, such an individual should be considered talented at all. Certainly, the subsequent development and deployment of this characteristic can result in unexpected and non-linear changes in development and performance (Abbott et al., 2002) reflecting a more accurate, 'dynamic conception' of talent. Simonton (1999) offers further support for this and proposes that talent is not a static entity but emerges over time both endogenously and in reaction to environmental factors (Simonton, 2001). Simonton's model of talent development accounts for the multiple factors that influence talent and suggests that these factors (e.g., innate ability, environmental factors, motivation, and learning strategies) interact in a multiplicative manner. Even if a young athlete has the physical attributes to succeed in sport, their potential to develop is also dependent on other determinants of success such as commitment, motivation, and the availability of developmental opportunities (Abbott & Collins, 2004; Baker & Horton, 2004).

Generic or specific skills – examining environmental and stage related differences

It would be naive to ignore context-specific differences that undeniably exist across performance domains. Such differences notwithstanding, a number of researchers have identified several generic features of the talent development process (Martindale et al., 2005; MacNamara et al., 2010b). For example, there is significant evidence to suggest that the same psychological characteristics are important regardless of performance domain (Gould et al., 2002; Jones, 2002). As such, TID processes that promote PCDEs not only encourage and facilitate athletes to achieve their potential in their current performance domain but also allow for the 'cross fertilization' of talent into other domains at later stages of development (Moore et al., 1998 and more recent talent transfer approaches). Even if an athlete does not change domain, PCDEs will help them adapt their performance to the different situations and contexts inherent in their activity (Abbott & Collins, 2004) and the broad range of 'other stuff' challenges (such as the 'joys' of an adolescent lifestyle), which can be equally powerful derailers.

The long-term health benefits of promoting and developing PCDEs in children are equally significant. The PCDEs that underpin development in achievement domains also seem to be the same psychological characteristics that promote uptake of, and adherence to, a physically active lifestyle. Thus, these psychological factors influence an individual's capacity to be physically active and underpin the competence and determination to make appropriate health and exercise choices; the operational mechanism of these factors may well be evidenced by the examination of other 'bridging' constructs such as self-determination (Wang & Biddle, 2007) or self-regulation (considered in the next section). Thus, the systematic development of PCDEs offers significant broader benefit, given for example the growing physical inactivity levels of youth and the health risks associated with this inactivity. In short, from both performance and educational perspectives, there appears to be substantial benefit from the systematic development and facilitated deployment of these generic skills.

However, it seems highly likely that the deployment of PCDEs may be complicated by the dynamic, individualized, and complex nature of the pathway to excellence (Abbott et al., 2005). A key finding of MacNamara et al.'s studies (2010a, 2010b) concerned the differential deployment of PCDEs relative to the individual's age, focus, stage of development/level of maturation, and performance domain. Simply put, the behavioral component of the PCDE may look different *depending on* the challenges faced by the individual at that particular point in their development. As such, it is important to recognize that young athletes will interpret PCDEs differently to their adult counterparts (Abbott & Collins, 2004). Illustrating this, there appears to be an understandable and necessary shift in responsibility from significant others (e.g., parents, teachers, coaches) promoting and reinforcing PCDEs in the early years, towards self-initiated and autonomous behaviours as athletes develop. At one end of the continuum, significant others use various means of reinforcement to regulate the actions of the performers. For example, coaches, teachers, and parents are largely responsible for young athletes' early motivation to practise and compete in their activity. As performers progress towards elite status, however, there is (or at least, should be) less emphasis on reinforcement from others and elite athletes are required to self-regulate their behaviour to a much larger extent. This shift in responsibility is important given that, at an elite level, responsibility for generating and maintaining motivation rests with the performers and not with the coach or parent (Young & Medic, 2008).

Moving towards self-regulation

Essentially, the differential deployment of PCDEs can be understood from a self-regulation perspective (Karoly, 1993). Self-regulated learners have the skills to self-monitor their progress, manage their emotions, focus on self-improvement, and seek help and support from others when necessary (Petlichkoff, 2004). Conversely, performers without these skills do not take personal responsibility for their own development but instead rely on others and attribute failures to maladaptive reasons.

Both these standpoints find interesting partial resonance in the ideas of Dweck's 'Growth Mindset'. Dweck (2008) identified two sets of beliefs that people have about their own intelligence, and suggested that these implicit beliefs provide a perspective that influences each individual's view of the world (Dweck, 1986). Individuals hold either an entity theory of intelligence (termed a fixed mindset) or an incremental theory of intelligence (termed a growth mindset). Research has repeatedly shown that a growth mindset fosters positive attitudes towards practice and learning, leads to a hunger for feedback, and a greater ability to deal with setbacks (Dweck, 2008). Critically, given the demands of high-level participation in any domain, a self-regulated athlete who possesses a growth mindset has the ability to initiate and persist at tasks that are not inherently motivating or interesting, though nonetheless important for development.

The ability to effectively cope with the stressors of development and adapt to the challenges faced, specifically increased autonomy and responsibility over one's development, is a key component of successful development (Côté & Hay, 2002). Exploring such challenges, Jonker and colleagues (Jonker, Elferink-Gemser, & Visscher, 2010) highlight the importance of reflection as a self-regulative skill and further propose that a sophisticated sense of self-reflection should help talented athletes acquire and consolidate the required knowledge, skills, and experiences during their 'development' years that can subsequently aid their progression to elite levels of performance. The self-reflection process is seen as an important component of both effective talent (cf. MacNamara & Collins, 2010) and talent development environments (Martindale et al., 2005). Reflecting these contentions, it may be that PCDEs represent the ways in which constructs such as the growth mindset are realized. If so, and once again, explicit development is to be strongly recommended.

Given that expertise involves the accumulation of years of deliberate practice, sacrifices, and effort, Holt and Dunn's (2004) suggestion that youth soccer players who develop discipline, commitment, resilience, and social support are more likely to successfully transition to professional adult soccer is hardly surprising (cf. van Yperen, 2009). What is interesting though is Holt and Mitchell's (2006) later finding that youth soccer players who failed to make the transition to professional soccer lacked volitional behaviour and the self-determination to succeed. This finding corroborates Toering and colleagues' (Toering, Elferink-Gemser, Jordet, & Visscher, 2009) proposition that self-regulative strategies distinguish youth players who successfully transition to elite sport and those who do not. The former group appear to have developed self-regulative strategies that enable them to reflect effectively on the learning process and thus learn more efficiently than their less successful peers (Jonker et al., 2010). Self-regulation involves processes that enable individuals to control their thoughts, feelings, and actions and consists of aspects of planning, self-monitoring, evaluation, reflection, effort, and self-efficacy (Baumeister & Vohs, 2004). Zimmerman (2000) describes self-regulation as the extent to which individuals are meta-cognitively, motivationally, and behaviourally proactive participants in their own learning process. In fact, the process of learning how to cope independently is one of the main developmental tasks of adolescence. Reinforcing the importance of self-regulatory processes, Anshel and Porter (1996) suggest that athletes who fail to self-regulate are less likely to achieve elite status or perform to their potential.

In sum, self-regulation appears to be the strategy of choice in terms of development in sport. When athletes self-regulate, they take responsibility for their own learning, display self-discipline, commitment, and resilience, and seek social support when necessary (cf. Ommundsen & Lemyre, 2007; Toering et al., 2009; Zimmerman, 2000). The ability to maximize developmental opportunities is underpinned by this transition to self-regulation, illustrated by athletes' ability to plan how they want to improve (Glaser & Chi, 1988), reflect on differences between where they are and where they want to get to (Chen & Singer, 1992), and remain motivated and focused on long-term development (Martindale, Collins & Daubney, 2005). Given that self-regulation appears to be an important factor in development, coaches and talent development programs must consider how they can encourage aspiring elites to gain self-control over their thoughts, feelings, and actions (Baumeister & Vohs, 2004). For example, coaches should encourage athletes to plan, self-monitor, and self-evaluate rather than exerting external control over these processes by telling athletes what they should work on (Toering et al., 2009). In essence, and reflecting the differential deployment of PCDEs described previously, a shift in the source of regulation (Cleary & Zimmerman, 2001), or what Glasser (1996) describes as a 'change of agency' from coach to athlete is required.

Promoting PCDEs in talent development environments

Although psychological skills training is often included in support programs aimed at elite performers, we contend that a more effective approach is to systematically incorporate these skills into talent development processes, with a specific contextual orientation to imminent events. Such a periodized emphasis will be different to the usual focus on peaking towards competition but, we suggest, more appropriate and effective for the most important issue, namely the young athletes' progression in their activity. Anticipating developmental challenges and providing opportunities to develop and refine the PCDEs to overcome them in advance (and providing remedial steps as necessary) would seem to hold considerably more promise, in terms of talent development and retention, than trying to address these issues mid-crisis. It also provides a perfect 'learning environment' in that developing performers can hone their skills on meaningful and personally relevant real-life challenges rather than in the public glare of competition with its associated 'stick' (e.g. social stigma, ego challenge) for all but the most perfect outcomes. Finally, teaching such generic skills a priori may aid the transition of athletes 'cut' from elite sport pathways, facilitating talent transfer (Vaeyens et al., 2008) or life after sport (Alfermann & Stambulova, 2007; Sinclair & Orlick, 1993). As such, further investigation of these factors is useful from both a specific (this sport) and generic (ability to transfer to other activities) performance perspective, together with a much broader educational agenda encompassing achievement after sport and lifelong physical activity participation (Bailey et al., 2010).

The importance of exposing young athletes to specialized coaching to accelerate their progress is well documented. Traditionally this has been dominated by physical, technical, and tactical approaches to training. Interestingly, however, several investigations have also examined how coaches and teachers can also develop mental skills and characteristics in young athletes (e.g., Gilbert, Cote, & Mallet, 2006; McCallister, Blinde, & Weiss, 2000), albeit with mixed results. Such outcomes are hardly surprising, however, and certainly do not question the veracity of the objectives or processes involved. For example, although the coaches in these studies valued psychological and mental skills, and attempted to teach these skills to their athletes, this was not always conducted in a systematic or intentional manner. Furthermore, the skill level of the coach mediated the ease with which these psychological skills were taught. Skilled coaches typically use a variety of well-thought-out and articulated strategies (e.g., team meetings, modelling behaviour, feedback) to teach psychological skills (Gilbert et al., 2001). Conversely, less skilled coaches taught psychological skills in an ad-hoc manner. Aspiring elites would benefit from coaches who carefully consider and prioritize PCDEs as part of their educational focus. Instead of the traditional focus on environmental (e.g., early specialization, enrichment programs), physical, and/or anthropometric factors, TID models should consider, monitor, and develop all the components that interact to determine an individual's capacity to develop.

There are examples in the literature of how effective development environments promote and reinforce the appropriate deployment of PCDEs as part of their holistic approach to development (MacNamara et al., 2010a, 2010b; Martindale et al., 2005). For example, the ability to engage in quality practice has been shown to be a requisite of effective development. The coaches in MacNamara et al.'s (2010b) study encouraged this behaviour by clearly explaining the purpose of the training and checking this understanding through questioning and probing. The coach reinforced the desired behavior (i.e., the ability to engage in quality practice) as part of his/her holistic educational focus. In line with evidence elsewhere in the literature, the coaches in this study employed strategies including setting clear standards and expectations (Gould et al., 2002), providing encouragement and support (Martindale et al., 2005), emphasizing effort and persistence as hallmarks of excellence (Martindale et al., 2005), modelling positive behaviours (Gould, Collins, Lauer, & Chung 2007), and providing social support (Connaughton, Wadey, Hanton, & Jones, 2008; Wolfenden & Holt, 2005). The coaches employed these strategies to create learning climates through which the aspiring elites acquired and refined the PCDEs pertinent to their development in sport (Subotnik & Knotek, 2007). This strategy is characteristic of award winning coaches' perspectives on the development of psycho-behavioral skills (Gould et al., 2007). Reflecting this, Seligman and co-authors (Seligman, Steen, Park, & Peterson, 2005) suggest that it is important to foster challenging, sustainable, and nurturing climates that enhance the development of these emerging psycho-behavioural skills.

Conclusion

This chapter argues for the role of psychology as the most influential factor in the development process (Abbott & Collins, 2004). Since this development process is non-linear, complex, and dynamic, it is vital that aspiring elites are provided with the skills needed to negotiate their own, highly individualistic pathways to excellence (Abbott *et al.*, 2005; MacNamara & Collins, 2010). Readers are referred to Abbott *et al.*'s technical report (2007) or MacNamara (2011) for examples of how these PCDEs may be operationalized and developed.

Finally, we should acknowledge that there are several emerging and parallel evolutions of similar ideas, focused on the development of young athlete characteristics that can facilitate progress up the performance ladder; for example, much of the work on the somewhat 'amorphous construct' of mental toughness. In this chapter, we have largely 'kept to our own', offering an emphasis on PCDEs against a large and varied literature of supporting ideas. We hope that this conscious decision to stay away from the different 'brand names', in an attempt to maintain clarity and enhance applicability, has not detracted from the overall message.

References

Abbott, A., & Collins, D. (2002). A theoretical and empirical analysis of a 'state of the art' talent identification model. *High Ability Studies*, *13*, 157–78.

—— (2004). Eliminating the dichotomy between theory and practice in talent identification and development: Considering the role of psychology. *Journal of Sports Sciences*, *22*, 395–408.

Abbott, A., Button, C., Pepping, G., & Collins, D. (2005). Unnatural selection: Talent identification and development in sport. *Nonlinear Dynamics, Psychology and Life Science*, *9*, 61–88.

Abbott, A., Collins, D., Martindale, R., & Sowerby, K. (2002) *Talent identification and development: An academic review*. Edinburgh: Sport Scotland.

Abbott, A., Collins, D., Sowerby, K., & Martindale, R. (2007). *Developing the potential of young people in sport*. A report for Sportscotland by University of Edinburgh.

Alfermann, D., & Stambulova, N. (2007). Career transitions and career termination. In G. Tenenbaum & R. C. Eklund (Eds), *Handbook of sport psychology* (3rd edn, pp. 712–36). New York: Wiley.

Anshel, M. H., & Porter, A. (1996). Examining the self-regulatory cognitive and behavioural strategies of elite and non-elite male and female swimmers. *International Journal of Sport Psychology*, *27*, 321–36.

Bailey, R., Collins, D., Ford, P., Pearce, G., MacNamara, A., & Toms, M. (2010). *Participant development in sport: An academic review*. A research report commissioned by SportCoach UK.

Bailey, R., & Morley, D. (2006). Towards a model of talent development in physical education. *Sport, Education and Society*, *11*, 211–30.

Baker, J., & Horton, S. (2004). A review of primary and secondary influences on sport expertise. *High Ability Studies*, *15*, 211–28.

Baumeister, R. F., & Vohs, K. D. (2004). *Handbook of self-regulation: Research, theory, and applications*. New York: Guilford Press

Bloom, B. S. (Ed.) (1985). *Developing talent in young people*. New York: Ballantine Books.

Chen, D., & Singer, R. N. (1992). Self-regulation and cognitive strategies in sport participation. *International Journal of Sport Psychology, 23*, 277–300.

Cleary, T. J., & Zimmerman, B. J. (2001). Self-regulation differences during athletic practice by experts, non-experts, and novices. *Journal of Applied Sport Psychology, 13*, 61–82.

Connaughton, D., Wadey, R., Hanton, S., & Jones, G. (2008). The development and maintenance of mental toughness: Perceptions of elite performers. *Journal of Sport Sciences, 26*, 83–95.

Côté, J., & Hay, J. (2002). Children's involvement in sport: A developmental perspective. In J.M. Silva & D.E. Stevens (Eds) *Psychological foundations of sport* (pp. 484–502). Boston: Allyn & Bacon.

Durand-Bush, N., & Salmela, J.H. (2002). The development and maintenance of expert athletic performance: Perceptions of world and Olympic champions. *Journal of Applied Sport Psychology, 14*, 154–71.

Dweck, C. S. (1986) Motivational processes affecting learning. *American Psychologist, 41*, 1040–48.

—— (2008). *Mindset: The new psychology of success*. New York: Ballantine Books.

Ericsson, K. A., & Charness, N. (1994). Expert performance: Its structure and acquisition. *American Psychologist, 49*, 725–47.

Freeman, J. (2001). *Gifted children grown up*. London: David Fulton Publishers.

Gilbert, W., Côté, J., & Mallett, C. (2006). Developmental paths and activities of successful sport coaches. *International Journal of Sports Science and Coaching, 1*, 69–76.

Gilbert, W. D., Gilbert, J. N., & Trudel, P. (2001). Coaching strategies for youth sports. Part 1: Athlete behavior and athlete performance. *Journal of Physical Education, Recreation and Dance, 72*, 29–33.

Glaser, R. & Chi, M. (1988). Overview. In M. Chi, R. Glaser, & M. Farr (Eds), *The nature of expertise* (pp. xv–xxvii). Hillsdale, NJ: Erlbaum.

Glasser, R. (1996). Changing the agency for learning: Acquiring expert performance. In Ericsson, K. A. (Ed.) *The road to excellence: The acquisition of expert performance in the arts & sciences, sports and games*. Mahwah, NJ: Erlbaum

Gould, D., Collins, K., Lauer, L., & Chung, Y. (2007). Coaching life skills through football: A study of award winning high school coaches. *Journal of Applied Sport Psychology, 19*, 16–37.

Gould, D., Damarjian, N., & Medbery, R. (1999). An examination of mental skills training in junior tennis coaches. *Sport Psychologist, 13*, 127–43.

Gould, D., Dieffenbach, K., & Moffett, A. (2002). Psychological characteristics and their development in Olympic Champions. *Journal of Applied Sport Psychology, 14*, 172–204.

Gould, D., Finch, L., & Jackson, S. (1993). Coping strategies used by national figure skating champions. *Research Quarterly for Exercise and Sport, 64*, 453–68.

Holt, N., & Dunn, J. (2004). Toward a grounded theory of the psychosocial competencies and environmental conditions associated with soccer success. *Journal of Applied Sport Psychology, 16*, 199–219.

Holt, N. L., & Mitchell. T. (2006). Talent development in English professional soccer. *International Journal of Sport Psychology, 37*, 77–98.

Johnson, M. B., Tenenbaum, G., Edmonds, W. A., & Castillo, Y. (2008). A comparison of the developmental experiences of elite and sub-elite swimmers: similar developmental histories can lead to differences in performance level, *Sport, Education and Society, 13*, 453–75.

Jones, G. (2002). Performance excellence: A personal perspective on the link between sport and business. *Journal of Applied Sport Psychology, 14*, 268–81.

Jones, M. I., & Lavallee, D. (2008). Character development and sportsmanship. In D. Lavallee, M. J. Jones, & J. M. Williams (Eds), *Key studies in sport and exercise psychology* (pp 245–57). Columbus, OH: McGraw-Hill.

Jonker, L., Elferink-Gemser, M., & Visscher, C. (2010). Differences in self-regulatory skills among talented athletes: The significance of competitive level and type of sport. *Journal of Sports Sciences, 28*, 901–08

Kane, J. E. (1986). Giftedness in sport. In G. Gleeson (Ed.), *The growing child in competitive sport*. London: Hodder and Stoughton.

Karoly, P. (1993). Mechanisms of self-regulation: A systems view. *Annual Review of Psychology, 44*, 23–52.

Kunst, G. & Florescu, C. (1971). *The main factors for performance in wrestling*. Bucharest: National Sports Council.

Lens, W., & Rand, P. (2000). Motivation and cognition: Their role in the development of giftedness. In K. A. Heller, F. J. Mönks, R. J. Sternberg & R. F. Subotnik, (Eds), *International handbook of giftedness and talent*, (pp. 193–202). London, UK: Elsevier.

Lohman, D. F. (1999). Developing academic talent: The roles of experience, mentoring, motivation, and volition. In N. Colangelo & S. Assouline (Eds), *Talent Development III: Proceedings from the 1995 Henry B. & Jocelyn Wallace National Research Symposium on talent development* (pp. 315–27). Scottsdale, AZ: Gifted Psychology Press.

Martindale, R., Collins, D., & Daubney, J. (2005). Talent development: A guide for practice and research within sport. *Quest, 57*, 353–75.

MacNamara, Á. (2011). Psychological characteristics of developing excellence. In D. Collins, A. Abbott, & H. Richards (Eds), *Performance psychology for physical challenge*, (pp. 43–60) London: Elsevier.

MacNamara, Á. & Collins, D. (2010). The role of psychological characteristics in managing the transition to university. *Psychology of Sport and Exercise, 11*, 353–62

MacNamara, Á., Button, A., & Collins, D. (2010a). The role of psychological characteristics in facilitating the pathway to elite performance. Part 1: Identifying mental skills and behaviours. *The Sport Psychologist, 24*, 52–73.

—— (2010b). The role of psychological characteristics in facilitating the pathway to elite performance. Part 2: Examining environmental and stage related differences in skills and behaviours. *The Sport Psychologist*, 24, 74–96.

McCallister, S., Blinde, E., & Weiss, W. (2000). Teaching values and implementing philosophies: Dilemmas of the youth sport coach. *International Sport Journal, 4*, 9–26.

Moore, P., Collins, D. J., Burwitz, L., & Jess, M. (1998). *The development of talent study (DOTS)*. London: English Sports Council.

Nieuwenhuis, C. W., Spamer, E. J., & van Rossum, J. H. A. (2002). A prediction function for identifying talent in 14 to 15-year old female field hockey players. *High Ability Studies, 13*, 21–33.

Noble, K. D., Subotnik, R. F., & Arnold, K. D. (1996). A new model for adult female talent development: A synthesis of perspectives from remarkable women. In K. D. Arnold, K. D. Noble, & R. F. Subotnik (Eds), *Remarkable women: Perspectives on female talent development* (pp. 427–39). Cresskill, NJ: Hampton Press.

Ollis, S., MacPherson, A., & Collins, D. (2006). Expertise and talent development in rugby refereeing: an ethnographic enquiry. *Journal of Sports Sciences, 24*, 309–22.

Ommundsen, Y, & Lemyre, P. N. (2007). Self-regulation and strategic learning: The role of motivational beliefs and the learning environment in physical education. In J. Liukkonen, Y. Auweele, D. Alfermann, B. Vereijken, & Y. Theodorakis (Eds), *Psychology for physical educators: Student in focus* (pp. 141–73). Champaign, IL: Human Kinetics.

Orlick, T. & Partington, J. (1998). Mental links to excellence. *The Sport Psychologist*, *2*, 105–30.

Perleth, C., & Heller, K. A. (1994). The Munich longitudinal study of giftedness. In R. F. Subotnik & K. D. Arnold (Eds), *Beyond Terman: Contemporary longitudinal studies of giftedness and talent* (pp. 77–114). Norwood, NJ: Ablex Publishing.

Petlichkoff, L. (2004). Self-regulation skills in children and adolescents. In M. Weiss (Ed.), *Developmental sport and exercise psychology: A lifespan perspective* (pp. 273–92). Morgantown, WV: Fitness Information Technology.

Pitsiladis, Y., & Scott, R. (2005). The makings of the perfect athlete. *The Lancet*, *366*, S16-S17.

Renzulli, J. S. (1986). The three-ring conception of giftedness: A developmental model for creative productivity. In R. Sternberg & J. Davidson (Eds), *Conceptions of giftedness*, (pp. 53–92). New York: Cambridge University Press.

Rose, J., & Jevne, R. F. J. (1993). Psychosocial processes associated with athletic injuries. *The Sport Psychologist*, *7*, 309–28.

Schoon, I. (2000). A life span approach to talent development. In K. Heller, F. Mönks, R. Sternberg & R. Subotnik (Eds), *International handbook of giftedness and talent*, (2nd ed., pp 213–25). Oxford: Elsevier.

Seligman, M. E. P, Steen, T., Park, N., & Peterson, C. (2005). Positive psychology progress: Empirical validation of interventions. *American Psychologist, 60*, 410–21.

Simonton, D. (1999). Talent and its development: An emergenic and epigenetic model. *Psychological Review*, *106*, 435–57.

Simonton, D. K. (2001). Talent development as a multidimensional, multiplicative, and dynamic process. *Current Directions in Psychological Science*, *10*, 39–43.

Sinclair, D. A., & Orlick, T. (1993). Positive transitions from high-performance sport. *The Sport Psychologist*, *7*, 138–50.

Subotnik, R. F., & Knotek, S. (2007). A positive psychology approach to developing talent and preventing talent loss in the arts and sciences. In R.Gilman, E. S. Hueber, & M (Eds), *Handbook of positive psychology in schools*. (pp 433 – 446) New York: Routledge.

Tebbenham, D., Moore, P., Collins, D., Burwitz, L., Abbott, A., & Arnold, J. (1999). The developmental nature of supporting talent: Transitional experiences of British performers. *Journal of Sports Sciences*, *16*, 93.

Toering, T. T., Elferink-Gemser, M. T., Jordet, G., & Visscher, C. (2009). Self-regulation and performance on elite and non-elite youth soccer players. *Journal of Sports Sciences*, *27*, 1509–17.

Toms, M. (2005). *The developmental socialisation of young people in club sport: An ethnographic account*. Unpublished PhD Thesis, Loughborough University.

Vaeyens, R., Lenoir, M., Williams, A. M., Philippaerts, R. (2008). Talent identification and development programmes in sport: Current models and future directions. *Sports Medicine*, *38*, 703–14.

van Yperen, N. (2009). Why some make it and others do not: Identifying psychosocial factors that predict career success in professional adult soccer. *The Sport Psychologist*, *23*, 317–29.

Wang, C. K. J., & Biddle, S. J. H. (2007). Understanding young people's motivation toward exercise: An integration of sport ability beliefs, achievement goal theory, and self-determination theory. In M.S. Hagger & N.L.D. Chatzisarantis (Eds), *Intrinsic motivation and self-determination in exercise and sport* (pp. 193–208). Champaign, IL: Human Kinetics.

Waskiewicz, Z., & Zajac, A. (2001). The imagery and motor skills acquisition. *Biology of Sport*, *18*, 71–83.

Whitehead, S. & Biddle, S. J. (2008). Adolescent girls' perceptions of physical activity: A focus group study. *European Physical Education Review*. *4*, 243–62.

Wolfenden, L. E., & Holt, N. L. (2005). Talent development in elite junior tennis: Perceptions of players, parents, and coaches. *Journal of Applied Sport Psychology, 17,* 1–19.

Yang, N., MacArthur, D. G., Gulbin, J. P., Hahn, A. G., Beggs, A. H., Easteal, S., & North, K. (2003). ACTN3 genotype is associated with human elite athletic performance. *American Journal of Human Genetics, 73,* 627–31.

Young, B. W., & Medic, N. (2008). The motivation to become an expert athlete: How coaches can promote long-term commitment. In D. Farrow, J. Baker, & C. MacMahon, (Eds), *Developing sport expertise: Researches and coaches put theory into practice* (pp. 43–59). New York: Routledge.

Zimmerman, B. J. (2000). Attaining self-regulation: A social cognitive perspective. In M.Boekaerts, P. R. Pintrich, & M. Zeidner (Eds), *Handbook of self-regulation* (pp. 13–39). San Diego, CA: Academic Press.

4

ENVIRONMENTAL INFLUENCES ON EARLY DEVELOPMENT IN SPORTS EXPERTS

Sean Horton

One hundred and forty years ago Francis Galton launched the scientific investigation into high achievement (Galton, 1869), and the ensuing debate over the relative contributions of 'nature' and 'nurture' has continued virtually unabated since that time. Galton highlighted three primary components to achieving excellence, namely *innate capacity*, *zeal*, and *the power to work hard*. The preceding chapter focuses on the first of these tenets – innate capacity. This chapter will focus on the latter two – zeal, and the capacity for hard work. In addition to these two important variables, there are a number of other environmental factors that help to shape talent development. Some of these, like access to good coaching, or a supportive family environment, are reasonably obvious. Others, like one's place and date of birth, are less so. As the evidence suggests, however, seemingly innocuous events like the day we were born can have a dramatic effect on our ultimate success.

Training factors – the power to work hard

While Galton conducted some of the earliest investigations into talent and performance, Anders Ericsson is the name most associated with the study of expert performance today. His work has been profiled in a number of recent best-selling books, including Geoff Colvin's *Talent is Over-rated* and Malcolm Gladwell's *Outliers*. Ericsson grew up in post-Second World War Sweden, a country with strong social programs and egalitarian ideals, which influenced his approach to the study of talent (Ericsson, 2007). Ericsson's notions of the importance of 'nurture' over 'nature' were reinforced by his early research. One of his most noteworthy studies examined the memory of a young student, an undergraduate of average intelligence who, within a short period of time, developed a prodigious capacity for remembering numbers (Chase & Ericsson, 1981).

Every day for an hour, this student (referred to as 'SF' in the study) sat in a small office while Ericsson read him lists of numbers – at a rate of one number per second. At the conclusion of each set of numbers SF was required to recite them back in the same sequence. When SF began this task, he was no better than the average person, maxing out at around seven numbers, which is consistent with short-term memory limitations. Two hundred and fifty days, and 250 hours of practice later, SF had progressed to the point where he could remember over 80 numbers. How did he do it? SF was a competitive runner, so he developed a system of grouping the numbers into running times. For example, 20,457 would become 2:04:57 – an excellent time for the marathon. This allowed him to combine individual numbers into much larger chunks, helping him to bypass the limitations of his short-term memory. The fact that SF was able to successfully teach his system to another student – in this case a female runner – helped to convince Ericsson that no special abilities were needed for the development of memory skill. Of particular interest, however, was that SF's skill was specific to numbers; when his memory skills were tested on other items (i.e., words, or individual letters of the alphabet) his memory span reverted to 'normal'.

This phenomenon, where an expert shows a distinct skill advantage in a specific area, but performs very much like an average person when the task is altered slightly, is referred to as 'domain specificity'. Classic experiments with chess players displayed this concept convincingly (e.g., Chase & Simon, 1973). In these experiments, Grandmasters who were given a few seconds to glance at a chessboard in a typical 'mid-game' position were able to reproduce the position on a second board almost in its entirety. If, however, the chess board depicted a random placement of chess pieces, Grandmasters performed no better than beginners.

Perhaps Ericsson's most noteworthy study was an attempt to ascertain how much time it takes to achieve this kind of expertise (Ericsson, Krampe, & Tesch-Römer, 1993). Ericsson and his colleagues examined three separate groups of musicians differentiated by skill level. The top-tier violinists were training for careers as international soloists. The second-tier violinists were training to be professional musicians in orchestras, while the third-tier were preparing to be music teachers. What Ericsson *et al.* discovered was that the skill level of each group corresponded to the number of hours of practice they had put in over the course of their lives. The top-tier violinists had accumulated 10,000 hours of practice by the age of 20, which was 2,000 hours more than the second-tier group and fully twice the number of practice hours compiled by the music teachers. Practicing 10,000 hours to become an expert has proven to be remarkably consistent across a variety of fields, and has become virtually a prescription for achieving excellence.

Importantly, Ericsson notes that the sheer number of hours was not a perfect predictor of expertise. In fact, practice without full concentration might actually impair performance. Therefore, the best gauge of expertise in any field was the number of hours of what he called 'deliberate practice' that have been accumulated. Ericsson *et al.* (1993) defined deliberate practice as activity that required substantial effort, was not inherently enjoyable, was highly relevant to and would result in maximal improvement in performance. In other words, this type of practice is hard. Moreover, Ericsson *et al.* found that engaging in this type of practice could only occur for a limited amount of time per day due to fatigue and burnout considerations.

Ericsson's approach suggests that, in order to acquire 10,000 hours of deliberate practice, focusing on one specific activity from an early age is a distinct advantage. Indeed, there are many examples of eminent performers who practiced copious amounts at a young age and went on to achieve formidable success (e.g., Mozart in music, Tiger Woods in golf), although this type of early specialization has also been linked to potentially negative consequences, including overuse injuries and burnout (Baker, 2003; Wiersma, 2000). A number of researchers (e.g., Côté, Baker, & Abernethy, 2003) have, as a result, advocated a more diversified approach for young athletes. They recommend that children sample a variety of different activities in order to build basic motor skills before specializing in their main sport in their mid-to-late teens. Importantly, Baker and colleagues (Baker, Côté, & Abernethy, 2003) provided evidence of numerous athletes who had sampled many different sports as children and still reached an elite level as adults.

Ten thousand hours is a phenomenal amount of time to spend practising the piano, or swimming laps in a pool, or hitting golf balls on a driving range. To take this out of the realm of the purely abstract, 10,000 hours equates to three hours a day, seven days a week, 365 days a year, for ten years. Sustaining motivation over this length of time becomes a crucial issue, particularly when the kind of effortful, concentrated, deliberate practice that Ericsson describes is not always fun; hence the recommendation that young children sample numerous activities prior to specializing fully in one main endeavour. An intriguing exception to this general recommendation may be child prodigies. Ellen Winner (1996) has studied such children, and she describes one common feature that many of them share – a 'rage to master'. For such children, their desire to master their chosen activity becomes more important than anything else, even things like socializing with friends. This rage to master is what propels them through years of gruelling training. Winner believes that infusing that kind of passion in a child is impossible, that it has to come from within. While you can force a child to work harder, she argues, you cannot instil the passion.

Instructional resources and family support

If we accept that (1) excellence in most endeavours involves an immense investment of one's time, and that (2) simple exposure to the domain is insufficient – practice needs to be highly purposeful and relevant in order for an athlete to make systematic progress – it follows that working with a competent coach who can help design practice sessions becomes an important ingredient to success. In many sports, once an athlete reaches a certain level, a coach often constructs a high percentage – in some cases virtually 100 per cent – of an athlete's practice time. Consequently, the ability of the coach to create an environment that fosters optimal learning becomes one of the most significant keys to athlete development.

There is a huge discrepancy in the way coaches use available practice time. An examination of high-level junior ice hockey practices found that players were only active for 50 per cent of the time they were on the ice (Starkes, 2000). This is in stark contrast to practice sessions conducted by an expert volleyball coach, during which players were active for 93 per cent of the time (Deakin & Cobley, 2003). The ability to maximize time in practice sessions is one hallmark of coaching excellence.

In addition to efficient use of time, expert coaches offer demonstrably superior instruction (Rutt-Leas & Chi, 1993). Studies have shown that expert coaches are very precise in their assessment and specific in their recommendations for improvement, whereas novice coaches tend to be more superficial and vague in their analyses. Therefore, at some stage it is important for athletes to gain access to a highly qualified and competent coach. At what age this becomes necessary, however, is an area of ongoing debate. Parents often go to great expense to obtain an expert coach as early as possible, thinking it will provide an edge for their child. Some researchers have questioned this approach, arguing that coaches for young children do not need to be technical experts in their sport (Côté *et al.*, 2003). Instead, they suggest it is more important that coaches are simply really good with kids. Creating an environment that is supportive and encouraging, where kids are safe and having fun, will foster intrinsic motivation resulting in continuing involvement by the child. Côté and colleagues suggest that it is not until later in a child's sporting development that they require a coach who is considered an 'expert'.

Benjamin Bloom's (1985) classic work *Developing Talent in Young People* explored the early training and the family environments of individuals who had achieved considerable success in their particular field. Examples are provided from a variety of professions, including sports, music, and medicine. Bloom described how, despite the diverse nature of the activities, there were stages of development they all shared. Côté (1999) both corroborated and developed these findings in a study specific to high-level athletes and their early development. As children they *sampled* a variety of activities for a number of years before *specializing* in a few during adolescence, and ultimately *investing* in one main activity. This progression may help to counteract the risks of injury and burnout that are associated with specializing at too young an age in a particular sport.

Both Bloom (1985) and Côté (1999) highlighted the importance of family and their roles in supporting a child on their journey to excellence. The role of parents and coaches changed fairly dramatically during each of these three (sampling, specializing, investing) stages. In early stages of involvement, parents provided leadership in a number of ways, from initially enrolling their child in the activity, to providing instruction or coaching, to arranging transportation and access to facilities. As the child moved from sampling to specializing to finally investing significant amounts of time and energy in one main endeavour, expert coaches took on an increasingly prominent role, while parental involvement in day-to-day training decreased substantially. The nature of parental support changed to an emphasis on financial and emotional aspects as parents helped to mitigate the pressures that are part of being an elite performer.

Culture

While the hours an athlete trains along with the support of both parents and coaches are crucial aspects to skill acquisition, there are other broad, societal factors that have a powerful, yet often under-appreciated influence on talent development. As a prime example, one's country of origin plays a tremendous role in a person's exposure to sports, and consequently, the various resources and training facilities that are available. In Canada, a large percentage of children will learn to ice skate at a young age, due to the high cultural value placed upon ice hockey in the country. Hockey players are treated as national heroes, and games receive generous attention in the national media. In any international event there is an expectation that Canada will emerge victorious; anything less is considered something approaching a national tragedy. In Brazil, it is football that commands national attention. Brazilian football players carry the weight of the nation's expectations, much like Canada's hockey players. Due to a combination of social, cultural, and financial factors, millions of Brazilian children play the sport, and in all likelihood, Brazil will continue to be a soccer powerhouse for decades to come.

In Kenya a similar dynamic is at work, but for long-distance running. Kenyan runners have dominated distance events for over two decades. In the last 20 Boston marathons (1991–2010), Kenyan runners have won all but three of the men's events (two of the three not won by Kenyans were won by Ethiopian runners, a country that borders Kenya). This dominance has led to suggestions that East Africans are blessed with a genetic predisposition for distance running. Such a suggestion, however, tends to discount contributing social factors. Kenyan runners are revered in their home country, much like Canadian hockey players and Brazilian footballers. For many Kenyan children, running is seen as a potential escape from poverty. While it would seem somewhat preposterous to attribute Canadian hockey or Brazilian football prowess to genetic factors, speculation as to East African genetic advantages specific to running are taken more seriously. Leading researchers investigating such questions note the equivocal nature of the findings, however, and suggest that we perhaps undervalue the tremendous social and cultural components of long-distance running that are so influential in East African nations (Pitsiladis, Bale, Sharp, & Noakes, 2007).

Birthplace effect

In addition to the country and culture, the actual city in which one grows up also plays a remarkably large role in an athlete's development. Size matters when it comes to cities. Compelling data from North America suggest that if you were born in a city that has between 50,000 and 100,000 residents, your chances of becoming an elite athlete increases substantially compared to a city that is either much larger, or much smaller. Côté and colleagues looked at the birthplaces of professional athletes from a variety of sports, including hockey, baseball, golf, soccer, and basketball, and found that a disproportionate number of them either were born in, or spent their developmental years in cities this size (Côté, MacDonald, Baker, & Abernethy, 2006).

Just 1 per cent of the US population reside in cities between 50,000 and 100,000 residents, yet cities of this size produce 16.8 per cent of major-league baseball players, 11 per cent of PGA Tour golfers, and 17.2 per cent of Americans who make it to the National Hockey League. In stark contrast, 10 per cent of the US population live in very large cities of 5 million or more. Thus, we would expect, all things being equal, that approximately 10 per cent of professional athletes would come from cities of this size. In actuality, the number is far smaller. Less than 2 per cent of American baseball players come from cities of over 5 million residents. For golf and hockey, it is less than 1 per cent (Côté et al., 2006). A key dividing line is 500,000; cities larger than this produced fewer professional athletes than expected, cities smaller than 500,000 produced more, with cities of 50–100,000 seemingly ideal.

While the precise reasons for the birthplace effect remain a bit of a mystery, researchers have forwarded some theories, which lie primarily around the manner in which children are first exposed to sports. In very large cities there is often a plethora of facilities, but they can be expensive (i.e., golf course memberships) or getting to and from them can involve significant travel time. In addition, there is lots of competition in a big city – children participating in sports are often little fish in a very large pond, making it more difficult to stand out from the crowd (Seaton, Marsh, & Craven, 2009).

Smaller cities, on the other hand, may have fewer barriers for children to get involved in sports. Facilities, whether they are baseball fields, ice rinks, or golf courses, are likely cheaper, and getting to them may be easier. Furthermore, there may be less competition for accessing these resources and/or gaining a spot on the local team. In a smaller city, it is much easier to be a big fish. This potentially leads to attention from parents or coaches who notice a child's talent or enthusiasm for a sport and encourage it by providing extra support or instruction. Thus begins a virtuous circle in which more plentiful opportunities to participate, combined with a supportive psycho-social environment (i.e., support from parents/coaches) results in increased motivation on the part of the child, particularly if they start to see themselves as competent or 'talented'.

Seaton and colleagues have explored the 'Big fish, little pond effect' in educational settings, and have found a distinct relationship between academic self-concept and the level of the school or class a student attends (Seaton et al., 2009). Students in high-ability schools or classes suffer from a poorer academic self-concept than those of similar abilities who are in mixed-ability classes. If everyone around you is a high achiever, your own self-concept may suffer. We likely see a similar phenomenon in sports. While it is necessary to eventually compete with and against the best in your field if you aim to achieve an elite level, spending your earliest years somewhat protected from an overly competitive environment may have important psychological and developmental benefits.

In general, smaller cities, for whatever combination of reasons, turn out more elite athletes than large cities, but can a city be too small? The research by Côté and colleagues suggests that Canadian towns with fewer than 1,000 people produced a disproportionately small number of NHL players. While 28.5 per cent of Canadians live in towns of this size, only 5 per cent of NHL players came from these towns. This suggests that a city needs a critical mass to foster the development of successful athletes. Very small cities may lack facilities, or lack knowledgeable coaches to work with children, or even a sufficient number of children to field a team.

The Relative Age Effect

In addition to *where* you were born, *when* you were born is another important determinant of your ultimate success. If you want to play ice hockey at the professional level, the odds improve if you were born in January. Throughout the history of the NHL, more players have January birthdays than any other month. The month with the fewest birthdays? December (Diamond, 2000). The explanation for this is surprisingly simple; hockey organizes players into age groups according to the calendar year. As a consequence, a child born in early January can be virtually a full year older than a child born in late December. Overall, children who are born early in the year, in January, February, and March in particular, are at a distinct advantage when it comes to high achievement in the game (Barnsley & Thompson, 1988; Barnsley, Thompson, & Barnsley, 1985).

There is a name for this phenomenon – it's called the Relative Age Effect (RAE). It is widespread in hockey and other sports, in which children born early in the year are over-represented on elite teams. Cobley and colleagues (Cobley, Baker, Wattie, & McKenna, 2009) examined 14 sports in 16 countries and consistently found these age effects. Hockey is the sport that has received the most research attention thus far (31.3 per cent of studies conducted), followed closely by soccer (30.9 per cent). Baseball (13.4 per cent), basketball (6.1 per cent), and volleyball (5.7 per cent) were ranked three through five in terms of studies conducted; Cobley *et al.*'s research confirmed significant RAEs for each of these sports.

While hockey tends to advantage children born in January, February, and March, soccer players in Brazil and Germany are at an advantage if they are born in August, September, and October, due to a 'cut-off' date of 1 August in those countries (Musch & Grondin, 2001). There is nothing magical about January – it is simply the cut-off national hockey organizations have chosen for grouping players. Changing the cut-off date will change which kids have the advantage. Powerful evidence in support of the somewhat arbitrary yet important nature of cut-off dates comes from Helsen, Starkes, and Van Wickel (2000) and Musch and Hay (1999) who investigated how changes in the date affected subsequent player distributions. For example, the Belgian Soccer Federation changed its cut-off date from 1 August to 1 January in 1997. Prior to 1997, players born in August, September, and October were over-represented in youth elite leagues, as these were the oldest players on a relative basis. Post 1997, with a new cut-off date of 1 January, the distribution shifted so that players born in January, February, and March were over-represented at the elite level.

A few specific theories have been proposed for the emergence of RAEs and are generally inter-related in nature (Cobley *et al.*, 2009; Weir, Smith, Paterson, & Horton, 2010). Maturation rates appear to be an important influence, as 10 or 11 months difference in age can afford a child a substantial advantage in terms of height, weight, and co-ordination. Eleven months represents a big chunk of life for someone who is only nine years old. These size or strength advantages often translate into better performance on the playing field or the ice rink, and prove to be important when coaches are sizing players up for all-star teams or elite leagues. Coaches think that they are selecting the most talented players for their teams, but in fact, they are often just selecting the older kids. Coaches are confusing talent with age.

Nevertheless, being identified by parents or coaches as 'talented' at a young age soon reaps rewards; more ice time, better coaching, more games and practices. All of a sudden, what had been a very small advantage in size and strength is now a considerable advantage due to more opportunities to play and practise. In addition, being identified as talented may boost a child's self-esteem and motivation to continue playing and training. The virtuous circle, so similar to what we see in the birthplace effect, has begun.

Another factor that may help to explain the RAE is the competitiveness of the domain. Generally, RAEs are found in sports that are highly popular (e.g., ice hockey in Canada, cricket in Australia, soccer in England). The more popular the sport and the more it is culturally valued, the more likely youth will be 'profes-sionalized' – where participants are identified and streamlined at a very young age based on their perceived talents. The greater the number of participants a sport attracts, and the more competition for spots on elite developmental rosters, the increasing likelihood that early height, weight or motor co-ordination advantages will play a role (Cobley *et al.*, 2009).

Men's and women's ice hockey in Canada exemplifies the relationship between RAE and the competitiveness of a domain. An RAE exists in women's hockey in Canada, although it is weaker than that found in the men's game (Weir *et al.*, 2010). While men's hockey has a long and storied history, women's hockey has emerged as a mainstream sport much more recently. Indeed, opportunities to play at a competitive level were fairly limited as recently as 25 years ago, when 13-year-old Justine Blainey took her quest to play on the local boys' team all the way to Canada's Supreme Court. The initiation of the women's world championship in 1990 and the inclusion of women's hockey in the Olympics in 1998 resulted in an explosion in participation rates in the country. Female participation is, however, still dwarfed by male participation rates. Recent numbers from Hockey Canada display that young women are outnumbered almost six to one by male players, and this may be the primary reason that the RAE is more firmly established in the male game (Weir *et al.*, 2010).

Sport maturity

The example of men's and women's hockey in Canada suggests that the popularity of the sport and the number of participants are factors to consider, and likely affect how difficult it is to reach an elite level. New sports, or those with fewer competitors, may provide athletes with the opportunity to reach elite status with fewer than 10,000 hours of practice. Furthermore, recent research has explored the notion of 'transfer' to determine how much training in one sport may be applicable to a different sport. In support for this concept, Baker and colleagues found that athletes who participated in a variety of sports at a young age required fewer than 10,000 hours to reach elite levels in the sports of basketball, field hockey, and netball (Baker et al., 2003).

Bullock and colleagues put this to the test in the sport of skeleton (Bullock, Gulbin, Martin, Ross, Holland, & Marino, 2009). Skeleton was reintroduced to the 2002 Winter Olympic Games after a 54-year absence. The researchers conducted a talent identification campaign that targeted elite athletes, albeit with no experience in skeleton. Using 'deliberate programming' – a holistic approach that incorporated state-of-the-art equipment, coaching, and training techniques – they developed an Olympic athlete who competed in the women's skeleton event in 2006 in Turin. After just 100 hours of sport-specific practice, this athlete placed thirteenth in the Olympic Games.

It is important to note, however, that the athletes who adapted most quickly to skeleton were experienced surf life-savers, a water sport in which the demands closely resemble those of skeleton. Each of these athletes had more than ten years' experience specific to surf life-saving and had competed nationally or internationally. Thus, the researchers were able to facilitate the transfer of an elite athlete into a similar sport that was, by international sporting standards, relatively uncompetitive. In fact, the researchers estimated that, at the outset of their talent identification campaign, there were fewer than 100 registered women skeleton athletes worldwide. Of those 100, less than half had World Cup competition experience (Bullock et al., 2009). It remains to be seen whether this kind of transfer is possible in more established sports with a richer history. For sports like soccer, tennis, or golf, all of which have been played for over 100 years and have millions of participants around the globe, something approaching 10,000 hours to achieve excellence is perhaps a much more realistic expectation, irrespective of one's sporting background.

Concluding thoughts

One of the most interesting and pertinent debates in the talent development literature is the extent to which children need to specialize at a young age. The 10,000 hour/ten year rule suggests the earlier the better, particularly in sports for which peak performance occurs while one is still relatively young. However, the consequences of early specialization are sometimes profound in terms of a child's long-term physical and psychological health. Hence the recent interest in two alternative, and related, concepts: *sampling*, in which children partake in a number of different activities in order to build a broad base of motor skills, and *transfer* – the extent to which capacities developed in one sport may be applicable to another.

Available evidence suggests that both early specialization and sampling can lead to elite performance, and normally it falls to parents to guide children on the path they feel is most appropriate. One fascinating test case of early specialization took place in Hungary in the game of chess. Laszlo Polgar, who is a psychologist by profession, felt that early, intensive specialization was the key to achievement in any field. Polgar was convinced that genius is 99 per cent hard work and 1 per cent talent. Even before starting his own family he penned a book, entitled *Bring up Genius*. Polgar subsequently had three daughters and introduced them all to chess at a young age. The daughters were home-schooled, and spent hours every day immersed in chess. All three were spectacularly successful players. The eldest, Susan, became the number one ranked woman in the world and the first woman ever to achieve Grandmaster status. The youngest, Judit, quickly surpassed her older sister, taking over the number one ranking (a position she still holds as this book goes to press). She became the youngest Grandmaster in history – male or female – at age 15, eclipsing the record that was held by Bobby Fischer. Judit has been rated as high as eighth in the international men's rankings.

The Polgar sisters appear to be living proof of their father's theories. Others, however, are less sure. Some question Lazlo's assertion that genetics played no role in his daughters' success. Others question the motivational aspect, arguing that chess and the sisters was like an arranged marriage that worked out well (Flora, 2005). As part of an extensive story in *Psychology Today* on the Polgar family, Flora (2005) interviewed Ellen Winner (introduced earlier in this chapter) who has written about prodigies and their 'rage to master'. Winner thinks Laszlo Polgar got lucky: 'You can force your kids to work harder, but you can't get them to have that level of passion. The sisters could have just as easily rebelled against Laszlo.'

Expert performance – how much of it is luck?

Good fortune undoubtedly plays a role, particularly with respect to one's genetic make-up. Knowledge of the myriad of environmental factors involved in attaining expert performance affords a measure of power, however, as these are elements over which we can assert some control. Lazlo Polgar may have gotten lucky with the success of his daughters, but to a considerable extent he made every effort to take luck *out* of the equation. The Polgar sisters faced substantial financial and cultural obstacles to achieving chess pre-eminence. They grew up in a small apartment in Hungary during the communist era, with modest financial resources. In addition, women faced explicit discrimination in the game; females were not considered to be genetically and/or temperamentally suited to chess. Indeed, when Susan first qualified for the men's world championship the chess authorities attempted to block her participation. In spite of these obstacles, Lazlo Polgar created an environment that resulted in his daughters flourishing. By providing early, intensive training, and by taking control of their schooling, Polgar shaped their early experiences to a remarkable degree. Perhaps just as important, his daughters attribute their enthusiasm and love for the game to his ability to ignite their interest in chess when they were children.

Investigations into the childhoods of those who become high-level performers (e.g., Bloom's *Developing Talent in Young People*) provide important insights into the kinds of early experiences that experts across various domains all share. These tend to involve (a) early exposure to the activity, (b) wholehearted parental support and (c) enthusiastic and competent coaching. Awareness of specific factors concerning training and coaching, in addition to the broad cultural and societal forces at work (e.g., relative age and birthplace effects), provides opportunities to both take advantage of available resources and to combat potential barriers.

References

Baker, J. (2003). Early specialization in youth sport: A requirement for adult expertise? *High Ability Studies, 14*, 85–94.

Baker, J., Côté, J., Abernethy, B. (2003). Sport specific training, deliberate practice and the development of expertise in team ball sports. *Journal of Applied Sport Psychology, 15*, 12–25.

Barnsley, R. H., & Thompson, A. H. (1988). Birthdate and success in minor hockey: The key to the NHL. *Canadian Journal of Behavioural Science, 20*, 167–76.

Barnsley, R. H., Thompson, A. H., & Barnsley, P. E. (1985). Hockey success and birthdate: The RAE. *Canadian Association for Health, Physical Education, and Recreation, 51*, 23–28.

Bloom, B. S. (Ed.) (1985) *Developing talent in young people*. New York: Ballentine.

Bullock, N., Gulbin, J., Martin, D., Ross, A., Holland, T., & Marino, F. (2009). Talent identification and deliberate programming in skeleton: Ice novice to winter Olympian in 14 months. *Journal of Sports Sciences, 27*, 397–404.

Chase, W. G., & Ericsson, K. A. (1981). Skilled memory. In J. R. Anderson (Ed.), *Cognitive skills and their acquisition* (pp. 141–89). Hillsdale, NJ: Lawrence Erlbaum Associates.

Chase, W. G., & Simon, H. A., (1973). Perception in chess. *Cognitive Psychology, 4*, 55–81.

Cobley, S., Baker, J., Wattie, N., & McKenna, J. (2009). Annual age-grouping and athlete development: A meta-analytical review of relative age effects in sport. *Sports Medicine, 39*, 235–56.

Colvin, G. (2008). *Talent is over-rated*. New York: Penguin.

Côté, J. (1999). The influence of the family in the development of talent in sports. *The Sport Psychologist, 13*, 395–417.

Côté, J., Baker, J., Abernethy, B. (2003). From play to practice: A developmental framework for the acquisition of expertise in team sports. In J. Starkes & K. A. Ericsson (Eds) *Expert performance in sports: Advances in research on sport expertise* (p. 89–110). Champaign: Human Kinetics

Côté, J., MacDonald, D., Baker, J., & Abernethy, B. (2006). When 'where' is more important than 'when': Birthplace effects on the achievement of sporting expertise. *Journal of Sports Sciences, 24*, 1065–73.

Deakin, J. M., & Cobley, S. (2003). An examination of the practice environments in figure skating and volleyball: A search for deliberate practice. In J. Starkes & K. A. Ericsson (Eds) *Expert performance in sports: Advances in research on sport expertise* (pp. 251–72). Champaign: Human Kinetics.

Diamond, D. (Ed.) (2000). *Total hockey*. New York: Total Sports Publishing.

Ericsson, K. A. (2007). Deliberate practice and the modifiability of body and mind: toward a science of the structure and acquisition of expert and elite performance. *International Journal of Sport Psychology, 38*, 4–34.

Ericsson, K. A., Krampe, R. T., & Tesch-Römer, C. (1993). The role of deliberate practice in the acquisition of expert performance. *Psychological Review, 100*, 363–406.

Flora, C. (2005). The grandmaster experiment. *Psychology Today.* http://www.psychology today.com/articles/200506/the-grandmaster-experiment (accessed 20 August 2010).

Galton, F. R. S. (1869) *Hereditary genius: An inquiry into its laws and consequences.* New York: D. Appleton and Company.

Gladwell, M. (2008). *Outliers: The story of success.* New York: Little, Brown & Company.

Helsen, W. F., Starkes, J. L., & Van Winckel, J. (2000). Effect of a change in selection year on success in male soccer players. *American Journal of Human Biology, 12*, 729–35.

Musch J., & Grondin, S. (2001). Unequal competition as an impediment to personal development: A review of the relative age effect in sport. *Developmental Review, 21*, 147–67.

Musch, J., & Hay, R. (1999). The relative age effect in soccer: Cross-cultural evidence for a systematic discrimination against children born late in the competition year. *Sociology of Sport Journal, 16*, 54–64

Pitsiladis, Y., Bale, J., Sharp, C., & Noakes, T. (2007). *East African running.* London: Routledge.

Rutt-Leas, R. & Chi, M. T. H. (1993). Analyzing diagnostic expertise of competitive swimming coaches. In J.L. Starkes & F. Allard (Eds) *Cognitive issues in motor expertise.* (pp. 75–94). Amsterdam: Elsevier Science Publishing.

Seaton, M., Marsh, H. W., & Craven, R. G. (2009). Earning its place as a pan-human theory: Universality of the big-fish-little-pond effect across 41 culturally and economically diverse countries. *Journal of Educational Psychology, 101*, 403–19.

Starkes, J. L. (2000). The road to expertise: Is practice the only determinant? *International Journal of Sport Psychology, 31*, 431–51.

Starkes, J. L., Deakin, J. M., Allard, F., Hodges, N., & Hayes, A. (1996). Deliberate practice in sports: What is it anyway? In K.A. Ericsson (Ed.) *The road to excellence: The acquisition of expert performance in the arts and science, sports and games.* (pp. 81–106). Hillsdale, NJ: Erlbaum.

Weir, P. L., Smith, K., Paterson, C., & Horton, S. (2010). Canadian women's ice hockey – Evidence of a relative age effect. *Talent Development and Excellence, 2*, 209–17.

Wiersma, L. D. (2000). Risks and benefits of youth sport specialization: perspectives and recommendations. *Pediatric Exercise Science, 12*, 13–22.

Winner, E. (1996). The rage to master: The decisive case for talent in the visual arts. In K. A. Ericsson (Ed.) *The road to excellence: The acquisition of expert performance in the arts and sciences, sports and games* (p. 271–301). Hillsdale, NJ: Erlbaum.

5

IDENTIFYING AND DEVELOPING SKILL EXPERTISE

Understanding current limits and exploring future possibilities

Damian Farrow

The effortless skill displayed by sport's elite is constantly admired by those in the stands. Such skill belies the effort the individual has invested in the sport and the resources channelled into the athlete over their sporting career. Not surprisingly, those at the coalface of the talent development pathway, coaches and parents of emerging talent, are increasingly leaving no stone unturned in their efforts to guarantee their protégé will be the next star. However, the tools and processes available to identify and develop talent are generally still in embryonic stages relative to many other disciplines of sport science and medicine. This chapter seeks to outline the progress and challenges that exist within the identification and development of skill.

The chapter is divided into four main sections commencing with an introduction to the theoretical underpinnings of skill acquisition and expertise research. This is followed by a critique of this body of research as it applies to talent identification and talent development respectively. The final section then discusses the key methodological issues from this research as a means of informing future research and practice directions. In particular, I highlight the steps still required before we gain a more complete picture of the processes underlying talent identification and development.

Theoretical underpinnings

The most obvious way for learners to bridge the gap between themselves and experts is through practice. There are a myriad of cognitive learning theories explaining motor skill acquisition (e.g., Anderson, 1982; Fitts & Posner, 1967; Shiffrin & Schneider, 1977). A unifying feature of these theories is that they typically propose skill learning to be a step-by-step process characterised by initially high levels of cognitive effort followed by gradual progression to automatic control. This sequential practice experience is typically one where initially rapid improvements in skill performance are made, before more significant practice investment is required to make relatively smaller gains. Early learning is characterised by controlled processing of the motor skill where controlled processing is (a) attention demanding, (b) step by step, (c) slow, and (d) under the volitional control of the performer (Schneider & Shiffrin, 1977; Shiffrin & Schneider, 1977). These characteristics are reflected both in a novice learner's uncoordinated movement attempts despite significant attention being devoted to the task, as well as the instructional approach of the coach who typically will attempt to minimise information overload through the use of brief instruction. After extensive practice automated control may occur which is (a) largely without attention demands, (b) parallel, (c) fast, and (d) unpreventable, in that the processing is unable to be consciously altered (Schneider & Shiffrin, 1977; Shiffrin & Schneider, 1977). Again this is readily observed by spectators attending any elite sports event where the athletes are seen to control their skills effortlessly and seemingly with time and attentional capacity in surplus. All these cognitively grounded theories of skill acquisition share a common conceptual framework, which emphasises the development of an experience-based means of acquiring what appears to be eventual automaticity in decision making and skilled movement (Singer & Janelle, 1999).

Building on the foundations of early skill acquisition and cognitive psychology research, study into expertise became established in the late 1960s. Much of the initial impetus to study sport expertise stemmed from the success of initial investigations into chess expertise by de Groot (1965) and Chase and Simon (1973). For instance, Chase and Simon (1973) provided some of the first empirical support for the presumption that performance differences between individuals could be explained by time spent training (Baker & Cobley, 2008). Examining the perceptual–cognitive capacities of Grandmaster and lower level chess players led to the establishment of the *ten-year rule of necessary preparation*. Put simply, without this significant investment in practice, sufficient skill acquisition to become an expert would be unlikely, whether the domain was chess, music, or sport. It is apparent from such conclusions that expertise research has progressed the century-old nature–nurture debate once commonly used to explain elite performance. While in some instances the importance of environmental factors has been highlighted, most seek to integrate both biological and environmental factors (see Baker & Davids, 2007).

Since Chase and Simon's pioneering work, the general aim of expertise research has been to experimentally identify and then understand components of performance that reliably distinguish between expert and novice performers in a particular skill domain. Expertise expresses itself in numerous aspects of human performance including perception, cognition, and motor execution. Irrespective of the domain investigated, experts have been consistently found to process and retrieve task-specific information differently (more effectively) than lesser skilled individuals.

Talent identification

The application of skill acquisition and motor expertise research is often intuitively linked to talent identification processes by practitioners. However, empirically there has been relatively little effort by researchers to systematically examine this connection, at least not directly. A key reason for this is that researchers recognise the limitations of attempting to identify skillful individuals early in their sporting careers. Skill is a highly trainable component of performance and it can be expected that individuals will develop at different rates of learning.[1] Making early decisions on the identification of talent is fraught with the danger of unwittingly excluding performers with great potential but who have yet to demonstrate their skill capabilities due to maturational or other influences (i.e., see Chapter 4, which discusses the influence of the RAE). However, some work relying on cross-sectional designs have investigated the skill development of component abilities, such as perceptual-cognitive skills like decision making, thought to be critical in adult, elite performance.

One of the more robust findings of the sport expertise literature is that expert performance is extremely sports specific, and potentially task specific, and consequently does not emerge on generalised measures of performance (Helsen & Starkes, 1999; Starkes & Deakin, 1984). This finding led to the distinction between hardware and software components of performance. 'Hardware' typically relates to genetic or 'hard-wired' characteristics of individuals such as optometric parameters (e.g., visual acuity, depth perception) and neural processing abilities (e.g., reaction time, fast information processing) that may contribute to performance. Despite the superficial appeal of a 'hardware' basis for expert performance, individual differences in 'hardware' seemingly do not relate to an individual's level of expertise (e.g., Helsen & Starkes, 1999). In contrast, 'software' refers to sport-specific information-processing capacities such as pattern recognition, knowledge retrieval, and anticipation. These capacities have been found to explain more of the variance between expert and lesser skilled performers, and importantly are amenable to training (e.g., Helsen & Starkes, 1999). While the simplicity of the hardware–software dichotomy means it is now seldom used, it nevertheless provides a useful heuristic for organising the existing research knowledge as to what perceptual, cognitive, and motor characteristics of performance separates, and equally does not separate, expert from novice performers.

Perceptual contributions to sport expertise are typically attributed to (a) improved selective attention to relevant information sources at the expense of irrelevant information, (b) enhanced recognition of context-specific patterns (e.g., offensive or defensive structures), and (c) more sophisticated feature analysis processes. Cognitive or decision-making performance is facilitated by the experts' superior task-specific knowledge-base relative to lesser skilled performers, particularly the development of larger, more elaborate, and better organised, rule-based procedures for information search, retrieval, and action planning. Similarly, an expert's movement execution is typically explained in terms of the development of enhanced control of the skill within a competitive context. In a talent identification context this is typically demonstrated via the skilled performer's capacity to execute the primary skills of the sport more proficiently than lesser skilled players (Pienaar, Spamer, & Steyn Jr, 1998). Coupled with this observation, dual task measurement approaches have also been used to demonstrate differences between performers whom on the surface seem to be of a similar skill level. The dual-tasking method requires an athlete to perform two tasks simultaneously – a primary task for which the attention demand is assessed (usually a core skill of the sport examined), and a secondary (dual) task (such as responding to auditory prompts), for which performance changes are measured and implications drawn regarding the level of attention required to maintain primary task performance (Abernethy, 1988a). In contrast to the success of dual-task measurement in demonstrating skill differences, there is little evidence demonstrating a relationship between generic tests of motor skill (e.g., jumping, running, and throwing) and expert sports-specific skill performance, primarily because of the violation of the principle of specificity (Henry, 1961). For more complete reviews of the components of sport expertise see Starkes and Ericsson (2003).

While there is an extensive collection of research detailing the contribution of various components of performance to expertise, there is comparatively limited research that has attempted to understand these component processes with both a multi-dimensional and developmental focus. A typical example of multi-dimensional work completed is that of Helsen and Starkes (1999) who subjected semi-professional soccer players (expert group) and kinesiology students with some soccer experience (intermediate group) to a battery of non-soccer specific tasks (e.g., reaction time, visual acuity in response to a generic stimulus) as well as soccer specific skills tests (e.g., perceptual, decision-making, and movement responses to tactical soccer patterns). Analyses revealed that it was the sport-specific tasks rather than non-specific qualities that contained the key attributes that discriminated the expert players from the intermediately skilled players. In particular, the experts possessed superior perceptual and decision-making skill as evidenced by faster response speed and accuracy in solving tactical game situations. This was accompanied by fewer visual fixations suggesting they could extract key information more effectively than the intermediate participants. A final contributing factor was the motor component of reduced ball–foot contact time for the expert players as they kicked the ball in response to the situations presented. The parameters, experimental design, and findings of Helsen and Starkes are consistent with a range of other multi-dimensional studies that have been completed (e.g., Elferink-Gemser, Visscher, Lemmink, & Mulder, 2004; Farrow, 2010; Starkes, 1987; Ward & Williams, 2003).

When the above components of performance are considered across the developmental spectrum through cross-sectional examination of age and experience, the powerful role of practice is again emphasised. For instance, perceptual skills that are known to be critical for expert performance in adults have been demonstrated to improve, not with maturation or chronological age alone but due to experience with, and exposure to, vast amounts of task-relevant practice. Abernethy (1988b) investigated the effect of skill and chronological age on anticipatory performance in badminton through the cross-sectional examination of groups of experts and novices ranging in age from 12 years to adult age. The experts, unlike the novices, showed a progressive increase in the use of early movement pattern information before racquet-shuttle contact (a key source of anticipatory skill) as they got older, although it was only at the adult level that the anticipatory performance of the experts was significantly superior to that of the age-matched controls. Tenenbaum, Sar-El and Bar-Eli (2000), in a comparable study of anticipatory skill in tennis, reported that while expert–novice differences in anticipation were evident from as early as 8–11 years of age, the magnitude of skill-related differences was greatest after some 6–7 years of accrued experience. Ward and Williams (2003) examined the relative contribution of visual, perceptual, and cognitive skill to the development of expertise in soccer. Groups of elite and sub-elite soccer players ranging in age from 9 to 17 years completed a battery of tests thought to be critical to expert performance based on previous research. Similar to Helsen and Starkes, their analyses revealed that tests of general visual function did not consistently discriminate between skill groups at any age. In contrast, sport-specific tests of anticipatory performance were most valuable in discriminating across skill groups, whereas pattern recall skill was most predictive of age. In contrast to the majority of previous research, Ward and Williams reported that elite players as young as nine years of age could predict the involvement of key players in a pattern of play. This result was interpreted to suggest that these young players possessed adult-like memory capabilities when generating appropriate decision-making solutions.

In summary, there are a range of performance components that can distinguish experts from lesser skilled performers; however it is also apparent that these capacities are relatively plastic and developed through extensive task-specific practice. Furthermore, some qualities may not emerge until relatively late in the developmental process. For example, Nevett and French (1997) demonstrated that the perceptual-cognitive ability of young baseball players was constrained by their physical capabilities. Those players who did not have the physical throwing skill to throw the ball from the outfield to home-base did not generate this throwing option as a possible solution to a tactical situation, whereas older players who were able to throw this distance successfully selected this as the most desirable option. The key message for coaches and applied sports practitioners is that talent identification based on skill capacities is at best an extremely difficult task and at worst has the capacity to de-select children who, with further practice and maturation, may still emerge as an expert performer.

Talent development

While identifying skillful talent early in a career is a difficult proposition, much can be learned from the practice experiences of expert performers. Consequently, a significant research effort has been devoted to identifying and understanding the primary and secondary factors thought critical to the development of talent (cf. Baker & Horton, 2004). This chapter will limit its discussion to the practice conditions necessary for skill development by reviewing an emerging body of research that has relied upon the retrospective analysis of the developmental history profiles of past and current elite performers. The common practice habits and environment underlying the skill development of these elite performers have been used to empirically support theoretical predictions concerning the nature and type of practice that needs to be undertaken to become an expert performer. This work has also been translated into recommendations for practitioners.

Practice or play? Or both?

A common experimental approach when seeking to gain insight into the talent development pathways of sport experts has been to examine the practice histories of both expert and less successful athletes using tools such as interviews, training diaries, and questionnaires (Starkes & Ericsson, 2003; Williams & Ericsson, 2005). The outcome of this work has led to the development of two different perspectives on the development of talent, namely the Theory of Deliberate Practice (Ericsson, Krampe, & Tesch-Romer, 1993) and the Developmental Model of Sport Participation (DMSP) (Côté, 1999) (see Table 5.1).

Deliberate practice

The Theory of Deliberate Practice was developed by psychologist Anders Ericsson and colleagues (Ericsson, Krampe, & Tesch-Römer, 1993; Ericsson, 2003). Deliberate practice is considered to have occurred when a well-defined task with an appropriate difficulty level for the particular individual is completed with access to informative feedback, and opportunities for repetition and corrections of errors. Such practice requires effort, generates no immediate rewards, and is motivated by the goal of improving performance rather than inherent enjoyment. This approach maintains that the amount of such practice is monotonically related (i.e., linear) to task performance such that deliberate practice has the same effect on performance

TABLE 5.1 Differences between deliberate play and deliberate practice. Recreated from Côté, Baker and Abernethy (2007).

Deliberate play	Deliberate practice
Done for its own sake	Done to achieve a future goal
Enjoyable	Not the most enjoyable
Pretend quality	Carried out seriously
Interest on the behaviour	Interest on outcome of the behaviour
Flexibility	Explicit rules
Adult involvement not required	Adult involvement often required
Occurs in various settings	Occurs in specialised facilities

regardless of whether it is the first hour of training or the ten thousandth hour. This position was established on data that revealed that expert level musicians spent greater than 25 hours per week engaged in specific practice activities (i.e., training alone) whereas less successful musicians spent considerably less time (e.g., amateurs < two hours per week) in such activities. These weekly differences in practice obviously accumulated over years of practice such that the expert musicians had accrued over 10,000 hours of deliberate practice by age 20 while the amateur musicians had accumulated only 2,000 hours at the same age.

While Ericsson's position has also been substantiated in some sport settings (e.g., Helsen, Starkes, & Hodges, 1998; Helsen, Hodges, Van Winckel, & Starkes, 2000; Hodges & Starkes, 1996) these researchers have also offered some modifications to the original theory, at least regarding how it applies to sport. For instance, they have defined deliberate practice activities as highly enjoyable and high in concentration as opposed to those that are not inherently enjoyable, or require effort. In addition, squad or team practice, rather than practice alone (or individually with a teacher), has been identified as being most predictive of skill level in team environments (c.f., Ericsson *et al.*, 1993; Helsen *et al.*, 1998).

Of critical relevance to coaches and practitioners is what deliberate practice represents in a sports setting. A golfer simply hitting a bucket of balls at the driving range is not deliberately practising, unless he is engaged in attempting to improve an element of his swing (e.g., alignment). When this issue is resolved, his practice attention then needs to switch to another critical element that again evokes high concentration and effort. Practice should be a continual striving to lift performance to a new skill level such that plateaus in learning do not occur.

Deliberate play

An alternate view of talent development has been provided by the work of Jean Côté and colleagues (Côté, 1999; Côté, Baker, & Abernethy, 2007; Côté & Hay, 2002). The Developmental Model of Sport Participation (DMSP) suggests that sporting experts not only accrue large amounts of deliberate practice but also engage, from an early age, in vast amounts of 'deliberate play'. Deliberate play involves activities defined as 'early developmental physical activities that are intrinsically motivating, provide immediate gratification and are specifically designed to maximize enjoyment' (Côté *et al.*, 2007, pp. 185–86). Most prominent in the early sampling years (ages 6 to 12 years), examples of deliberate play include informal neighbourhood games, like street basketball and hockey, or backyard games like cricket and soccer. Rules and equipment are adapted to meet any specific contextual needs and are monitored by the participants or sometimes an adult if present. Like the deliberate practice approach, practice hours spent in deliberate play during development are thought to be critical in determining whether expertise ultimately emerges.

Baker, Côté, and Abernethy (2003) examined the developmental activities of expert decision makers from a range of Australian team sports. They found that the participation profiles of the expert performers with non-expert decision makers from the same sports was relatively similar until approximately 12 years of age, after which time the experts significantly decreased their *sampling* of other activities and began to *specialise*. Similarly, the number of hours of sport-specific training remained similar between the two groups until approximately ten years into their careers, where the experts then began to *invest* in their primary sport and consequently amassed significantly more practice hours than the non-experts. However, the number of hours accrued was well short of the 10,000 hours of deliberate practice reported by Ericsson.

The implications for coaches and practitioners seeking to apply the DMSP model are readily apparent. Using stages modified from Bloom (1985), Côté proposed that the talent development pathway toward elite performance consists of three distinct stages: the sampling years (childhood; age 6 to 12), the specialising years (early-adolescence; age 13 to 15) and the investment years (late adolescence; age 16+). During the sampling years, children should be encouraged to participate in a variety of sports with the focus being primarily on deliberate play activities. The specialising years involve engagement in fewer sporting activities, both organised and unorganised, that are more competitive in nature. Finally, during the investment years the athlete needs to demonstrate a commitment to only one structured sport activity. Consistent with progression through these three stages, deliberate play predominates early development, while both play and practice occur in the specialising years before ultimately a transition to deliberate practice occurs in the investment years.

Play and practice

Ultimately there are numerous pathways to expert sport performance. This is best exemplified in Côté's current DMSP model (see Côté *et al.*, 2007), which demonstrates that the deliberate practice pathway is required if one is interested in becoming an expert in early specialisation sports where elite performance is achieved in pre-puberty, such as in women's gymnastics. However, for other sports a more participation-focused pathway is still a viable option, particularly if the potentially negative psycho-social consequences of early specialisation are considered (Baker, 2003). It is apparent that a range of sport-specific factors such as the international competitive depth of the sport and cultural context will play a significant role in shaping the preferred developmental pathway (Ward, Hodges, Starkes & Williams, 2007; see also Chapter 4). Hence a primary message to those involved in talent development programming is the need to consider any available empirical data specific to one's own sport context when seeking to implement a particular pathway.

Methodological issues driving future directions

Until very recently, the predominantly laboratory-based research investigating performance components such as anticipation and its age-related development (as detailed in the talent identification section) and the research on the practice and developmental histories of experts (as detailed in the talent development section) have largely occurred independently with little regard for the need to integrate the two methodologies (Weissensteiner, Abernethy, Farrow & Müller, 2008). Convergence of these two methodological approaches is a fertile area for future research as it has the capacity to provide greater understanding of both the capacity for talent identification and more importantly the developmental trajectory of particular skills. A recent example is provided by Weissensteiner *et al.* (2008) who examined the link between the anticipation skills of cricket batsmen and their developmental practice histories. Skilled and lesser skilled batsmen, ranging in age from 14 years of age to adults, completed a batting anticipation task and a structured interview, in which their accumulated hours of experience in organised and unorganised sporting activities were estimated. The skilled adult and U20 players demonstrated an ability to use kinematic information available in a bowler's action pre-ball release to anticipate the delivery type. This capacity was not evident among the younger players or lesser skilled batsmen. The developmental history question- naires revealed that skilled players of all ages were distinguishable in terms of their accumulated hours of cricket-specific experience, yet this practice/experience was only modestly related to the player's demonstrated anticipatory skill when independent of the player's age. While a number of methodological considerations are of importance in fully interpreting these findings (some of which are detailed below) clearly the above findings provide a much richer explanation of the devel- opment of the specific component skill.

A key methodological challenge facing both skill learning and expertise researchers is the need to capture the skill in its true context. Traditional skill acquisition research has long suffered when applied to the real-world sports setting. It has relied on the use of designs involving complete learners performing simple laboratory-based tasks, which are practised over a short learning phase and accompanied by a similarly short retention period (see Table 5.2).

Quite rightly, practitioners have questioned the applicability of such findings in real-world settings. While expertise research is usually much closer in design to the needs of the practitioner, the issue of task representation is still a challenge. Put simply, the capability of the researcher to design an experimental task that captures the essence of the real-world task so that an expert performer may appropriately utilise their skills is critical. Coupled to this issue is the need for expertise researchers to adopt more multi-dimensional designs (as described earlier) if we are to gain a more complete picture of how the various components of expert performance are developed over time.

The majority of researchers examining talent development have relied primarily upon retrospective reports of practice history provided by athletes. Not only are such reports suspect to issues of recall accuracy, almost absent from such reports is detail related to the microstructure of practice (Deakin & Cobley, 2003; Singer & Janelle, 1999). For example, the frequency, type, scheduling, and organisation of practice relative to stage of skill development is seldom reported or considered. While some researchers have attempted to address this shortcoming in recent times

TABLE 5.2 Some of the advantages and disadvantages when attempting to identify adaptive learning mechanisms using practice history profiles and traditional learning studies. Recreated from Williams and Ericsson (2005).

Retrospective Practice History Profiles	*Traditional Learning Studies*
• Provides a description of the general structure of activities leading to expert performance. • Overemphasis on the macro rather than micro structure of practice. • Limited attempt to identify specific practice activities (and strategies) that contribute to the development of skills. • Absence of control groups. • Potential concerns with validity of retrospective estimates of practice hours.	• Enables the validity of specific practice activities and instructional procedures to be examined under controlled laboratory conditions. • Overemphasis on using simple and novel tasks leading to concerns in generalising findings to real-world learning activities. • Short-term training interventions, mainly with novice rather than expert participants. • Limited attempts to record process-tracing measures of learning. • Often absence of transfer and/or retention tests, particularly involving realistic stressors such as anxiety and fatigue.

(see Deakin & Cobley, 2003; Ward *et al.*, 2007) their definition of microstructure of practice still only relates to a broad category of activities completed in a session (team, individual, matchplay-competition, routines etc . . .) as opposed to the organisation and scheduling of such activities (practice trial organisation and structure, nature of coach instruction and feedback). Clearly this microstructure of practice is influential in the learning and development of a performer (e.g., Williams & Hodges, 2005) and has the potential to provide more information on a preferred developmental pathway than simply a record of practice hours accumulated. Similar to recent expertise research that has used the practice history profiles to aid in the explanation of component skill performance (e.g., Weissensteiner *et al.*, 2008), the longitudinal and prospective recording of practice microstructure in established talent development pathways, while not without its own difficulties, is a logical step toward improving the link between the theory and practice of talent identification and development.

The implementation of prospective, longitudinal research designs is perhaps the greatest challenge to all talent identification and development researchers. Such designs where an individual or group of participants are tracked on a range of measures over their career from novice to expert are relatively rare due to the logistical issues associated with their implementation. Notably, the small likelihood of any of the novice performers actually becoming expert! Consequently, the data discussed in this chapter have been collected using predominantly cross-sectional designs. Such approaches are based on the assumption that the features that distinguish adult experts manifest themselves in younger performers also, hence providing encouragement to those who wish to attempt to identify talent early. However, early talent is still not a guarantee of expertise as many factors (e.g., maturation) will act as constraints on the developmental process (Vaeyens, Matthieu, Williams & Philippaerts, 2008). A logical compromise as highlighted by Abernethy, Thomas and Thomas (1993) is the use of quasi-longitudinal designs where expert and novice performers (in particular children) are tracked over the course of a competitive season. Such an approach provides the benefits of the cross-sectional approach, plus it starts to tap into some of the prospective, longitudinal design advantages. Similarly, an emerging research direction within national sports institutes is the systematic tracking of emerging talent over the course of a competitive season, scholarship period and Olympic cycle, albeit usually in the absence of a control group. With the above issues in mind, practitioners should be aware of the constraints and limits of any recommendations presented from existing research. However, they should equally be buoyed by the significant progress in our understanding of expertise, and the ongoing collective effort of skill acquisition and expertise researchers in developing a more complete understanding of talent identification and development in the skill domain.

Notes

1   It is timely to distinguish between usage of the terms 'skill' and 'ability' as they are often used interchangeably in non-scientific discussion. In the context of skill acquisition, an ability is genetically determined and largely unmodified by practice or experience, whereas a skill is a capacity such as being able to hit a tennis ball that can be easily modified by practice (see Schmidt, 1991).

References

Abernethy, B. (1988a). Dual-task methodology and motor skills research: Some applications and methodological constraints. *Journal of Human Movement Studies, 14,* 101–32.

—— (1988b). The effects of age and expertise upon perceptual skill development in a racquet sport. *Research Quarterly for Exercise and Sport, 59,* 210–21.

Abernethy, B., Thomas, K. T., & Thomas, J. T. (1993). Strategies for improving understanding of motor expertise (or mistakes we have made and things we have learned!!). In J. L. Starkes & F. Allard (Eds) *Cognitive issues in motor expertise* (pp. 317–56). Amsterdam: Elsevier Science Publishers.

Anderson, J. R. (1982). Acquisition of cognitive skill. *Psychological Review, 89,* 369–406.

Baker, J. (2003). Early specialization in youth sport: A requirement for adult expertise? *High Ability Studies, 14,* 85–94.

Baker J., & Cobley, S. (2008). Does practice make perfect? The role of training in developing the expert athlete. In D. Farrow, J. Baker, & C. MacMahon. (Eds), *Developing sport expertise: Researchers and coaches put theory into practice* (pp. 29–42). Oxford: Routledge.

Baker, J., & Davids, K. (2007). Introduction: Nature, nurture and sport performance. *International Journal of Sport Psychology, 38,* 1–3.

Baker, J., & Horton, S. (2004). A review of primary and secondary influences on sport expertise. *High Ability Studies, 15,* 211–28.

Baker, J., Côté, J., & Abernethy, B. (2003). Learning from the experts: practice activities of expert decision-makers in sport. *Research Quarterly for Exercise and Sport, 74*, 342–47.

Bloom, B. S. (1985). *Developing talent in young people.* New York: Ballantine.

Chase, W. G., & Simon, H. A. (1973). Perception in chess. *Cognitive Psychology, 4*, 55–81.

Côté, J. (1999). The influence of the family in the development of talent in sport. *The Sport Psychologist, 13*, 395–417.

Côté, J., & Hay, J. (2002) Children's involvement in sport: A developmental perspective. In J. M. Silva & D. Stevens (Eds) *Psychological foundations in sport* (pp. 484–502). Boston, MA: Merrill.

Côté, J., Baker, J. & Abernethy, B. (2007). Practice and play in the development of sport expertise. In R. Eklund & G. Tenenbaum (Eds) *Handbook of sport psychology* (3rd Edn), (pp. 184–202), Hoboken, NJ: Wiley.

Deakin, J. M., & Cobley, S. (2003). A search for deliberate practice: An examination of the practice environments in figure skating and volleyball. In J. L. Starkes, & K. A. Ericsson (Eds), *Expert performance in sports* (pp. 115–36). Champaign, IL: Human Kinetics.

de Groot, A. (1965). *Thought and choice in chess.* The Hague: Mouton.

Elferink-Gemser, M. T., Visscher, C., Lemmink, K. A. P. M., & Mulder, T. W. (2004). Relation between multidimensional performance characteristics and level of performance in talented youth field hockey players. *Journal of Sports Sciences, 22*, 1053–63.

Ericsson, K.A. (2003). Development of elite performance and deliberate practice: An update from the perspective of the expert performance approach. In J. L. Starkes & K. A. Ericsson (Eds) *Expert performance in sports* (pp. 49–84). Champaign, IL: Human Kinetics.

Ericsson, K. A., Krampe, R. T., & Tesch-Römer, C. (1993). The role of deliberate practice in the acquisition of expert performance. *Psychological Review, 100*, 363–406.

Farrow, D. (2010). A multi-factorial examination of the development of skill expertise in high performance netball. *Talent Development & Excellence, 2*, 123–35.

Fitts, P., & Posner, M. (1967). *Human performance.* Belmont, CA: Brooke/Cole.

Helsen, W. F., & Starkes, J. L. (1999). A multidimensional approach to skilled perception and performance in sport. *Applied Cognitive Psychology, 13*, 1–27.

Helsen, W. F., Hodges, N. J., Van Winckel, J., & Starkes, J. L. (2000). The roles of talent, physical precocity and practice in the development of soccer expertise. *Journal of Sports Sciences, 18*, 727–36.

Helsen, W. F., Starkes, J. L., & Hodges, N. J. (1998). Team sports and the theory of deliberate practice. *Journal of Sport and Exercise Psychology, 20*, 12–34.

Henry, F. M. (1961). Specificity vs generality in learning motor skill. In R. C. Brown & G. S. Kenyon (Eds) *Classical studies in physical activity* (pp. 331–40). Englewood Cliffs, NJ: Prentice-Hall.

Hodges, N. J. & Starkes, J. L. (1996). Wrestling with the nature of expertise: A sport specific test of Ericsson, Krampe and Tesch-Römer's (1993) theory of 'Deliberate Practice'. *International Journal of Sport Psychology, 25*, 1–25.

Nevett, M., & French, K. (1997). The development of sport-specific planning, rehearsal, and updating of plans during defensive youth baseball game performance. *Research Quarterly for Exercise & Sport, 68*, 203–14.

Pienaar, A. E., Spamer, M. J., & Steyn Jr, H. S. (1998). Identifying and developing rugby talent among 10-year-old boys: A practical model. *Journal of Sports Sciences, 16*, 691–99.

Schmidt, R. A. (1991). *Motor learning and performance.* Champaign, IL: Human Kinetics.

Schneider, W., & Shiffrin, R. M. (1977). Controlled and automatic human information processing: I. Detection, search and attention. *Psychological Review, 84*, 1–66.

Shiffrin, R. M., & Schneider, W. (1977). Controlled and automatic human information processing: II. Perceptual learning, automatic attending, and a general theory. *Psychological Review, 84*, 127–90.

Singer, R. N., & Janelle, C. M. (1999). Determining sport expertise: From genes to supremes. *International Journal of Sport Psychology, 30,* 117–50.

Starkes, J. L. (1987). Skill in field hockey: The nature of the cognitive advantage. *Journal of Sport Psychology, 9,* 146–60.

Starkes, J. L., & Deakin, J. (1984). Perception in sport: A cognitive approach to skilled performance. In W. F. Straub & J. M. Williams (Eds) *Cognitive sport psychology* (pp 115–28). Lansing, NY: Sports Science Associates.

Starkes, J. L., & Ericsson, K. A. (Eds). (2003). *Expert performance in sports.* Champaign, IL: Human Kinetics.

Tenenbaum, G., Sar-El, T., & Bar-Eli, M. (2000). Anticipation of ball location in low and high-skill performers: a developmental perspective. *Psychology of Sport and Exercise, 1,* 117–28.

Vaeyens, R., Matthieu, L., Williams, A. M., & Philippaerts, R. M. (2008). Talent identification and development programmes in sport. *Sports Medicine, 38,* 703–14.

Ward, P., & Williams, A. M. (2003). Perceptual and cognitive skill development in soccer: The multidimensional nature of expert performance. *Journal of Sport & Exercise Psychology, 25,* 93–111.

Ward, P., Hodges, N. J., Starkes, J. L. & Williams, A. M. (2007). The road to excellence: Deliberate practice and the development of expertise. *High Ability Studies, 18,* 119–53.

Weissensteiner, J., Abernethy, B., Farrow, D., & Müller, S. (2008). The development of anticipation: A cross-sectional examination of the practice experiences contributing to skill in cricket batting. *Journal of Sport & Exercise Psychology,* 30, 663–84.

Williams, A. M., & Ericsson, K. A. (2005). Perceptual-cognitive expertise in sport: Some considerations when applying the expert performance approach. *Human Movement Science, 24,* 283–307.

Williams, A. M., & Hodges, N.J. (2005). Practice, instruction and skill acquisition in soccer: Challenging tradition. *Journal of Sports Sciences, 23,* 637–50.

6

DEVELOPING TALENT IN ATHLETES AS COMPLEX NEUROBIOLOGICAL SYSTEMS

Ian Renshaw, Keith Davids, Elissa Phillips and Hugo Kerhervé

Although attempts to formalize talent identification and development processes have become more popular across the world, the efficacy of such programmes has been scrutinized (Abbott *et al.*, 2005; Gullich, 2007; Vaeyens *et al.*, 2009). This chapter proposes that sports performance evolves as an emergent dynamic system where the performance landscape is constantly shifting. The implication of this view is that predicting athletes who may be defined as 'talented' or 'expert' in the future is inordinately challenging. Rigid, over-structured talent identification and development programmes that fail to consider interacting individual, environmental and task constraints underpinning sports performance (see Renshaw, Davids & Savelsbergh, 2010), are unlikely to succeed. Traditional approaches tend to over-emphasize anthropometric and physiological measures so that potentially talented individuals are initially excluded or de-selected from programmes, due to limited assessments of talent potential based on current performance (Abbott *et al.*, 2005; Phillips, Davids, Renshaw & Portus, 2010). In this chapter we argue that the focus in sport needs to eschew early identification of expert athletes towards the development of skilled, highly adaptive performers. We start by considering why sports adopt early talent identification processes despite it being a flawed approach. We next highlight theoretical ideas on how modeling talent development as a non-linear, emergent process can provide a more effective and efficient system. Such an approach can create a productive 'talent' population with a greater chance of matching individuals and sports, reducing wastage.

The status quo: talent identification and selection as the focus

Despite empirical evidence that early talent selection struggles to identify future champions in great numbers (e.g. Vaeyens *et al.*, 2009), many sports continue to adopt a model of early specialization. The early specialization model is intuitively appealing for often cash-poor sports administrators because it enables them to focus limited financial and coaching resources on the putative talented 'few' deemed to possess the necessary traits and characteristics needed to achieve expertise. Additionally, administrators are concerned with protecting their 'market share' of talented athletes in their sport, with a fundamental assumption that sports are competing for a limited talent pool.

Strong support for early specialization appeared in the theory of deliberate practice (Ericsson, Krampe & Tesch-Römer, 1993). The belief that expertise acquisition requires 10,000 hours of practice is widely accepted in the sport community (e.g., Coyle, 2009; Gladwell, 2008; Syed, 2010). Adopting the tenets of deliberate practice is a powerful tool for coaches to use to 'motivate' performers to undertake more practice hours, although increasing evidence questions the concept (e.g., Abbott *et al.*, 2005; Gullich, 2007; Simonton, 1999; Vaeyens *et al.*, 2009).

Early talent selection strategies, allied to a deliberate practice methodology, have had limited success as administrators have often adopted monotonic linear models of talent development, which fail to capture the emergent nature of expertise acquisition due to the interactions between an individual's genes and the environment (e.g., Simonton, 1999). Abbott *et al.* (2005) suggested five reasons why early talent selection does not work. First, predicting the future level of a genetically driven sub-component of performance is virtually impossible due to nonlinear processes of system development. Second, performance is multi-factorial with a number of different constraints on talent development, not just an individual's genetic structure. Third, a focus on discrete performance measures such as physiological or anthropometric variables only provides a fraction of the information about a person's adaptability and development potential. Fourth, selection often occurs during childhood when performance can be affected by unstable characteristics during transitional periods such as puberty or adolescence. Finally, not enough emphasis is given to factors that underpin successful *development* towards one's potential. Given these concerns, what does research tell us about the development trajectories of current experts? We consider this question next.

Talent development from a dynamic systems perspective

Recently, sports expertise was conceptualized from a dynamical systems theoretical perspective (Phillips, Davids, Renshaw, & Portus, 2010). This theoretical model proposed that expert skill acquisition emerges through interactions between specific individual, task and environment constraints. It suggests that the range of interacting constraints impinging on each athlete is unique and shapes the acquisition of expertise, resulting in the expectation of varying developmental pathways between individuals. In talent development, individual performer constraints include mental and physical (physiological and anthropometric) characteristics. Task constraints were considered specific to a sports discipline for each developing athlete, while environmental constraints included socio-cultural factors, like family support, access to facilities and cultural trends in sport participation. Useful discussions of key ideas and concepts of the constraints model (Newell, 1986), are provided in Davids, Button and Bennett (2008) and Renshaw, Davids and Savelsbergh (2010).

Individual–environment synergies shape talent development

In contrast to focusing solely on individual factors, some researchers have qualitatively examined environmental backgrounds and competencies that exist among elite athletes (e.g., Gould, Dieffenbach & Moffett, 2002; Durand-Bush & Salmela, 2002; Holt & Dunn, 2004). One important finding regards similarities and differences in development, suggesting that experts can adopt different pathways and strategies during expertise acquisition (Durand-Bush & Salmela, 2002; Phillips *et al.*, 2010a). This is because intrinsic dynamics of developing experts are shaped by genetic and environmental constraints. The differential effects of environmental constraints on phenotypic gene expression means that expert levels of performance in athletes with apparently 'less favourable' genetic dispositions is still possible, given access to appropriate skill acquisition environments (Baker & Horton, 2004). Alternatively, genetically gifted athletes may fail to achieve expert status without a rich environment for acquiring and practising skills. Rich learning environments do not necessarily imply a need for purpose-built, state of the art training facilities (see Araújo *et al.*, 2010; Phillips *et al.*, 2010a). In fact, there is evidence of sporting champions emerging from the most basic learning and performance environments in 'talent hotbeds', whether in countries, small towns or individual sports clubs. For example, Brazil creates champion footballers, while in Australia the over-representation of champions from country areas is well known and described as the 'Wagga-Wagga effect'. Alternatively, the hotbed might be an individual sporting club such as the Spartak tennis club in Moscow that produced 20 world ranked women from 2005–07. In New Zealand five national standard performers emerged at the same time from Grey Street in Kamo, a small town of 1,000 people situated two hours north of Auckland (Jones, 1998). Interestingly, these performers reached elite level in five diverse sports (e.g., rugby union, equestrianism, table tennis, cricket and motor racing). All these examples demonstrate the importance of studying the range of unique constraints that shape future athlete performance and behaviour. The implication is that making predictions on future expert performers is extremely difficult due to the diverse and varying nature of sport performance contexts (Davids & Baker, 2007).

Changing performance landscapes and developmental trajectories of current experts

The importance of environment–individual interactions underpinning talent development has been highlighted as well as the need for practitioners to understand how performance environments change over different time-scales. Modelling talent development as a dynamic performance system results from constantly changing environments; a 'common optimal pathway' to performance expertise is unlikely, due to the capacity of structurally distinct parts of complex movement systems to achieve different outcomes in varying contexts (Davids, Button *et al.*, 2008). This concept (termed degeneracy) characterizes the sub-systems of each individual performer, and the effect of interactions between environmental and personal constraints on a learner's intrinsic dynamics. It signifies how expert performers can develop different functional performance solutions (Davids *et al.*, 2008; Renshaw *et al.*, 2010).

These arguments and analysis of extant data suggest the need for less reliance on early talent selection and hours of deliberate practice in a target sport as a strategy for identifying and developing future experts. Evidence for this view comes from retrospective analyses of developmental histories of experts and investigation of success rates of talent systems. Gullich (2007) reported that analysis of the Russian and German talent ID programmes revealed low to moderate success rates. Some studies have identified the time of sport specialization as key to expertise acquisition. In 1977, Olympic Gold Medalist David Emery asked: 'What Makes a Champion?', and revealed that the mean age of specialization for champions in a range of sports was 15 years. Currently, this mean age still appears to be at the upper end of the specialization phase (Côté *et al.*, 2003). Indeed, Vaeyens *et al.* (2009) suggested that an early onset and extended involvement in discipline specific training and competition during adolescence is not necessary for subsequent international selection in athletics. Athletes who entered training programmes *later* were more likely to win Olympic medals, possibly due to performance advantages gained via increased participation opportunities in other sports. A higher proportion of World Class athletes have trained (61 per cent vs. 48 per cent) and competed (47 per cent vs. 37 per cent) in an alternate sport in a ratio of 1:2 training sessions (of the target sport), up to 10 years of age and 1:3 training sessions from 11 to 14 years of age.

In our work (e.g., Phillips, Davids, Renshaw, & Portus, 2010a) we examined developmental trajectories of expert fast bowlers in cricket to identify key components in fast bowling expertise development. Eleven international fast bowlers (2,400 test wickets in over 630 international matches) were interviewed. Results revealed that unique interacting constraints underpinned their development, and the pathway to expertise could be construed as a messy, noisy and nonlinear process leading to unique, nonlinear trajectories of development. Specifically, data illustrated experts' ability to continually adapt behaviours under multifaceted ecological constraints. The key role of unstructured practice activities, optimizing learning processes, strong support networks, and effects of cultural constraints were highlighted in fast bowling development. An interesting finding concerned the distinction between 'place of birth' and 'place of development' effects in the context of fast bowling development (Phillips *et al.*, 2010a), with the latter potentially mediating the former. Expert bowlers reported that birth date effects may have been mediated by opportunities to play with older, more experienced players in challenging, yet supportive environments. Often these opportunities were inherently embedded in the performance landscape (e.g., for 'country' based cricketers who by necessity played against men at younger ages), or were deliberately created (e.g., for more talented young bowlers in the major conurbations). Exposure to adult competition was always undertaken in sympathetic environments where experienced older players created a controlled, supportive, mentored, learning programme. This environment contrasts with the 'survival of the fittest' structures apparent in many current talent 'de-selection' development systems (Abbott *et al.*, 2005). Importantly, from a talent development perspective, exposure to adult practice and performance environments made sure players were continually challenged and always on the edge of performance stability, forcing them to constantly adapt their behaviours and increase performance levels.

Although experts spoke about their high levels of general structured and unstructured cricket participation throughout adolescence, there was a relatively late focus on fast bowling for many individuals, with the majority not specializing in fast bowling until their late teens. Several experts were not even involved in structured cricket until late in their teens. This perception contradicts the need for high levels of early deliberate practice and later specialization may actually benefit young players by protecting them from high workloads during periods of vulnerability in growth spurts (Lee, 1982).

To summarize, these findings highlight the inefficiency of apportioning the majority of resources in high performance sport into talent identification programmes, at least as these programmes are currently structured. Due to the nonlinearity of interactions between individual athletes and the environment, predicting future champions is a challenging process because sport performance is constantly evolving. These ideas suggest that a greater emphasis should be placed on talent development rather than on theoretically flawed and wasteful attempts to identify talent early. How then should talent development programmes be designed? In the following section we highlight a number of principles upon which to base talent development programmes.

The role of meta-stability in acquiring expertise

When conceptualizing individual athletes as self-organizing dynamical systems, development can be viewed as a process of dynamic stability, rather than an inevitable linear march towards maturity (Smith & Thelen, 2003). It is important for practitioners to understand that athletes are sensitive to change since at various times both stability and flexibility are useful. Developing athletes cannot display too much stability in their behaviours, since being in a state of deep equilibrium might be dysfunctional in dynamic performance landscapes (Kauffman, 1995). For example, plateaus in performance can emerge as a result of team players participating in a competition that is below their level. Another example is when individual players spend too long performing at a level where they are not stretched to be successful, for instance when a racket sport player repeatedly plays against a limited number of training partners or only practises or competes at a venue that has unique physical characteristics.

The relative stability or instability of emerging expert athletes over time means that they are more or less receptive to change at specific periods of development. New behaviours and performance levels can emerge out of fluctuations created by periods of system instability. Control parameters, which guide system changes, may reside within the individual (e.g., strength or self-confidence), the environment (e.g., exposure to a different coach) or tasks (e.g., a more intense practice game).

These ideas suggest how, in the acquisition of expertise, small alterations in experience, practice and/or development, combined with small variations in genetic structure, might induce continuous and abrupt changes in the set of possible behaviours available to a developing athlete. The level of change caused by a specific event is sometimes difficult to predict and will be determined by the intrinsic dynamics (current predispositions) of the individual. As a result there is considerable indeterminacy by which athletes achieve similar performance outcome levels. As self-organizing systems they remain poised on the edge of stability and instability ready to produce creative movement solutions to performance challenges (Phillips *et al.*, 2010; Kauffman, 1995). The fluctuations caused by small (or large) changes in individual, environmental and task constraints in a developing system's organization can create performance instabilities, which may be detrimental or functional in assisting transitions in expertise with practice and experience. For example, instabilities and transitions (e.g., an injury or a traumatic experience if pushed to high performance environments before being ready) can move the athletic system to a less or more adapted state.

Crucial to designing individualized development programmes is identifying when behavioural patterns are stable or unstable and more open to change (Smith & Thelen, 2003). In this *co-adaptive* model, phase transitions (e.g., sudden changes) in system behaviour are most prevalent in meta-stable regions where co-evolving system components (e.g., an athlete's emotions, beliefs, physical characteristics, knowledge) compete to modify his/her performance landscape. Systems are said to be in meta-stable regions when conditions are equally poised to facilitate system stability and instability on the edge of transition from one state to another (Davids & Araújo, 2010). For example, the visual perception system is dynamic and capable of undergoing instantaneous change as observed from responses of individuals to perceptual illusions such as the Duck-Rabbit or the Reversible Figure-Vase illusions (Gross, 1996).

Applications for talent development

When multi-stable self-organizing systems, such as a developing expert, are poised in a state near this meta-stable region, nonlinearities might also create individual differences. Different types of behaviour can emerge depending on changes in relevant system control parameters and even very small differences in developmental histories. Such variations can amplify and lead to large individual differences in the ultimate level of individual attainment and the individual pathways to expertise (Smith & Thelen, 2003), raising some important issues about attempting to identify future champions. The implication is that sometimes apparently minor changes to individual, task or environmental constraints can result in regressions, giant leaps or paradigm shifts in performance leading to transitions along the expertise pathway. For example, a minor change in technique, a change of coach, an opportunity to play at a higher level due to injury to another athlete, or interaction with a previous champion could act as a catalyst or 'tipping point' (Gladwell, 2008) in a developmental pathway.

In simplistic terms, designing learning environments that push individual athletes to the edge of criticality can lead to the emergence of unique performance solutions. Learners can harness similar processes that drive evolutionary systems, but on different timescales, as a neurobiological system will always strive to behave in a functionally adaptive way to satisfy the specific confluence of performance constraints acting on it (Davids & Araújo, 2010). In practice, variability in the system of a developing athlete can be useful to exploit in facilitating a transition to a new state of expertise in sport. This process involves designing learning tasks with multiple performance solutions and performers are required to explore the practice environment to enhance their decision-making and action capabilities. Creating learning scenarios where opportunities for action are rich and varied can enhance exploratory activities, and lead to the emergence of more adaptive behaviours and functional performance solutions for individuals and teams. This approach leads to the creation of different ways to achieve the same outcome goals. During learning individuals are taught to cope successfully when a preferred performance solution is prevented by changes in task constraints (e.g., an opponent's actions), individual constraints (e.g., fatigue) or environmental constraints (e.g., weather or pitch conditions). At a team level, a good example of the need to find an alternative solution exists if a team's attacking strategy of always passing the ball to a key 'playmaker' was neutralized (by close marking of opponents), requiring the team to find new ways to solve the problem.

Identifying when developing experts are in critical regions is not easy and there are considerable challenges in predicting developmental potential (Smith & Thelen, 2003). However, expert coaches have significant levels of experiential knowledge in assessing an athlete's intrinsic dynamics, creating timely learning interventions that prevent too much stability in performance. Deliberately creating instability in practice environments leads to the development of performers with high levels of adaptability who can choose from a range of stable functional movement patterns. Research on nonlinear pedagogy has provided ideas on how practitioners can enhance learning design to enhance practice for developing experts (Chow *et al.*, 2009; Davids *et al.*, 2008: Renshaw, Chow, Davids, & Hammond, 2010; Renshaw, Davids & Savelsbergh, 2010).

Harnessing the evolutionary strategy of co-adaptation to induce performance paradigm shifts

The challenge for coaches and sport scientists is to identify when individual athletes enter meta-stable regions or critical periods while developing expertise so that performance paradigm shifts in expertise and skill acquisition may be triggered. By exposing athletes to meta-stable regions of the performance landscape during talent development, potential experts can discover new modes of behaviour to satisfy interacting constraints. New modes of performance are likely to emerge as novel solutions to performance problems, as developing athletes co-adapt responses to challenging constraints imposed by opponents, coaches or performance environments. For example, after the famous 'turn' away from defenders, performed by Johan Cruyff at the 1974 Football World Cup, millions of young players began to imitate and practise the move in training.

Creating meta-stability in children's sport

Backyard games (an Australian term meant to reflect the informal practice environments of children in backyards, streets and local parks) have been viewed as an ideal foundation for the development of expertise because they allow young players to devote hours of holistic unstructured practice, which enable the development of often unique skills, requisite mental toughness and the physical conditioning that underpinned expertise (Araújo *et al.*, 2010; Cannane, 2009; Cooper, 2010; Renshaw & Chappell, 2010).

During informal practice, the unique environments of individuals underpin the emergence of playing styles that are often the later signatures of experts (see Cannane, 2009). For example, it has been noted that the great Australian batsman, Neil Harvey, was proficient on turning pitches because he had to develop fast footwork to cope with ball deviations caused by a childhood spent batting on the cobblestone streets near his house. Similarly, Steve and Mark Waugh's trademark batting flicks through midwicket emerged as a result of a sloped front yard pitch that made these shots highly productive. Perhaps a key factor in these informal learning environments is that without the presence of adults, children are free to experiment and make mistakes without having to face adult criticism. Learning in these informal performance environments leads to players developing the intrinsic motivation needed for the significant amounts of play and practice necessary to develop high level performance skills (Renshaw & Chappell, 2010).

In summary, informal learning experiences have more to offer than just fun. For those responsible for talent development programming, harnessing the ideas and principles of backyard games can provide holistic development of emotional, physical, technical, tactical, and mental skills as well as the leadership and social skills needed for later success (Cooper, 2010).

Meta-stability in expert development systems

To summarize so far, co-adaptation is an evolutionary strategy that can be applied to exemplify how constraints might influence the process of athletic talent development by forcing developing experts to find new functional performance solutions. The process occurs naturally as a sport develops (i.e. through technique, rules and equipment changes or as athletes pose each other new performance problems through the competitive process). New solutions to performance problems emerge as talented individuals learn how to assemble creative movement solutions during practice.

The developmental strategy of seeking to move athletes to a meta-stable region of the performance landscape might provide a platform for the creation of new, more adaptive, modes of action to satisfy emerging task and goal constraints of the performance environment. For example, in high jump early athletes used a scissor technique to jump with the inside leg leading, followed closely by the other leg in a scissoring motion. The scissors action then progressed to the western roll and the Fosbury Flop, which represents a good example of the meta-stable region in the sport of high jumping. The Fosbury Flop was a performance solution that emerged coinciding with the use of raised, softer landing areas in modern times. Directing the body over the bar, head and shoulders first and sliding over on one's back, would have likely led to injury without modern landing mats.

The story of how Dick Fosbury 'flopped' is an interesting one and highlights that innovators who come up with creative solutions often need to have the personality traits that insulate them from criticism or attempts to make them conform to the norm. Fosbury's coach was less than enamoured with his new way of jumping and forbade him from practising the technique in training. However Fosbury was not easily put off and refined his revolutionary technique in competition at weekend meets when his coach was absent (Lee, 2007).

A similar story concerns the greatest batsman ever seen in world cricket: Sir Donald Bradman. When he first broke into the New South Wales team, Bradman was advised that he would need to change his unorthodox grip as it would not work at this new higher level. Bradman politely refused the advice and the infamous test average of 99.94 suggests that he may have been right (Chappell, 2010)!

Performance paradigm shifts have been created by: (i) equipment changes (e.g., the change from bamboo to fibre glass pole vaults leading to the world record increasing from around 4.5 m to 6.14 m by Bubka in 1993); (ii) changes to playing surfaces (e.g., such as playing international hockey matches on artificial turf instead of grass); and (iii), rule changes such as the turnover law in rugby union or the distance of the three-point line in the Olympics versus the NBA.

In elite sport, the drive for success means that performers are constantly being challenged to co-adapt to succeed. Through co-adaptation players need to add new skills or strategies to continue to present opponents with new problems. Essentially, players have to adapt or up-skill themselves to adapt to innovative strategies developed by opponents or new challenges posed by new opponents.

Meta-stability in action

A key to designing effective learning environments that harness meta-stability is providing representative practice tasks that facilitate couplings between key information sources and movements (Davids *et al.*, 2008; Renshaw *et al.*, 2010). Replicating performance environments during practice provides opportunities for learners to attune to key perceptual information sources (e.g., information from opponents' actions) (Beek *et al.*, 2003). However, in attempts to control the myriad variables that underpin performance, coaches can be prone to over-complicate training by, for example, decomposing tasks or designing activities that are not reflective of competition demands.

Representative practice: the battle zone

Earlier we discussed the importance of informal practice environments in under-pinning the development of expertise. Here we propose how coaches might harness key properties of these practice environments. We argue that, by using a constraint-led approach in learning design, coaches can maintain the representativeness of tasks, while creating high levels of intensity necessary to drive players to new performance levels. The efficacy of using games to enhance performance is obvious and is reflected in growing interest in pedagogical approaches such as Teaching Games for Understanding, Games Sense and the constraints-led approach (Bunker & Thorpe, 1982; Chow *et al.*, 2009; Renshaw *et al.*, 2010). For many coaches, replicating the structure of games is straightforward but a major challenge is often creating the same levels of intensity as observed in competition. Recently, a game-centred approach was introduced at the Cricket Australia/AIS Centre of Excellence in Brisbane, Australia under the guidance of the head coach at the time, Greg Chappell. Traditionally, playing games has not been a key feature in cricket practice sessions with most training being based on 'net practice'. The initial task was to find a way to create games that required players to function at high levels of intensity, such as *centre wicket practice*. However, coaches believed that this approach was limited, with fielders disengaged from the bat–ball 'competition'. The idea of putting a low 'net' on the 30m circle was considered, as it meant that all players would be constantly challenged and engaged emotionally, mentally, technically and physically in the practice games. The practice area became known as the 'Battle Zone', to reflect that this strategy is as much a concept as a physical space (see Figure 6.1). Battle Zone game design is based on adopting a constraints-led approach in a Nonlinear Pedagogy (Chow *et al.*, 2009; Davids *et al.*, 2008; Renshaw *et al.*, 2010), with coaches manipulating constraints to facilitate the opportunity for players to explore new ways of performing (Renshaw & Chappell, 2010). For example, coaches can develop game scenarios by awarding more runs for hitting or bowling balls into specific zones, or by having batters play games with different equipment such as a narrow bat or a different make of ball. A final point about the advantages of the Battle Zone is that performance assessment provides highly functional

FIGURE 6.1 The Battle Zone. The 'Battle Zone' practice area is created by putting a low 'net' on the 30 m circle. The Battle Zone is as much a concept as a physical space and was designed to ensure that all players are constantly challenged and engaged emotionally, mentally, technically and physically in the practice games. Battle Zone game design is based on adopting a constraints-led approach in a Nonlinear Pedagogy.

and relevant performance data on which to plan individualized development programmes.

The idea that coaches could design practice for developing experts to force them to the edge of stability to create higher levels of performance is captured in the story of John Amaechi, the former NBA centre. Amaechi reports that when he arrived at Penn State University he was far and away the best player on the team. Consequently, to challenge him, his coach recruited a 'walk-on' who only came on court to 'double-team' him when his team were on attack. As a result, Amaechi was forced to develop his game:

> I had to create time and space that scarcely seemed to exist. It pushed me past my limits, forcing me to think faster, sharper, deeper and with far greater creativity. In turn, my limits just kept expanding.
>
> *(Syed, 2010, p. 83)*

Providing performers with multiple opportunities to explore and solve problems for themselves is in line with Bernstein's (1967) definition of practice as 'repetition without repetition'. Creating variability in practice is essential to the learners' discovery processes and produces flexible and adaptable performers who invent novel adaptations to solve typical motor problems.

The role of movement variability in successful co-adaptation

The functional role of variability in expert performance may have an important role to play in expert skill acquisition in sports. This idea is supported by data reported by Morriss, Bartlett and Fowler (1997) who examined variability of men's javelin throwing in the 1995 World Athletics Championships. They found that the finalists from the event exhibited a range of movement solutions, which was reliant on different upper body contributions to projectile release speed. The silver medallist demonstrated linear shoulder movements (shoulder horizontal flexion and extension), whereas the winner of the event utilized shoulder rotation movements combined with higher velocity elbow flexion (18 per cent > any other competitor).

These data indicated that the notion of 'universal' optimal movement solutions for a specific performance task is inappropriate given the complex and degenerate nature of neurobiological systems (Glazier & Davids, 2010). Dynamical systems theorists have suggested that common optimal movement patterns for all performers probably do not exist and that variability is an intrinsic feature of skilled motor performance, providing flexibility to adapt performance in dynamic environments (Glazier & Davids, 2010). Talent identification programmes face a number of challenges given the nonlinear processes of development and difficulties in predicting future performance of individuals with often unstable genetic and environmentally driven variables. Elite level sport is a dynamical system that is continually evolving due to rule changes, new training methods and performance strategies. Over the long term, assessing future performance capacity becomes an even more complex issue when trying to predict what a sport will look like in five to ten years time. For example, predicting some of the technological advances that are continually changing the nature of sport seems impossible. Rather, there is a need for talent ID programmes to create flexible learning environments that provide performers with the opportunity to adapt to constant change. In the final two sections of the chapter we introduce new models for consideration by providing some ideas for individualized learning design and talent development systems.

Talent development as a nonlinear process: an adaptive transitional development model

Creating opportunities for athletes to compete against higher grade opponents is important for creating phase transitions as players are pushed away from stable performance solutions and forced into regions of meta-stability requiring adaptability to more demanding competitive environments. However, in some professional sports (e.g., association football or rugby union) these opportunities are largely limited to athletes stepping up to higher levels of competition or training in higher grade squads. This traditional group-based Step-Wise Sequential Model creates a number of challenges in developing talent. First, the difference in standard between performance levels means that selection is often based on guesswork as assessment of performance potential is often based on the whim of coaches (Christensen, 2009).

In this sort of system the coach can be reliant on statistical data or second hand evaluations (e.g., by the media), which may be more or less useful since these methods do not necessarily reveal data about the psychological attributes of the athlete. For example, a promoted athlete may face a number of psychological barriers including being momentarily overawed or intimidated by playing against more experienced performers, perhaps experiencing low self-confidence and high levels of anxiety. Second, lower initial performance levels might be initially predicted as the new player takes time to adapt to the increase in skill demands (perceptually, technically, decision-making). Third, selectors are more likely to make selection mistakes due to a lack of detailed knowledge about individual performers leading to a preference for players who do not have the requisite qualities to succeed. Finally, because of the limited opportunity to compare players at different levels, players with the potential to be successful at higher levels may have to play for a long time before they get their chance at the higher level. This effect implies that their performance might become too stable, reaching a plateau. Subsequently, when they do get their chance they might struggle to adapt to the new demands.

The previous discussion highlights that the over-riding issue for the Step-Wise Sequential Model is that the match between the intrinsic dynamics of performers and the 'new' task constraints (of the higher level) is largely dependent on the size of the step between two levels. The height of the step can be influenced by cultural constraints that influence the structure of performance pathways. A potential way of solving this problem is to design competition structures that create an overlap of playing talent between performance levels. Creating a system where players perform at two or even three levels promotes skill acquisition by moving performers to meta-stable regions of their performance landscape. This approach, termed the Adaptive Transitional Developmental Model (ATDM), is much more individually focused and may go some way to solving the problems inherent in the Step-Wise Sequential Model (see Figure 6.2).

Below are some of the assumptions/advantages of adopting an ATDM approach:

- Provides opportunity to learn by playing with and against the best players. This would include off-field behaviours and preparation.
- A number of players playing at two levels means that the step up for up and coming players is less severe as they have played against a selection of the 'better' players in competition.
- The time required to adapt to the higher standard is likely to be shorter.
- Promoted players may be more confident when promoted as they have played against (and most importantly had some success against) some of the players at lower level.
- Up and coming players are less intimidated and not overawed by better players as they are familiar with them.
- There is a greater chance of selectors choosing the right players as their performance can be assessed when they play against players from the higher levels (in their current level).

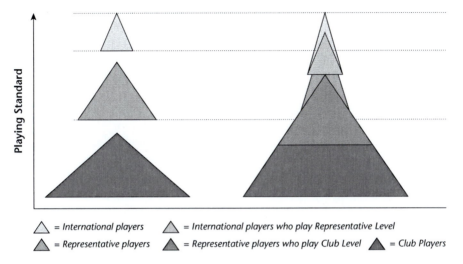

FIGURE 6.2 Talent Development Programmes. (a) *Step-Wise Sequential Model* demonstrating the separation between performers who play at each level and highlighting that there is a 'step-up' to the next level and (b) the *Adaptive Transitional Developmental Model* which shows the overlap of performers at each playing level.

- Provides opportunity to move players up for a short period and then back down again, giving them a taste of the requirements of the higher level.
- If a player fails at the higher level it can be a good thing as they know they can go back to the lower level and work on the areas of need.
- The greater movement between levels means that players can be given an early chance to be exposed to higher levels.

Playing 'down' a level:

- Gives the player the opportunity to take risks without significant consequences: to create new adaptive solutions.
- Creates mental toughness as expectation levels are higher as has to fight off the challenges of the 'new kid on the block.'
- Means that the better player has to become a team player and help the more junior partner. At appropriate moments this can involve protecting the player or giving them the chance to lead; act as a role model (in all aspects of performance); pass on knowledge that cannot be found in books.

Conclusion

In this chapter we have argued the need to enhance understanding of talent development processes in athletes as complex emergent systems, rather than emphasize the early identification of talent espoused in traditional approaches. Our aim was to provide a comprehensive theoretical rationale as guidance in designing talent development programmes. This theoretical rationale is based on understanding the acquisition of expertise in sport as a nonlinear process where the individual is a sub-component of a complex system. Our theoretical analysis criticizes the *organismic asymmetry* (Davids & Araújo, 2010; Dunwoody, 2006) inherent in the traditional 'athlete-centric' approach to understanding talent without a detailed consideration of the role of the environment. This focus on attributing regulation of behaviour to organismic structures and processes, at the expense of consideration of the individual–environment relationship as an interrelated basis for explaining human behaviour (Davids & Araújo, 2010), is a weakness in the psychology literature and limits the ability to identify talent or consider the most appropriate ways to develop talent. We have discussed how environmental constraints (cultural and physical), task constraints (changes in equipment technology, sport rules, playing surfaces) and individual constraints (as individuals develop new techniques, strategies or training methods) can interact to shape the emergence of talent. Clearly, when the future performance landscape cannot be defined in great detail, it becomes virtually impossible to identify the make-up of the future expert. We concluded by discussing some practical examples that elucidate these ideas across different sports. Key messages include the need to place a greater focus on inclusivity at grass roots level with a greater emphasis on providing high quality coaching based on representative practice for all children involved in programmes. The importance of early involve-ment in multiple sports means that children are better equipped to make sporting career choices later, leading to a better fit between the task dynamics of key actions in a specific sport and their own intrinsic dynamics. The implication of these ideas is that talent selection should be left until much later in an individual's development at a time closer to the age for peak performances. An important message through the chapter is that coaching programmes should be focused on individualization, eschewing the notion of a common optimal template for an expert in a particular sport. In emergent complex systems variability in performance and talent devel-opment is inherent due to system degeneracy. The role of phase transitions and rate limiters in nonlinear talent development is important and when systems reach a meta-stable region of the landscape characterizing athletic performance, rich and creative patterns of skilled behaviour can emerge as evidenced in the history of sport. The upshot of these ideas is that coaching in talent development programmes should adopt an athlete-centred, *hands-off* approach where learners are provided with environments where they can learn generic and sport specific skills, rather than be prescriptively taught putatively optimal movement patterns that are hypothesized to characterize all experts. In understanding developing experts as emergent complex systems, the key to developing talent is the encouragement of intelligent, motivated, highly adaptive individuals who are able to cope with the predictable and unpredictable changes in sport that come about as a result of changes in interacting environmental, task and individual constraints.

References

Abbott, A., Button, C., Pepping, G.-J., & Collins, D. (2005). Unnatural selection: Talent identification and development in sport. *Nonlinear Dynamics, Psychology, and Life Sciences, 9*, 61–68.

Araújo, D., Fonseca, C., Davids, K. Garganta, J., Volossovitch, A., & Brandão, R. (2010). The role of ecological constraints on expertise development. *Talent Development and Excellence, 2*, 165–80.

Baker, J. & Horton, S. (2004). A review of primary and secondary influences on sport expertise. *High Ability Studies, 15*, 211 – 28.

Beek, P. J., Jacobs, D. M., Daffertshofer, A., Huys, R. (2003). Expert performance in sport: Views from the joint perspectives of ecological psychology and dynamical systems theory. In J. L. Starkes & K. A. Ericsson (Eds), *Expert performance in sport* (pp. 321–44). Champaign, IL: Human Kinetics.

Bernstein, N. A. (1967). *The control and regulation of movements.* London: Pergamon Press.

Bloom, B. S. (1985). *Developing talent in young people.* New York: Ballantine.

Bunker, D., & Thorpe, R. (1982). A model for the teaching of games in the secondary schools. *The Bulletin of Physical Education, 18*, 5–8.

Cannane, S. (2009). *First tests: Great Australian cricketers and the backyards that made them.* Sydney: ABC Books.

Chappell, G. S. (2010). Personal communication, May 21.

Chow, J., Davids, K., Button, C., Renshaw, I., Shuttleworth, R., & Uehara, L. (2009). Nonlinear Pedagogy: Implications for teaching games for understanding (TGfU). In T. Hopper, J. Butler & B. Storey (Eds) *TGfU . . . Simply good pedagogy: Understanding a complex challenge* (pp. 131–43). Ottawa: Physical Health Education Association (Canada).

Christensen, M. K. (2009). 'An eye for talent': Talent identification and the 'practical sense' of top-level soccer coaches. *Sociology of Sport Journal, 26*, 365–82.

Cooper, P. (2010). Play and children. In L. Kidman & B. J. Lombardo (Eds), *Athlete-centred coaching.* (2nd edn, pp. 137–51). Worcester: IPC Print Resources.

Côté, J., Baker, J., & Abernethy, B. (2003). From play to practice: A developmental framework for the acquisition of expertise in team sports. In J. Starkes & K. A. Ericsson (Eds), *Expert performance in sports: Advances in research on sport expertise* (pp. 89–110). Champaign, IL: Human Kinetics.

Côté, J., Baker, J., & Abernethy, B. (2007). Practice and play in the development of sport expertise. In G. Tenenbaum & R. C. Eklund (Eds), *Handbook of sport psychology* (pp. 184–202). Hoboken, NJ: John Wiley & Sons.

Coyle, D. (2009). *The talent code.* London: Random House Books.

Davids, K., & Araújo, D. (2010). The concept of 'Organismic Asymmetry' in sport science. *Journal of Science and Medicine in Sport, 13*, 633–40.

Davids, K. & Baker, J. (2007). Genes, environment and sport performance: Why the nature-nurture dualism is no longer relevant. *Sports Medicine, 37*, 961–80.

Davids, K., Button, C., Bennett, S. (2008). *Dynamics of skill acquisition: A Constraints-led approach.* Champaign, Il: Human Kinetics.

Dunwoody, P. T. (2006). The neglect of the environment by cognitive psychology. *Journal of Theoretical Philosophical Psychology, 26*, 139–53.

Durand-Bush, N., & Salmela, J. (2002). The development and maintenance of expert athletic performance: Perceptions of World and Olympic Champions. *Journal of Applied Sport Psychology, 14*, 154–71.

Edelman, G. M., & Gally, J. A. (2001). Degeneracy and complexity in biological systems. *Proceedings National Academic Science U. S. A., 98* (24), 13763–68.

Emery, D. (1986). *Sporting excellence: What makes a champion*. London: Collins Willow.

Ericsson, K. A., Krampe, R. T., Tesch-Römer, C. (1993). The role of deliberate practice in the acquisition of expert performance. *Psychological Review, 100*, 363–406.

Gould, D., Dieffenbach, K., & Moffett, A. (2002). Psychological characteristics and their development in Olympic champions. *Journal of Applied Sport Psychology, 14*, 172–204.

Gladwell, M. (2008). *Outliers: The story of success*. Camberwell: Penguin Group.

Glazier, P., & Davids, K. (2010). Deconstructing neurobiological coordination: The role of the biomechanics-motor control nexus. *Exercise & Sport Science Reviews, 38*, 86–90.

Gross, R. (1996). *Psychology: The science of mind and behaviour* (3rd edn). Abingdon: Hodder & Stoughton.

Gullich, A. (2007). *Training – Support – Success: Control-related assumptions and empirical findings*. Saarbrucken: University of the Saarland [in German].

Holt, N. L., & Dunn, J. G. H. (2004).Toward a grounded theory of the psychosocial competencies and environmental conditions associated with soccer success. *Journal of Applied Sport Psychology, 16*, 199–219.

Jones, I. (1998). *Unlocked*. Auckland: Celebrity Books.

Kauffman, S. (1995). *At home in the universe: The search for laws of self-organization and complexity*. Oxford: Oxford University Press.

Lee, M. (Ed.). (1999). *Coaching children in sport: Principles & practice*. London: Spon Press.

Lee, J. (2007). *Dick Fosbury: Former Olympic high jumper*, http://speedendurance.com/2007/06/15/dick-fosbury-former-olympic-high-jumper/ (accessed 22 March 2011).

Morriss, C. J., Bartlett, R. M., & Fowler, N. (1997). Biomechanical analysis of the men's javelin throw at the 1995 world championships in athletics. *New Studies in Athletics, 12*, 32.

Newell, K. M. (1986). Constraints on the development of coordination. In M. G. Wade & H. T. A. Whiting, (Eds), *Motor skill acquisition in children: Aspects of coordination and control* (pp. 341–60). Amsterdam: Dordrecht: Martinus Nijhoff.

Phillips, E., Davids, K., Renshaw, I., & Portus, M. (2010). Expert performance in sport and the dynamics of talent development. *Sports Medicine, 40*, 1–13.

—— (2010a). The development of fast bowling experts in Australian cricket. *Talent Development and Excellence, 2*, 137–48.

Renshaw, I., & Chappell, G. S. (2010). A constraints-led approach to talent development in cricket. In L. Kidman & B. Lombardo (Eds), *Athlete-centred coaching: Developing decision makers* (2nd edn, pp. 151–73). Worcester: IPC Print Resources.

Renshaw, I., Chow, Ji-Yi, Davids, K. & Hammond, J. (2010). A constraints-led perspective to understanding skill acquisition and game play: A basis for integration of motor learning theory and physical education praxis? *Physical Education & Sport Pedagogy, 15*, 117–37.

Renshaw, I., Davids, K., & Savelsbergh, G. (Eds). (2010). *Motor learning in practice: A constraints-led approach*. London: Routledge.

Simonton, D. K. (1999). Talent and its development: An emergenic and epigenetic model. *Psychological Review, 106*, 435–57.

Smith, L. B., & Thelen, E. (2003). Development as a dynamic system. *TRENDS in Cognitive Sciences, 7*, 343–48.

Syed, M. (2010). *Bounce: How champions are made*. London: Forth Estate.

Vaeyens, R., Güllich, A., Warr, C. R., & Philippaerts, R. (2009). Talent identification and promotion programmes of Olympic athletes. *Journal of Sports Sciences, 27*, 1367–80.

International case studies of talent identification and development

7

TALENT IDENTIFICATION AND DEVELOPMENT IN WOMEN'S ARTISTIC GYMNASTICS

The Talent Opportunity Program (TOPs)

William A. Sands

USA Gymnastics has achieved unprecedented success in international competition in recent years; both men's and women's artistic gymnastics have garnered a number of World and Olympic medals. The following will be a description of the Talent Opportunity Program (TOPs) for Women's Artistic Gymnastics (vault, uneven bars, balance beam, floor exercise) in the United States. Although the US Men's Artistic program has an active and well-attended version of a talent identification (TID) program called 'Future Stars,' the women outnumber the men in national participation by over six to one. The two TID programs have different philosophies, with the men's more dependent on competition and the women more dependent on testing. However, the modern men's and women's artistic gymnastics national teams of USA Gymnastics have been viable at the world and Olympic level for more than a decade, with dozens of team and individual medals. Clearly, USA Gymnastics is one of the premiere national gymnastics programs in the world. As such, does the TID program for the women (TOPs) provide USA Gymnastics with an advantage over other nations that may not have a TID program in place? The development, implementation, and results of the TID program for women are described below.

Like most sports, gymnastics relied almost exclusively on competitive attrition to identify the best athletes. However, prior to the 1990s, during the Cold War, literature and rumors of intensive TID programs from the former Eastern Bloc were common (Gilbert, 1980; Bompa, 1985; Drabik, 1996). USA Gymnastics responded with various 'junior programs' that were widely variable in both objectives and management. During 1992, the USA Gymnastics Women's Artistic Gymnastics program began development of a TID program. The program was called the Talent Opportunity Program or TOPs. The initial approach was to seek and find youngsters between the ages of 6 and 12 years by canvassing physical education programs across the country, much as Bela Karolyi did in Rumania when he discovered Nadia Comaneche (Karolyi & Richardson, 1994). However, it was quickly realized that working through physical education was too expensive and difficult to organize. Moreover, it was quickly apparent that USA Gymnastics had ready access to thousands of potential athletes in gymnastics schools scattered across the country. There were numerous gymnastics schools, private businesses, across the nation that did not participate in high-level gymnastics for various reasons and likely had a wealth of untapped talent simply because the coaches were less trained, less familiar with high performance gymnastics, and the gymnastics school may not have had elite performance as part of its mission. The initial program was developed in order to assess performance variables that were under considerable genetic control and variables that were largely modifiable by training (Sands, 1993). The yearly iterations of the program have seen many modifications, particularly as the program shifted from the author's development and control to committee governance. The current TOPs program is described as:

> The Talent Opportunity Program is an identification system that is implemented under the direction of the Athlete Development Committee. Its purpose is to assist the coach with early identification of potentially talented athletes and to nurture and assist in the development of these athletes and their coaches and to pro-vide competitive opportunities.
>
> *(National Women's Program Committee, 2009)*

Program overview

History

The original program was written by the author in 1992 with a manual published in 1993 (Sands, 1993). The primary goal of the program was to identify young talented female gymnasts via physical abilities testing and gymnastics skills testing to provide these athletes with a more streamlined path to the elite level of performance than was currently available in the Junior Olympic Program (Geithner, Malina, Stager, Eisenmann, & Sands, 2002). The Junior Olympic Program is a very well-tested and important program for gymnastics competition and athlete development, but due to its many required levels, the path of a very talented young gymnast was often too long to be efficient. Thus, the TOPs program was set to allow a 'short-cut' for talented gymnasts. The initial testing was conducted in Indianapolis, IN during 1992. In 1992 there were approximately 54,000 athlete members of USA Gymnastics including men and women. This number grew to over 90,000 in the last athlete membership data set published in 2008. With the enormous rise in memberships and the fall of the Eastern Bloc, the setting was ripe for the development and implementation of a talent identification program that could rival what the Eastern Bloc had reportedly developed. The overall structure of the program is shown in Figure 7.1.

The initial program was ambitious with secondary goals of gathering enormous amounts of data on young gymnasts in a career-long approach to studying the

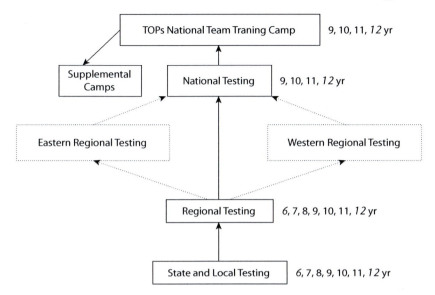

FIGURE 7.1 Overview of the TOPs program structure. Athletes begin at State and Local Testing. Note that the dotted lines indicate aspects of the program that were abandoned largely due to expense and time. Italicized ages (6 and 12) indicate that these ages were also abandoned. In addition, supplemental national training camps were begun due to the popularity of the program and a desire to include more athletes while keeping the TOPs National Team status intact.

longitudinal development of young female gymnasts. The secondary goal was abandoned shortly after the program's shift to committee governance in the mid-1990s. The implementation of the TOPs program has changed in a variety of ways since the shift. For example, 12-year-old athletes were eliminated in 2001, and 2007 saw the inclusion of a 'B' category for an additional national training camp followed by a 'Diamond Level' for younger athletes seven and eight years of age. Figure 7.2 shows the national participation of athletes in testing at the state and local level through 2008. Access to so many young and developing athletes and their coaches was unprecedented in USA Gymnastics and has continued to be a major program for the national governing body.

The tests

The initial program involved many tests that were ultimately abandoned. For example, pre-participation physicals were required using the format of Micheli and Yost (1984). Unfortunately, the ability and willingness of physicians to perform sport-related pre-participation physicals varied widely in terms of quality and expense (87 per cent of returned physical forms were incomplete), with some physicians charging hundreds of dollars and some simply signing the form and recording no medical information (Major, McNeal, & Sands, 1996). The pre-participation physicals were abandoned after two years. Many of the original tests

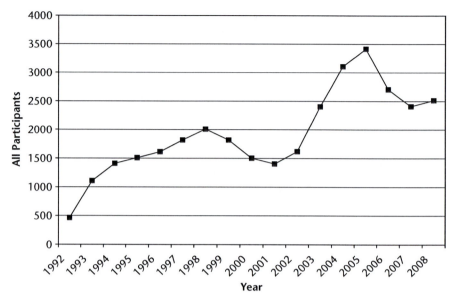

FIGURE 7.2 National participation in the TOPs program.

were also abandoned, largely because the testers could/would not comply with described protocols. Sadly, insufficient data were acquired for any of the tests to ascertain whether the tests could discriminate the talented from the highly trained or predict future gymnastics success. Thus, a great deal of effort was extended to the determination of tests that could be done fairly by coaches at the state and regional level. There was no opportunity for specialized equipment for testing beyond what was available in a typical gymnastics gym. These and other constraints ultimately led to abandonment of the following tests:

- pre-participation physicals;
- all anthropometry including weight and height;
- handstand push ups;
- medicine ball throws forward and backward;
- single leg balance tests;
- pull ups;
- push ups;
- broad jump;
- active flexibility of the lower extremities;
- drop jumps.

Gymnastics skill testing was fluid in that skills were added and deleted based on the most recent perceived needs of the TOPs athletes and the future national program. The current list of tests (National TOPs Testing, USA Gymnastics, www.usa-gymnastics.org) consists of the following:

- Handstand hold for 30 seconds, seven to eight year olds, and 60 seconds, nine to 11 year olds, time and score based on form and technique errors.
- 20m sprint, time only.
- Casts to handstand, on the low bar of the uneven parallel bars, repetitions and score based on form and technique errors.
- Rope climb via arms only, time to 12 feet (nine to eleven year olds) or six feet (seven to eight year olds), and a time deduction based on form and technique errors.
- Vertical jump and reach, performed standing near a flat wall, standing reach height is subtracted from jump height.
- Press handstand, starts in a straddle L position, repetitions and score based on form and technique errors.
- Leg flexibility test, forward splits performed on two vault boards placed with their low ends together and the athlete's crotch placed at the vault boards' junction, height of the crotch from the board low points, and score based on form and technique errors.
- Bridge test, the gymnast assumes a bridge or backbend position and then pushes with her feet to move her shoulders beyond her wrists, scoring is based on a vertical line from the armpits to the gymnast's wrists.
- Leg lift, on stall bars, the gymnast assumes a 90-degree bend at the hips and holds this position until she lifts her feet toward her hands. She must touch the bar with her hands or her feet must pass below the bar, then she returns to the 90 degree hip position and repeats, repetitions and score based on form and technique errors.
- Skill testing, the athletes perform various gymnastics skills on all events and are evaluated by certified judges. Skills are dictated based on age and frequently change due to national and international trends.

Scoring

All testing is conducted through USA Gymnastics with coaches performing all of the athlete testing. Coaches are trained to administer the tests, but there were/are complaints about fairness and different judgments based on varying regions, test interpretations, and accusations of cheating. Although relatively rare, these anomalies are handled by the National TOPs Program Director.

Scores are handwritten by each coach/tester on paper that is then turned in at the end of the testing to USA Gymnastics personnel. A mean and standard deviation are calculated for each test and individual athlete and test Z-scores are calculated. The Z-score permits the elimination of the problem of comparing tests conducted with different units of measurement (e.g., time in seconds versus repetitions versus a score judgment). Each athlete's individual test score is converted to a Z-score and then the average of the Z-scores for each athlete across all tests is used for further ranking. The number of athletes who move on to higher testing level or to the National TOPs Training Camp(s) are based on their rank and budgetary constraints of USA Gymnastics to support the event, provide uniforms, flights, and so forth.

Benefits to participants

Approximately 60–70 athletes, ages nine to eleven years, from the National Testing progress to the TOPs National Team Training Camp. The TOPs Training Camp attendees are considered TOPs National Team members, receive a uniform and the amenities of the camp. The coaches of the TOPs National Team members are invited to attend and most do. The seven to eight year old athletes who are too young to attend the TOPs National Team Training Camp achieve the privilege of having their coach invited to the camp to take part in observing the training, develop a social and information network of coaches and national coaching staffs, and take part in educational activities.

Does the program work?

There are three objectives for the TOPs program. These are: identification of talent, nurturing of talent, and education of talent.

Identification of talent

The TOPs program has had a total of 1,338 different athletes participate at the TOPs National Test Level from 1992 to 2009. The total number of athletes who have begun the assessment process at the most local levels has exceeded 25,000. Twenty-five of the 1,338 TOPs National Test Level athletes made it to the Senior National Team. The Senior National Team (15 years and older) (International Gymnastics Federation, 1997) is the team from which Olympic and World Championship competitors are selected. Thus, the likelihood of any National Test Level TOPs athlete making the Senior National Team during this 17-year period was approximately 2 per cent (25:1,338). There have been a total of 48 individual National Test TOPs athletes qualifying for the Junior National Team (as dictated by age and committee policy) (National Women's Program Committee, 2009). The likelihood of making the Junior National Team from the TOPs National Test Level during the same period was approximately 3.6 per cent (48:1,338). If an athlete from the National Level makes the Junior National Team, she is quite likely to move to the Senior National Team (approximately 80 per cent). Interestingly, the only analysis performed on the productivity of the TOPs program prior to this chapter was presented in 2002 (Geithner *et al.*, 2002). The 2002 analysis showed that the single best predictor of Senior National Team membership was being a member of the TOPs National Team. However, the most recent analyses show that the single best predictor of Junior and Senior National Team membership is the particular gymnastics schools where the athletes train. For example, a single gymnastics school produced more Senior National Team members during the period from 1992 to 2009 than did the TOPs program. This single gymnastics school contributed 43 of the 219 individual Senior National Team members (19.6 per cent, many athletes make the Senior National Team multiple years). In terms of Junior National Team members during the same 17 year period, the TOPs National Test Level produced

49 of the 318 (15.4 per cent) individual Junior National Team members; again, athletes can qualify for the Junior National Team multiple times. However, Junior National Team members are constrained by an upper age limit such that they have to move on to the Senior National Team if they have failed to qualify for either team. The largest contribution from a single gymnastics school to the Junior National Team was 29 athletes (29:318, 9.1 per cent). However, if the second highest Junior National Team member contributor is included; then these two schools slightly exceed the number of athletes (57:318, 17.9 per cent) contributed by the TOPs National Test Level athletes. Most gymnastics schools contribute one or two members of either Junior or Senior National Teams. For example, 55.1 per cent and 59.3 per cent of the total number of gymnastics schools contributed only one or two members to the Junior or Senior National Teams, respectively.

One of the goals of a TID program is to separate genetically determined performance characteristics (i.e., capabilities that cannot be easily changed but are important determinants of performance) from fitness characteristics (i.e., capabilities that respond well to intelligent training) (Roberts, 1986; Bouchard, Malina, & Perusse, 1997). The TOPs program has, for good or ill, elected to disregard this fundamental issue in favor of fitness tests and tests that are easy enough that coaches can administer them and no special testing equipment is required. For example, all anthropometric tests have been abandoned. Anthropometry, assessing size and shape, has been shown to be predictive of performance in national and international events (Claessens, Lefevre, Beunen, & Malina, 1999) with gymnasts being the smallest and lightest of all Olympic competitors (Malina, Bouchard, Shoup, Demirjian, & Lariviere, 1979). Observation of the TOPs National Level testing has shown that the size and shape of the athletes have largely coalesced to a small, lean, and light body type, mostly due to the fact that only this type of body can succeed in achieving a high rank in the TOPs program tests. However, it is also clear that given the low number of TOPs National Level athletes that make it to the Senior National Team, the fact that most national team athletes do not use the TOPs program as a path to National Team membership, the lack of sound test selection, and failure to enhance the sophistication of tests, one can only conclude that the TOPs program is successful in identifying those athletes who train specifically for the program and/or come from gymnastics schools that are already accomplished in producing high-performance gymnasts.

A number of challenging questions arise when evaluating the TOPs program in terms of TID. Certainly, the likelihoods listed above do not indicate that more recent TOPs participation is a powerful future performance predictor. However, among those who made the Senior National Team and were TOPs National Level athletes there are numerous World Championship and Olympic champions and medalists. At least five of the 26 Senior National Team athletes accounted for more than a dozen Olympic and World gold medals. In the rarefied world of national governing bodies and international sport, medal counts are often the only means by which a program is judged and medals are a powerful determinant of program viability.

A counter-argument to the efficacy of TID and TOPs is that the athletes that 'made it' probably would have been successful anyway, and the TOPs program may have only been a brief encounter. Unfortunately, one cannot replay the tape-of-time to determine how much of an influence the TOPs experience had on the athlete and her coaches. Moreover, there are a large number of Olympic and World Championship team members who did not use the TOPs experience or pathway to success, which indicates that TID from the TOPs program was neither necessary nor sufficient for national and international competitive success. Moreover, given the time and resources devoted to this TID program, one can justifiably wonder about expense versus outcomes. Olympic medals are staggeringly expensive, when assessed through a purely economic lens (Hogan & Norton, 2000).

In sum, the individual club and coach may exert a greater influence on the outcome of an athlete's performance and career than does this particular TID program. Although the TID program may confirm or verify that an athlete has special capabilities, the TOPs program rapidly changed from its initial search for talent to a competitive program that gymnastics schools trained specifically for and thereby taught to the test. As such, this practice emasculated the TID aspects of the program. This issue is exemplified by the fact that from 1992 to 2009, 37.5 per cent of the TOPs National Test Level athletes participated more than once and more than 15 per cent participated more than twice. One should question whether being 'identified' more than once makes any sense. Or, has the TOPs program simply become a goal in itself. While these issues are not harmful in themselves, the idea that TOPs is a TID program probably waters down the definition of the term as to make it useless. Moreover, one has to question the devotion of enormous financial, facility, time, and other resources to a program that demonstrates such a relatively small return in terms of international competitive productivity.

Nurturing talent

It makes little sense to identify talent and then have no means of supporting and nurturing that talent. The age group addressed by the TOPs program is much too young for international competition and the plaudits and pitfalls that accompany high level gymnastics. USA Gymnastics, and its leadership, know that a single contest, test, or event does not predict future performance with any certainty and will be unlikely to ever do so (Sands & McNeal, 2000). Moreover, there is a clear understanding that in order to win at the national and international level, the idea of TID must be particularly fluid ranging from rough verifications of talent versus no talent to determination of who is specifically ready and able to win in the decisive moment on the competitive floor of the Olympic Games or other important contest. TID is a process of detection of talent certainly, but also for nurturing talent that goes on continually and consciously among gymnastics coaches and administrative leadership. 'Talent' in this case is constrained to the immediate competition or competitive period. Team and individual athlete selection are based on a recent TID decision made by coaches, doctors, administrators, and others. Clearly, many have demonstrated that predicting the future of human events is a perilous task that almost never gets things right and that the further in the future one wants to predict the more perilous the predictions become (Gould, 1989; Shermer, 1995; Sands & McNeal, 2000).

There are examples of selecting athletes from one sport to participate in another sport and achieving some measure of success simply due to selection of requisite abilities (Bloomfield, 2003; Nunn-Cearns, 2007; Bullock *et al.*, 2009). However, gymnastics takes such an enormous amount of time to develop skills, strength, flexibility, and stamina that long-term commitment is necessary. Perhaps an unsurprising aspect of women's gymnastics is a type of 'athlete-poaching' that occurs by other sports in search of strong, flexible, agile, and mentally tough females. Female gymnasts have found success in sports such as weightlifting, diving, pole vaulting, aerial skiing, wrestling, and synchronized swimming. As such, gymnastics seems to develop athletes who not only succeed in gymnastics, but also in other sports.

Periodization and planning have become essential for modern gymnastics success whether the coach and administrators write down elaborate plans or the coach has the experience to keep it all in their head. Most athletes compete too often and gymnastics is not immune to this problem (Sands, Irvin, & Major, 1995; Issurin, 2008). Gymnastics has also been increasingly interested in planned recovery and the application of recovery modalities to enhance training and performance (Shazryl & Henley, 1991; Cooper, 1986; Sinyakov, 1982; Jemni, Sands, Friemel, & Delamarche, 2003).

Nurturing in the form of injury avoidance has probably become the single most important focus of modern gymnastics training (Sands, 2000). Gymnasts appear to suffer more than their share of injuries, particularly the athletes at the top (Caine, Cochrane, Caine, & Zemper, 1989; Caine, Lindner, Mandelbaum, & Sands, 1996). Injury prevention has therefore become a growth industry in terms of special matting, foam pits, special training apparatuses, trampolines, softer impacts, and many others (Daly, Bass, & Finch, 2001; Sands, 2002; Bieze Foster, 2007).

Education of talent

Coaches' education is practically nonexistent in the United States. There are very few coaching degrees offered from colleges and universities and most of these are not offered by academicians who were/are themselves top level coaches. Instead, most of these curricula are based on applied exercise science (Stone, Sands, & Stone, 2004) as if science alone is enough to make an expert coach. However, the education of coaches is as necessary as it is difficult and historically neglected. Perhaps the single most important contribution of the TOPs program has been in the education of young ambitious coaches.

Most gymnastics coaches are frantically trying to run a gymnastics school business while coaching gymnasts in competitions. These coaches are frequently traveling to competitions more than 30 or 40 weekends each year. Offering excellent coaches education workshops and seminars has often met problems because coaches simply do not come (Sands, 1990; Stone *et al.*, 2004). Coach attendance can be enhanced if the national governing body pays the coaches' expenses, but experience has shown that even covering expenses is often not enough to get coaches to take part in educational opportunities. Moreover, coaches don't tend to learn in ways that are typical of the academy. Coaches, by their own account, do not read scientific/medical journals, attend scientific/medical meetings, or participate in data acquisition to produce new knowledge themselves within their own training situations (Sands, 1990; Stone *et al.*, 2004). Coaches tend to acquire their information almost exclusively by experience, mentoring under a more senior coach and by attending local and regional clinics and seminars specifically for them (Sands, 1990). However, coaches will naturally choose to accompany their athletes to competitions, TOPs testing, and training camps.

The TOPs program provides an outstanding opportunity to bring ambitious young coaches together, introduce them to the national coaching staff, make them aware of the latest trends in gymnastics training and performance, and provide educational opportunities that are simply a part of the TOPs experience. Moreover, in spite of some shortcomings, the TOPs program provides a structure for the young coach making his/her first foray into elite level gymnastics. Although the TOPs program is not a guarantee of success the coach and athlete can explore, perhaps venturing ankle deep, into the world of high level gymnastics. By rubbing elbows with other ambitious coaches, seeing what their athletes are doing and how they are doing it, and becoming acquainted with the folklore and coaching wisdom of high-performance gymnastics – these coaches are getting an education that no book or course could possibly give them. Perhaps the greatest strength of the TOPs program is the access it provides to coaches who then go back and coach dozens or hundreds of young gymnasts better than they did before. As a result the TOPs program magnifies the benefits of education well beyond the athletes that a coach may bring to the program.

Conclusion

The idea that TID programs may save time and money while making the choice of the 'right' athletes with whom to work more efficient (Bompa, 1983; Bompa, 1985; Hogan & Norton, 2000) appears to be overestimated here. Neither time nor money appear to be saved, and the productivity versus expense of the TOPs program is questionable. However, the hidden and tangential benefits of nurturing and educating coaches and athletes are an important side-benefit of the TOPs program that may outweigh the issues of high level athlete performance prediction.

References

Bieze Foster, J. (2007). Efforts to reduce gymnastics injuries focus on spring floors. *Biomechanics, 14*, 11–12.

Bloomfield, J. (2003). *Australia's sporting success*. Sydney: University of New South Wales.

Bompa, T. O. (1983). *Theory and methodology of training*. Dubuque, IA: Kendall/Hunt.

—— (1985). Talent identification. *Science Periodical on Research and Technology in Sport*, February: 1–11.

Bouchard, C., Malina, R. M., & Perusse, L. (1997). *Genetics of fitness and physical performance*. Champaign, IL: Human Kinetics.

Bullock, N., Gulbin, J. P., Martin, D. T., Ross, A., Holland, T., & Marino, F. (2009). Talent identification and deliberate programming in skeleton: Ice novice to Winter Olympian in 14 months. *Journal of Sports Sciences, 27*, 397–404.

Caine, D., Cochrane, B., Caine, C., & Zemper, E. (1989). An epidemiologic investigation of injuries affecting young competitive female gymnasts. *American Journal of Sports Medicine, 17*, 811–20.

Caine, D. J., Lindner, K. J., Mandelbaum, B. R., & Sands, W. A. (1996). Gymnastics. In D. J. Caine, C. G. Caine, & K. J. Lindner, (Eds) *Epidemiology of sports injuries* (pp. 213–46). Champaign, IL: Human Kinetics.

Claessens, A. L., Lefevre, J., Beunen, G., & Malina, R. M. (1999). The contribution of anthropometric characteristics to performance scores in elite female gymnasts. *Journal of Sports Medicine and Physical Fitness, 39*, 355–60.

Cooper, B. (1986). Massage of the forearms for male gymnasts. *Sports Science and Medicine Quarterly, 2*, 4–5.

Daly, R. M., Bass, S. L., & Finch, C. F. (2001). Balancing the risk of injury to gymnasts: how effective are the counter measures? *British Journal of Sports Medicine, 35*, 8–20.

Drabik, J. (1996). *Children & sports training*. Island Pond, VT: Stadion Publishing Co.

Geithner, C. A., Malina, R. M., Stager, J. M., Eisenmann, J. C., & Sands, W. A. (2002). Predicting future success in sport: Profiling and talent identification in young athletes. *Medicine and Science in Sports and Exercise, 34*, S88.

Gilbert, D. (1980). *The miracle machine*. New York: Coward, McCann & Geoghegan, Inc.

Gould, S. J. (1989). George Canning's left buttock and the origin of species. *Natural History, 5*, 18–23.

Hogan, K., & Norton, K. (2000). The 'Price' of Olympic gold. *Journal of Science and Medicine in Sport, 3*, 203–18.

International Gymnastics Federation. (1997). *1997–2000 code of points women's artistic gymnastics*. Indianapolis, IN: International Gymnastics Federation.

Issurin, V. (2008). *Block periodization: Breakthrough in sport training*. Muskegon, MI: Ultimate Athlete Concepts.

Jemni, M., Sands, W. A., Friemel, F., & Delamarche, P. (2003). Effect of active and passive recovery on blood lactate and performance during simulated competition in high level gymnasts. *Canadian Journal of Applied Physiology, 28*, 240–56.

Karolyi, B., & Richardson, N. A. (1994). *Feel no fear*. New York: Hyperion.

Major, J. A., McNeal, J. R., & Sands, W. A. (1996). Physician compliance with physical examinations for national talent-selected female gymnasts age 6–11 years. *Proceedings of The North American Society for Pediatric Exercise Medicine, 1*, 70.

Malina, R. M., Bouchard, C., Shoup, R. F., Demirjian, A., & Lariviere, G. (1979). Age at menarche, family size, and birth order in athletes at the Montreal Olympic Games, 1976. *Medicine and Science in Sports, 11*, 354–58.

Micheli, L. J., & Yost, J. G. (1984). Preparticipation evaluation and first aid in sports. In L. Micheli, (Ed.) *Pediatric and adolescent sports medicine* (pp. 30–48). Boston, MA: Little, Brown, & Co.

National Women's Program Committee. (2009). *2010–2011 women's program rules and policies*. Indianapolis, IN: USA Gymnastics.

Nunn-Cearns, G. (2007). Testing the talent pool. *Modern Athlete & Coach, 45*, 5–8.

Roberts, D. F. (1986). Genetic determinants of sports performance. In R. M. Malina, & C. Bouchard, (Eds) *Sport and human genetics* (4 edn, pp. 105–21). Champaign, IL: Human Kinetics.

Sands, W. A. (1990). Survey of coaches – sport science and education. *Technique, 10*, 5–6.

—— (1993). *Talent opportunity program.* Indianapolis, IN: United States Gymnastics Federation.

—— (2000). Injury prevention in women's gymnastics. *Sports Medicine, 30*, 359–73.

—— (2002). *Gymnastics Risk Management: Safety Handbook 2002 Edition.* Indianapolis, IN: USA Gymnastics.

Sands, W. A., & McNeal, J. R. (2000). Predicting athlete preparation and performance: A theoretical perspective. *Journal of Sport Behavior, 23*, 1–22.

Sands, W. A., Irvin, R. C., & Major, J. A. (1995). Women's gymnastics: The time course of fitness acquisition. A 1-year study. *Journal of Strength and Conditioning Research, 9*, 110–15.

Shazryl, E., & Henley, D. (1991). Massage therapy utilization in a university gymnastics team training situation. *FIG Scientific/Medical Symposium Proceedings, 1*, 51–53.

Shermer, M. (1995). Exorcising LaPlace's demon: chaos and antichaos, history and metahistory. *History and Theory, 34*, 59–83.

Sinyakov, A. F. (1982). Restoration of work capacity of gymnastics. *Gymnastika, 1*, 48–51.

Stone, M. H., Sands, W. A., & Stone, M. E. (2004). The downfall of sports science in the United States. *Strength and Conditioning Journal, 26*, 72–75.

8

WHO ARE THE SUPERSTARS OF TOMORROW?

Talent development in Dutch soccer

Marije T. Elferink-Gemser and Chris Visscher

At the World Cup in South Africa in 2010, the Dutch team finished second (http://www.fifa.com). For weeks, Dutch streets and houses were orange (our national colour during sports events), and people celebrated this achievement as if 'we' were the champions. During the tournament, it seemed as if the Dutch team had almost 16 million coaches (the number of inhabitants in the Netherlands), for all pretended to know what to do to make it to the finals. In other words: we love soccer.

In this chapter, we first describe how youth soccer in general and talent development in particular is organized in the Netherlands. Second, we provide insight into several performance characteristics that distinguish the ultimately successful players making it to the professional level in adulthood from those who try but fail in reaching excellence. Finally, we pay attention to practical implications and give information for trainers, coaches, scouts, parents, and athletes.

Organization of Dutch youth soccer

The Netherlands has a sophisticated system of more than 27,000 sports clubs, including over 4.7 million people participating in organized sports, which is unique in the world (www.nocnsf.nl). Clubs of the same sport are united in one of 90 sports federations, such as the Royal Dutch Soccer Association (KNVB), and all sports federations are united by the Dutch Olympic Committee NOC*NSF. Soccer is the most popular sport in the Netherlands, with over a million active participants (Koninklijke Nederlandse Voetbal Bond, 2008). About half are youth players under 19 years, especially boys (n = 508,288 boys and n = 60,798 girls). Whereas soccer has been a typical sport for men in the past, lately more attention is paid to stimulate soccer in girls as well. Children can start playing soccer at one of the 3,417 soccer clubs from the age of five.

The KNVB's vision on youth soccer is that 'Soccer is learnt by playing soccer'. This means that children are introduced to the three major soccer team tasks, that is, offense, defense, and switching from on-the-ball situations to off-the-ball situations and vice versa. Exercises during practice are focused on game situations and therefore a link must exist with the real game. The focus is on the individual player: each can play soccer at his or her level, and attention is paid to age-typical characteristics. The KNVB distinguishes three phases in learning how to play soccer:

1. Age five to ten years (called mini-, F-, and E-pupils): the focus is on learning how to handle the ball and working together while playing small-sided games like four against four or seven versus seven.
2. Age 11–15 years (called D-pupils and C-juniors): the focus is on learning to play 11 against 11, deal with a larger field, the rules of the game and play in formations.
3. Age 16–19 years (called B-juniors and A-juniors): players must improve their task efficiency, handle the ball quicker, and specialize in the tasks they do best. Practice is focused on the game, players must play as a team, and learn to deal with pressure.

Two-year age categories are used for youth competitions; however, with respect to national representation teams, one-year categories are used. There are competitions at national, district, and regional levels for U13, U15, U17, and U19. For U11 and younger, we only have regional competitions. The clubs participating at the highest competition levels are mostly premier league soccer clubs.

Talent development programs

To develop talented players towards professional soccer in adulthood, professional clubs have talent development programs where soccer scouts observe youth players from the age of 11 (and sometimes younger) during regional competitions and invite those players who attract their attention to visit the club. At the club, the youth players participate in talent scouting days that involve a team of scouts, expert trainers, coaches, and staff deciding which players are subsequently invited to join the talent development program. The goal of the program is to develop professional players. In addition to talent development programs at premier league soccer clubs, the KNVB has district and national selection teams (see Table 8.1). As a rule, players in these teams are also part of a talent development program of a premier league club.

Players start the development program around the age of 12; however, there is a limited number of spots at the top and too many players are selected for too few spots in the first league. In addition, because the prediction of long-term success is extremely complex in which many factors (e.g., maturation) play a role, few of the initially selected players ultimately reach the top (e.g., Elferink-Gemser, Visscher, Lemmink, & Mulder, 2004, 2007; Vaeyens, Lenoir, Williams, & Philippaerts, 2008). Consequently, along the road to top level soccer, many players are released from

TABLE 8.1 Number of district and national selections of the Royal Dutch Soccer Association (KNVB) presented by age-category and status of matches.

District selections

Representation team	Number of representation teams per district	Number of representation teams in the Netherlands
Regional selections U12 and U13	10	60
Interregional selections U13 and U14	Differs per district	6–12
District selections U14 and U15	1	6
Amateur selections U14–U16	1	6

National selections

National selection team	Status
Netherlands U15 and U16	Friendly matches
Netherlands U17	European Championships
Netherlands U18	Friendly matches (year 'in between')
Netherlands U19	European Championships
Netherlands U21	World Championships
Netherlands U23	Friendly matches, Olympics
Netherlands first team	European Championships, World Championships, Olympics

the program. At the end of each season the trainers, coaches, and technical staff decide whether a player is allowed to continue in the talent development program, resulting in a relatively high rate of deselected players every year. Most of the deselected players return to a club playing soccer at a lower level of competition. The way back into a talent development program is extremely hard.

Studies on talent development

To gain insight into the performance characteristics that distinguish the successful talented players who make it to the professional level in adulthood from those who try but fail to reach excellence, we have followed talented youth soccer players over time by applying a longitudinal research design. This research is organized in our Center for Human Movement Sciences, especially in the Groningen Center for Talent Development and the Soccer Science Institute Groningen, both of which are part of the University of Groningen. We work together with four premier league clubs and have been following talented soccer players from two of these clubs over the last ten years. In our studies, we apply the model as depicted in Figure 8.1, which is modified after Newell (1986) and shows the hypothetical contribution of person-related, task-related, and environmental characteristics to sport performance in talented athletes.

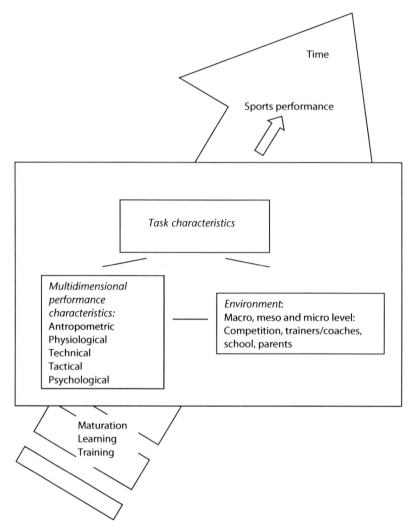

FIGURE 8.1 The development of a talented athlete's sport performance over time with the hypothetical contribution of person-related, task-related, and environmental characteristics to sport performance in talented athletes.

Depending on the task, in this case soccer-specific tasks in the field, an athlete needs a certain combination of person-related and environmental characteristics to be successful. Person-related characteristics are the multidimensional performance characteristics such as antropometric, physiological, technical, tactical, and psycho-logical factors (Elferink-Gemser *et al.*, 2004). Environmental characteristics apply to competition structure but also trainers, coaches, parents, school etc. The interplay between personal and environmental characteristics related to the task results in an athlete's sports performance. This changes over time and is influenced by maturation (Malina, Cumming, Kontos, Eisenmann, Ribeiro, & Aroso, 2005), learning and training of the athlete. As the road to the top is long, to be successful in sports, a talented athlete has to continuously improve his sports performance over time. While the performance level of an individual player increases over time, the level of complexity and refinement of elite soccer is also advancing. Over the years, the game of soccer has become faster and more complicated, requiring more of the players. In our studies, at the time of measurement, all players were part of a talent development program of a premier league club and consequently belonged to *the top 0.5 per cent* of all soccer players in their age category. Measurements of personal characteristics (multidimensional performance characteristics, e.g., antropometric, physiological, technical, tactical, and psychological factors), environmental characteristics as well as measures for maturation, learning, and training have been taken annually starting in season 2000–2001. An overview of the results is presented below.

Physiological characteristics in talented soccer players

Soccer can be characterized as a high-intensity, intermittent game in which both the aerobic and anaerobic energy systems play an important role (Reilly, 1997). During a 90-minute game, adult elite level players run 8 to 12 km at an average intensity close to the lactate threshold (Hoff, 2005) and aerobic metabolism provides about 90 per cent of the energy cost of a soccer match play (McMillan, Helgerud, MacDonald, & Hoff, 2005). Within this endurance context, a soccer player has to perform numerous bouts of explosive activity, such as jumping, kicking, tackling, turning, and sprinting, which are mainly covered by anaerobic metabolism (Mohr, Krustrup, & Bangsbo, 2003). However, great aerobic capacity is needed to recover from these high activity efforts (Spencer, Bishop, Dawson, & Goodman, 2005). To compete at the professional level, talented youth soccer players need to develop their intermittent endurance capacity in order to meet the demands of the game (Visscher, Elferink-Gemser, & Lemmink, 2006). They have to be able to perform high-intensity work repeatedly and to recover rapidly during periods of low-intensity exercise (Mohr *et al.*, 2003).

To examine the relationship between the development of intermittent endurance capacity in talented youth soccer players aged 14–18 and adulthood playing level (i.e., professional or non-professional), we followed 130 talented youth soccer players into adulthood (Roescher, Elferink-Gemser, Huijgen, & Visscher, 2010). The players were measured with the Interval Shuttle Run Test (ISRT; Lemmink, Visscher, Lambert, & Lamberts, 2004) when they were 14, 15, 16, 17, and 18 years old. Afterwards, we waited until the players reached the age of 20. At that age we identified them as either professional (n = 53) or non-professional (i.e., amateur) players (n = 77). Professional players were those who played in the selection of a premiere league club or the first team of a first division club. Non-professional or amateur players were those who played in the second team of a first division club or at the amateur level.

Intermittent endurance capacity improves with age in talented youth soccer players. At younger ages, no differences were found between later professionals and later amateurs. From 15 years of age, players who reached the professional level later on in their career showed a more promising development than their non-professional counterparts. This development was positively influenced by both soccer-specific and additional training. These results are similar to the develomental patterns in talented youth field hockey players in the same age band (Elferink-Gemser, Visscher, Van Duijn, & Lemmink, 2006).

Technical skills in talented soccer players

For the more crucial moments of a match, like winning possession of the ball, deceiving an opponent, or scoring a goal, technical skills are considered critical to performance in soccer (Bangsbo, 1994). Consequently, the velocity and accuracy of dribbling are of great importance in those vital moments of the game. It is therefore not surprising that the development of dribbling (i.e., sprinting while keeping control over the ball) is a central component in the development of young players (Huijgen, Elferink-Gemser, Post, & Visscher, 2010). The majority of dribbling actions involve acceleration, because players commonly cover short distances (e.g., Bangsbo, Mohr, & Krustrup, 2006). At the same time, dribbling regularly involves changes of direction (Young, McDowell, & Scarlett, 2001), which require acceleration and deceleration. To examine the relationship between the development of technical skill in dribbling in talented youth soccer players aged 14–18 and adulthood playing level (i.e., professional or non-professional), we followed 131 talented youth soccer players into adulthood (Huijgen, Elferink-Gemser, Post, & Visscher, 2009). We measured the players in their youth with the Shuttle Sprint and Dribble Test (ShuttleSDT; Lemmink, Elferink-Gemser, & Visscher, 2004) and waited until they reached the age of 20 to identify them as either professional (n = 54) or amateur players (n = 77). During adolescence (age 14–18), the peak and repeated dribbling performance of players who were ultimately successful was better than the players who were ultimately less successful. Successful players were on average about 0.3 seconds faster in peak dribbling on a 30m course containing three 180 degrees turns (average time around 9.5 seconds) and about one second faster in repeated dribbling (3 x 30m course; average time around 30 seconds). These time differences are considered essential in winning possession of the ball, dribbling around an opponent, or scoring a goal (Huijgen et al., 2009).

Tactical skills of talented soccer players

A player can have great endurance and a fabulous technique, but if he does not perform the right action at the right moment, he will probably not reach the top (Visscher, Elferink-Gemser, Richart, & Lemmink, 2005). Also in soccer, tactical expertise is a prerequisite for expert performance (Janelle & Hillman, 2003) and studies on tactical skills underline that athletes at a higher performance level consistently outscore players at a lower performance level on these measurements (e.g., Helsen & Starkes, 1999; Kannekens, Elferink-Gemser, & Visscher, 2009).

Tactical skills refer to the quality of an individual player to perform the right action at the right moment. Unlike physiologically based predictors of high level performance, tactical skills rely primarily upon cognitive skills that are typically categorized as declarative ('knowing what to do') or procedural knowledge ('doing it') (e.g., McPherson & Kernodle, 2003). Declarative knowledge has been defined as the knowledge of the rules and goals of the game (McPherson, 1994; Williams & Davids, 1995), whereas procedural knowledge describes the selection of an appropriate action within the context of game play (McPherson, 1994). In soccer, these elements of tactical skills can be further classified into 'on-the-ball' and 'off-the-ball situations' (Oslin, Mitchell, & Griffin, 1998). Compared to novices, talented players seem to not only know what to do during a game better than regional players but are also better in performing the right action at the right moment (Elferink-Gemser et al., 2010).

Moving along the learning continuum towards expertise, we made a comparison between elite and sub-elite youth players. Talented players (elite and sub-elite) all seem to have well-developed knowledge about procedures, the rules of the game, team mates and opponents, and ball actions. However, when it comes to the interpretation of a specific situation, to decide in a split second with opponents restricting time and space, to be at the right place at the right moment and to perform the right action at the right moment, elite players seem superior to sub-elite players (Elferink-Gemser, Kannekens, Tromp, Lyons, & Visscher, 2010). Given the importance of tactical skills as a predictor of future success, we assessed the tactical skills of 105 talented youth soccer players the moment they reached the end of the talent development program (mean age 17.8 ± 0.9) (Kannekens, Elferink-Gemser, & Visscher, 2010). Subsequently, we made a comparison between the players who reached the professional performance level in adulthood (n = 52) and those who became amateurs (n = 53). The players completed the Tactical Skills Inventory for Sports (TACSIS) with scales for declarative and procedural knowledge in either attacking or defensive situations. A logistic regression analysis identified the tactical skills that contributed to professional performance level in adulthood. *Positioning and deciding* appeared as the tactical skill that best predicts adult performance level. This is especially true for midfielders, with correct classification of elite youth players in the range of 80 per cent. For players scoring high on this skill the odds ratios indicated a 6.60 times greater chance that a player became a professional than players scoring low.

Training and learning

Because all players in these studies were part of the talent development program of a premiere league club, they had similar access to high-level trainers and coaches, training facilities and medical supervision resulting in an equal amount of soccer-specific training hours. Nevertheless, the successful ones seemed to be able to improve more within the same time constraints. A possible explanation for this phenomenon is a player's self-regulation (Toering, Elferink-Gemser, Jordet, &

Visscher, 2009). Self-regulation involves processes that enable individuals to control their thoughts, feelings, and actions (Baumeister & Vohs, 2004). Self-regulation is described by Zimmerman and colleagues (1989, 2006) as the degree to which individuals are metacognitively, motivationally, and behaviourally proactive participants in their own learning process. This means that individuals know how to attain their goal of performance improvement; they are motivated; and they take action to reach their goal. Self-regulatory processes will not immediately produce high levels of expertise, but can assist an individual in acquiring knowledge and skills more effectively (Zimmerman *et al.*, 2006). Youth soccer players who self-regulate well may improve their performance more, because they are more aware of their strong and weak points, better focused on making progress, and more capable of adapting their learning strategies to the requirements of practice/the game. Therefore, these players may develop faster and be better able to get the maximum out of their potential (Jonker, Elferink-Gemser, & Visscher, 2010).

From our longitudinal studies it seems that talented youth soccer players who ultimately make it to the top perform better than their less successful counterparts on a combination of performance characteristics (e.g., physiological, technical, and tactical skills). Successful players seem to have acquired better dribbling skills by the age of 14, develop their interval endurance capacity faster from the age of 15 and outscore less successful players on tactical skills at the age of 17. Nevertheless, one has to be careful in interpreting the scores of individual players based on only one test; it is possible to reach the professional level while scoring worse than the predicted curves for professionals. Therefore, it is of the utmost importance to present the total picture of a talented player's scores on his multidimensional performance characteristics favourably combined with information on environmental characteristics as well as on maturation, learning, and training to trainers, coaches, and staff.

Practical implications

From these studies practical implications and information for trainers, coaches, scouts, parents, and athletes can be derived. One has to realize that the development of a talented athlete's sport performance towards expertise is a long process in which many years of dedicated training have to be invested. Although the quality of training (i.e., training programs designed by highly skilled trainers and coaches) and the quantity of training (i.e., number of training hours) are important parameters, what an athlete gains from *each* training session seems even more important. To optimally benefit from training, a talented athlete needs to take responsibility for his own learning process. He has to reflect on his own performance and think about strategies to further develop his performance characteristics. These performance characteristics are multidimensional and trainers, coaches as well as scouts need to realize this. To reach expertise, talented soccer players are developing characteristics such as their interval endurance capacity, dribbling speed, and their skill at best positioning themselves on the field, making the right decisions. They do so, however, in their own unique way. Although on average the ultimately successful ones (i.e., the ones signing a professional contract) seem to have acquired better dribbling skills by the age of 14, develop their interval endurance capacity faster from the age of 15 and outscore later amateurs by their tactical skills at the age of 17, individual developmental curves differ from each other. This implies that for each player, the individual performance curves on each characteristic need to be depicted and followed over time. By comparing the scores of each player to his own earlier scores, as well as to the group, valuable practical information can be derived concerning talent development.

References

Bangsbo, J. (1994). Energy demands in competitive soccer. *Journal of Sports Sciences, 12*, S5-S12.

Bangsbo, J., Mohr, M., & Krustrup, P. (2006). Physical and metabolic demands of training and match-play in the elite football player. *Journal of Sports Sciences, 24*, 665–74.

Baumeister, R. F., & Vohs, K. D. (2004). *Handbook of self-regulation: Research, theory, and applications.* Guilford Press, New York.

Elferink-Gemser, M. T., Kannekens, R., Tromp, E. J. Y., Lyons, J., & Visscher, C. (2010). Knowing what to do and doing it: Differences in self-assessed tactical skills of regional, sub-elite, and elite youth field hockey players. *Journal of Sports Sciences, 28*, 521–28.

Elferink-Gemser, M. T., Visscher, C., Lemmink, K. A. P. M., & Mulder, Th. (2004). Relation between multidimensional performance characteristics and level of performance in talented youth field hockey players. *Journal of Sports Sciences, 22*, 1053–63.

—— (2007). Multidimensional performance characteristics and performance level in talented youth field hockey players: A longitudinal study. *Journal of Sports Sciences, 25*, 481–89.

Elferink-Gemser, M. T., Visscher, C., Van Duijn, M. A. J., & Lemmink, K. A. P. M. (2006). Development of the interval endurance capacity in elite and sub-elite youth field hockey players. *British Journal of Sports Medicine, 40*, 340–45.

FIFA (2009). World Football Ranking. www.fifa.com/worldfootball/ranking/lastranking/gender=m/fullranking.html (accessed 20 October 2010).

Helsen, W. F., & Starkes, J. L. (1999). A multidimensional approach to skilled perception and performance in sport. *Applied Cognitive Psychology, 13*, 1–27.

Hoff, J. (2005). Training and testing physical capacities for elite soccer players. *Journal of Sports Sciences, 23*, 573 – 582.

Huijgen, B. C. H., Elferink-Gemser, M. T., Post, W. J., & Visscher, C. (2009). Soccer skill development in professionals. *International Journal of Sports Medicine, 30*, 585–91.

—— (2010). Development of dribbling in talented youth soccer players aged 12–19 years: A longitudinal study. *Journal of Sports Sciences, 28*, 689–98.

Janelle, C. M., & Hillman, C. H. (2003). Expert performance in sport. Current perspectives and critical issues. In J. L. Starkes & K. A. Ericsson (Eds) *Expert performance in sports: Advances in research on sport expertise* (pp. 19–47). Champaign, IL: Human Kinetics.

Jonker, L., Elferink-Gemser, M. T., & Visscher, C. (2010). Differences in self-regulatory skills among talented athletes: The significance of competitive level and type of sport. *Journal of Sports Sciences, 28*, 901–8.

Kannekens, R., Elferink-Gemser, M. T., & Visscher, C. (2009). Tactical skills of world-class youth soccer teams. *Journal of Sports Sciences, 27*, 807–12.

—— (2010). Positioning and deciding: Key factors for talent development in soccer. *Scandinavian Journal of Medicine and Science in Sports.* Epub ahead of print. DOI 10.1111/j.1600–0838.2010.01104.x.

Koninklijke Nederlandse Voetbal Bond (2008). Over KNVB. www.knvb.nl/organisatie/academie/elearning (accessed 28 November 2008).

Lemmink, K. A. P. M., Elferink-Gemser, M. T., & Visscher, C. (2004). Evaluation of the reliability of two field hockey specific sprint and dribble tests in young field hockey players. *British Journal of Sports Medicine, 38,* 138–42.

Lemmink, K. A. P. M., Visscher, C., Lambert, M. I., & Lamberts, R. P. (2004). The interval shuttle run test for intermittent sport players: evaluation of reliability. *Journal of Strength and Conditioning Reasearch, 18,* 821–27.

Malina, R. M., Cumming, S. P., Kontos, A. P., Eisenmann, J. C., Ribeiro, B., & Aroso, J. (2005). Maturity-associated variation in sport-specific skills of youth soccer players aged 13–15 years. *Journal of Sports Sciences, 23,* 515–22.

McMillan, K., Helgerud, J., Macdonald, R., & Hoff, J. (2005). Physiological adaptations to soccer specific endurance training in professional youth soccer players. *British Journal of Sports Medicine, 39,* 273 – 277.

McPherson, S. L. (1994). The development of sport expertise: Mapping the tactical domain. *Quest,* 46, 223–40.

McPherson, S. L., & Kernodle, M. W. (2003). Tactics, the neglected attribute of expertise. Problem representations and performance skills in tennis. In J. L. Starkes & K. A. Ericsson (Eds) *Expert performance in sports: Advances in research on sport expertise* (pp. 137–67). Champaign, IL: Human Kinetics.

Mohr, M., Krustrup, P., & Bangsbo, J. (2003). Match performance of high-standard soccer players with special reference to development of fatigue. *Journal of Sports Sciences, 21,* 519–28.

Nederlands Olympisch Comité*Nederlandse Sport Federatie (NOC*NSF). (2010). http://nocnsf.nl/home (accessed 20 October 2010).

Newell, K. M. (1986). Constraints on the development of co-ordination. In M. Wade & H.T.A. Whiting (Eds) *Motor development in children: aspects of co-ordination and control* (pp. 341–60). Dordrecht: Martinus Nijhof.

Oslin, J. L., Mitchell, S. A., & Griffin, L. L. (1998). The game performance assessment instrument (GPAI): development and preliminary validation. *Journal of Teaching in Physical Education, 17,* 231–43.

Reilly, T. (1997). Energetics of high-intensity exercise (soccer) with particular reference to fatigue. *Journal of Sports Sciences, 15,* 257–63.

Reilly, T., Bangsbo, J., & Franks, A. (2000). Anthropometric and physiological predispositions for elite soccer. *Journal of Sports Sciences, 18,* 669–83.

Reilly, T., Williams, A. M., Nevill, A., & Franks, A. (2000). A multidisciplinary approach to talent identification in soccer. *Journal of Sports Sciences, 18,* 695–702.

Roescher, C. R., Elferink-Gemser, M. T., Huijgen, B. C. H., Visscher, C. (2010). Soccer endurance development in professionals. *International Journal of Sports Medicine, 31,* 174–79.

Spencer, M., Bishop, D., Dawson, B., & Goodman, C. (2005). Physiological and metabolic responses of repeated-sprint activities: Specific to field-based team sports. *Sports Medicine, 35,* 1025–44.

Toering, T. T., Elferink-Gemser, M. T., Jordet, G., & Visscher, C. (2009). Self-regulation and performance level of elite and non-elite youth soccer players. *Journal of Sports Sciences, 27,* 1509–17.

Vaeyens, R., Lenoir, M., Williams, A. M., & Philippaerts, R. M. (2008). Talent identification and development programmes in sport: Current models. *Sports Medicine, 38,* 703–14.

Visscher, C., Elferink-Gemser, M. T., & Lemmink, K. A. P. M. (2006). Interval endurance capacity of talented youth soccer players. *Perceptual and Motor Skills, 102,* 81–86.

Visscher, C., Elferink-Gemser, M. T., Richart, H., & Lemmink, K. A. P. M. (2005). Necessity of including tactical skills measurement in a field hockey talent development program. In N. Dikic, S. Zivanic, S. Ostojic, & Z. Tornjanski (Eds) *Book of Abstracts of the 10th Annual Congress of the European College of Sport Science in Belgrade, Serbia from 13–16 July 2005* (pp. 187–88).[aq40]

Williams, M., & Davids, K. (1995). Declarative knowledge in sport: A by-product of experience or a characteristic of expertise. *Journal of Sport and Exercise Psychology*, *17*, 259–75.

Young, W. B., McDowell, M. H., Scarlett, B. J. (2001). Specificity of sprint and agility training methods. *Journal of Strength and Conditioning Research*, *15*, 315–19.

Zimmerman, B. J. (1989). A social cognitive view of self-regulated academic learning. *Journal of Educational Psychology*, *81*, 329–39.

—— (1990). Self-regulated learning and academic achievement: An overview. *Educational Psychologist*, *25*, 3–17.

Zimmerman, B. J., Ericsson, K. A., Charness, N., Feltovich, P. J., & Hoffman, R. R. (2006). Development and adaptation of expertise: The role of self-regulatory processes and beliefs. In K. A. Ericsson, N. Charness, P. J. Feltovich., & R. R. Hoffman (Eds) *The Cambridge handbook of expertise and expert performance* (pp. 705–22). New York: Cambridge University Press.

9

TALENT IDENTIFICATION, SELECTION AND DEVELOPMENT IN UK JUNIOR RUGBY LEAGUE

An evolving process

Kevin Till, Chris Chapman, Steve Cobley, John O'Hara and Carlton Cooke

Rugby league football originated in the north of England in 1895, and is currently played worldwide with the game most popular in the UK, France, Australia and New Zealand (Meir, Newton, Curtis, Fardell, & Butler, 2001). Rugby league is physically demanding (Gabbett, King & Jenkins, 2008) with time-motion analysis demonstrating that players cover an average of 8.5km during senior professional (i.e., Super League) match play with an average work-to-rest-ratio of about 1:11, demonstrating the intermittent nature of the game (Sykes, Twist, Hall & Lamb, 2009). The average energy expenditure and heart rate during a senior semi-professional Australian game have been reported as 24 kcal/min (Coutts, Reaburn & Abt, 2003) and 166 beats/min (Gabbett, Kelly, Ralph & Driscoll, 2007) respectively.

In the UK, the Rugby Football League (RFL) is the sports governing body (see www.rfl.uk.com for more information), covering the sport between the community level (i.e., schools and amateur clubs starting at Under 7s annual-age category) to the full-time senior professional game (i.e., Super League) and international programme. A number of playing levels and representative selections occur across the game with Figure 9.1 providing an overview of the structure of junior rugby league within the UK. Rugby league in the UK has undergone significant change over the past few years, partially due to an extensive research programme focused on improving talent identification and player development. Between 2001 and 2008, the RFL used a Player Performance Pathway as its talent identification and development model. After 2008, this model was modified based on identified limitations. Below we discuss the previous model and the basis for developing the current model.

The RFL Player Performance Pathway

The Player Performance Pathway was a sustainable talent identification, selection and development process with the major aim of assisting the development of the

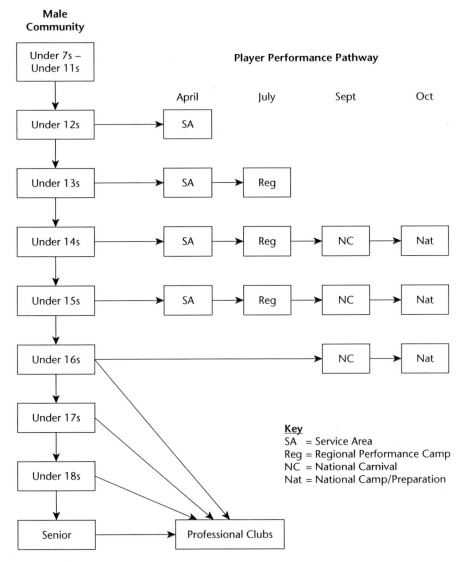

FIGURE 9.1 A model describing the developmental structure in UK rugby league (adapted from Till, Cobley, Wattie *et al.*, 2010).

most talented players and coaches to train, prepare and compete at all levels on the world stage. This chapter focuses on the identification, selection and development of talented junior players within the Player Performance Pathway between 12 and 16 years of age. This was the chosen group as after 16 years of age the identification, selection and development of talented players primarily rests with the professional clubs who offer players professional contracts. The selection stages used in the Player Performance Pathway for the Under 12–16 annual-age categories are shown in Figure 9.1 and included:

- *Service Area* – the first stage of selection and representation was to the Service Area programme (local district authority; e.g., Leeds, a city in Yorkshire). Selection was made from the community game (e.g., schools and amateur clubs) at under 12, 13, 14 and 15 age-categories, in which up to 28 Service Area teams competed against each other as part of an 'inter-service area' competition during the end of the playing season (i.e., May–June). This comprised of four to five games with each Service Area squad having up to 25 players.
- *Regional* – the second representative stage was to Regional level (county standard e.g., Yorkshire). Selection occurred at the under 13, 14 and 15 age-categories to Regional squads in Yorkshire ($n = 40$), North-West ($n = 40$), Cumbria ($n = 20$), North East ($n = 20$), Midlands ($n = 20$) and London and the South ($n = 20$). Regional selection resulted in selected players attending a four-day performance camp (occurring around July/August) to undertake specialised training, coaching and support.
- *National Carnival* – based on player performances at Regional camp, a Regional squad (i.e., 20 players approx.) was selected to compete in a National Carnival (around September at the start of a new season; i.e., Under 13s are now Under 14s). This was comprised of four teams (i.e., Yorkshire, North-West, Cumbria and Combined Regions – North East, Midlands, London and South).
- *National* – generally, through participation at the National Carnival, a player would then be considered and selected for the National Programmes (i.e., National Performance Camp/Link Programme = Under 14s, $n = 40$; National Preparation = Under 15s and 16s, $n = 24$). Selection at this level typically involved additional training with support provided throughout the following playing year.

For each season, a new process of selection and identification commenced for the Player Performance Pathway, in which all players within the junior participation structure became eligible again and reconsidered for selection at each of the respective stages.

The Player Performance Pathway selection criteria

Selection onto the Player Performance Pathway was typically made using a talent selection approach, which involved selecting players who demonstrated prerequisite standards of performance for inclusion in a particular team or squad (Mohamed *et al.* 2009). The RFL employed nine National Performance Analysts (PA) whose role was to identify and select players onto and within the Player Performance Pathway. The PAs were asked to observe players across the selection stages and comment on both their current playing ability and potential for the future, which was determined subjectively through the PAs' experience and knowledge on what enables a player to progress and succeed. No tests or measurements were used at this point of selection by the PAs. Whilst potential was an important factor in the process, the players had to demonstrate rugby league ability (i.e., technical and tactical rugby league skills and knowledge alongside physical, mental and lifestyle attributes) at the current time. Once players were identified, PAs continued to monitor a player's performance and provide regular feedback and reports to the player, his community coach and the RFL. All PAs were centrally contracted with the RFL and were provided with a programme of standardisation and moderation to ensure the quality of their selections and nominations. Moderation was essential to ensure consistency across the regions and included PA workshops on what to look for at each stage, and assessments through video and live observations. The PAs also reviewed each other's reports and assessments with each regional lead PA responsible for co-ordinating the programme.

The criteria used when selecting a player included physical, technical, tactical, mental and lifestyle attributes. Each criterion was considered differently dependent upon the stage of selection along the Player Performance Pathway. For example, at the Service Area stage, the focus was very much aligned to the physical, technical and tactical attributes. Due to the 'snap shot' nature of game observations at the Service Area stage, PAs and coaches were asked to view the player's physical attributes relative to playing the game (e.g. if a player had speed how did he utilise this in a game situation). Technical attributes were restricted to the core skills (e.g. grip, carry, catching, passing, play the ball, tackling, kicking and falling), whilst tactical attributes were assessed on the players' ability to recognise and react to situations with and without the ball (e.g. a defensive decision or line of carry with the ball). All players were nominated to a playing position which usually, but not always, corresponded to the position they played at Service Area.

On progressing to Regional Camp, PAs spent more time observing the individuals outside of the playing environment, and so other attributes were able to be observed and monitored. This included attitude toward training, approach to preparation and how the player responded off the field and in performance workshops alongside anthropometric and fitness testing. Similar attributes were observed from Regional Camp through to National Camp and National Preparation. Here PAs looked for a greater consistency in performance and the ability to continue to perform the necessary skills and techniques as the player progressed through the stages. A 'best versus the best' approach (i.e., the best players at each annual-age category competed against each other) was seen as the pinnacle of the pathway. A significant weighting was placed on 'rugby league ability' and those players who performed well in the field-based testing, were attentive in the workshops, listened to the coaches in sessions but were of a lower playing ability were not selected ahead of the others.

Player Performance Pathway training and support

The Player Performance Pathway aimed to provide a progressive continuum of high quality experiences for a player they could then apply when returning to respective stages of the game (e.g., community). The progression was considerate of the player's current playing level and age/stage of development. The programme was structured around the five key attributes involved in selection (technical, tactical, physical, mental and lifestyle development), titled the 'star' player. Service Areas across all age categories generally focused on core skills, Regional programmes developed the fundamentals of rugby league combining core skills in variable and random practice and National Programmes included positional specific training. Players were grouped according to their playing position and were provided with deliberate practice and situational scenarios aligned to this position. For example, forwards worked on timing, depth and lines around the play of the ball; pivots worked on lines from dummy half and kicking and the outside backs developed lines of support.

All programmes included technical coaching, fitness testing and anthropometric measurements, small sided games, formal assessments, one on one coach reviews and performance workshops including mental skills, nutrition and treatment of injury. As players progressed within the pathway, the coaching approach and content were further refined to include greater levels of physical contact and more sustained pressure. Players worked in structured situations where they were expected to make repeated efforts, be involved in decision making and continuously 'fix' game-based problems. The increase in pressure resulted from the level of contact, intensity and volume (number of plays or time of the scenario) of the session.

Emerging issues with the Player Performance Pathway

During the years where the pathway was active, several research studies were conducted (e.g., Till, Cobley, Wattie, O'Hara, Cooke, & Chapman, 2010; Till, Cobley, O'Hara, Chapman, & Cooke, 2010; Till, Cobley, O'Hara, Brightmore, Cooke, & Chapman, 2011). Collectively, these studies began to highlight some key issues associated with player identification, selection and development within junior rugby league. A summary of these key issues is provided below.

Relative Age Effects (RAEs)

Till, Cobley, Wattie *et al.* (2010) identified that RAEs (see Chapter 4) were highly prevalent across male rugby league in the UK. Significant uneven distributions of birthdate – relative to dates established for annual-age groups – favoured the selection of relatively older players. For junior players represented in the Player Performance Pathway, RAEs increased with each selection level (i.e. Under 13s – Service Area Q1 = 43.5 per cent, Q4 = 11.3 per cent; Regional Q1 = 52.2 per cent, Q4 = 5.8 per cent; National Camp Q1 = 60.0 per cent, Q4 = 2.5 per cent), where selection for a smaller number of places on a representative squad occurred. As an example, Figure 9.2 summarises the relative age distributions of junior rugby league players by combining the Under 13–15 age groups and categorising according to selection stage. Findings identified that relatively older males in all tiers of rugby league (i.e., junior participation, junior representative and senior professional) had a greater likelihood of participation and selection than their relatively younger peers. This discrepancy commenced at the earliest stages of the game and increased at every stage of the pathway.

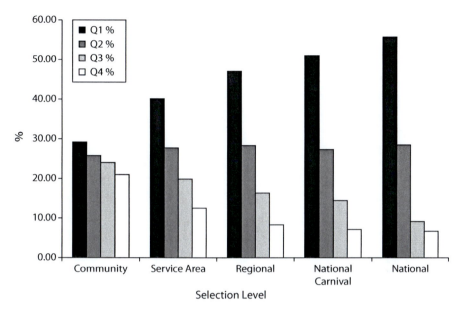

FIGURE 9.2 Relative age distributions of junior rugby league players in the Under 13–15 categories (combined) according to performance level (Till, Cobley, Wattie *et al.*, 2010).

Height, body mass and maturation

Till, Cobley, O'Hara *et al.* (2010) compared the height and body mass of Regional and National selected players (Under 13–15) with UK reference values. Comparisons were made at the fiftieth and ninety-seventh percentile (Freeman, Cole, Chinn, Jones, White & Preece, 1995) to see how many players were above the mean and within the top 3 per cent for aged matched height and body mass. Results found that 92.7 per cent and 30.7 per cent of Regional and 94.7 per cent and 33.1 per cent of National players were above the fiftieth and ninety-seventh aged matched percentiles for height respectively. For body mass, 96.3 per cent and 32.4 per cent of Regional and 97.4 per cent and 37.0 per cent of National players were above the fiftieth and ninety-seventh aged matched percentiles. For maturation status, the average age at Peak Height Velocity (PHV, otherwise known as the 'growth spurt') was 13.6 years for Regional and 13.5 years for National players. This represents an earlier age at Peak Height Velocity than represented in European boys of 13.8–14.2 years (Malina, Bouchard & Bar-Or, 2004). Findings on height, body mass and maturation demonstrate that selection to the Player Performance Pathway is biased towards the taller, heavier and earlier maturing player, suggesting that selected players are most likely to have benefited from earlier maturation, thereby providing a physical and performance advantage over similar aged grouped peers.

Physical performance characteristics

Fitness testing (Till *et al.*, 2011) comparing physical characteristics (e.g. height, speed, etc.) of players selected at the Regional and National selection levels revealed a clear association between growth and maturation with anthropometric and performance characteristics. When comparing test results between Regional and National selected players, differences were found for body fat, lower and upper body power, speed, agility and estimated aerobic power, with National players outperforming Regional players on all tests. However, when examining the results, differences between Regional and National players were only minimal (e.g. 0.05s for 30m sprint time), suggesting that although physical qualities were important for selection to the Performance Pathway, it is likely that a combination of physical attributes with technical skills and tactical knowledge determined National selection.

Playing position

Till, Cobley, O'Hara *et al.* (2010) considered player characteristics in relation to playing position, with position classified into four sub-categories ('Outside-Backs', 'Pivots', 'Props' and 'Backrow'). Generally, junior 'Props' and 'Backrow' positions were taller, heavier and possessed more body fat than 'Outside-Backs' and 'Pivots'. Physiological tests found 'Outside-Backs' as having a significantly greater vertical jump than any other playing position, with 'Props' and 'Backrow' scoring significantly higher in the 2kg medicine ball chest throw. 'Props' performed significantly worse on the speed, agility and estimated aerobic power tests. When analysing RAEs between playing positions, a general effect was evident across all positions, however RAEs were increased in the 'Props' position and decreased in the 'Pivots', most probably due to the increased physical demands of the 'Props' position in Rugby League compared with the 'Pivots'. This is further supported by the maturation status results, with 'Props' likely to contain the earliest maturing player (age at PHV = 13.3 years) and 'Pivots' containing the later maturing players (age at PHV = 14 years). This maturation difference, along with the anthropometric characteristics of respective positions, lends further support to the more pronounced selection bias in the 'Props' compared to the 'Pivot' positions. When comparing performance with maturation and development, 'Props' were the earliest maturing players but were actually the worst performing on the range of fitness tests. Therefore, if later maturing players were already in advance of early maturing players on selected performance tests, it is likely that further physical performance (e.g. speed) differences would develop as maturity into adulthood occurred.

Process of change – the new player development structure

In 2008, following the RFL's submission to Sport England for funding to assist in the delivery of its objectives and an 18-month consultation, which included research on cutting edge best practice, the RFL made a number of changes to the Player Performance Pathway. Whilst building on the positives of the existing pathway (e.g. providing a quality environment for the transition of many players to full international status), a modification was deemed necessary in order to address some of the known shortfalls (e.g. players performing under time frames and pressure, effect of injury on selection, selection of potential vs. performance), as well as address some of the key issues (e.g. selection of relatively older, larger and earlier maturing players; emphasis on physical performance), which arose out of the applied research.

The new pathway has now moved away from a discrete linear path of youth talent development, to a more holistic approach and one that encompasses all ages and environments. The main changes included:

- Increasing coaching opportunities and creating a wider talent pool for players.
- Reduction of competition, therefore removing overplaying and allowing more developmental opportunities.
- The focus on development and not representation.
- Players are not selected based on playing position as there are no team requirements.
- Coaching sessions are provided throughout the playing year instead of at the end of the playing season.
- The pathway is now linked to professional clubs scholarships so players are only involved in two programmes in a season instead of the previous five.
- Selection is based on relative age and training age.

Player development is now central to the strategies of all professional clubs as well as the RFL, and as such the alignment of club and governing body activity has been essential. This new approach, called the Player Development Pathway, incorporates a seven-stage model, including: school, community club, player development groups, scholarship, academy, first grade and elite training squads (see Table 9.1).

Player development is now recognised as a non-linear process, and whilst opportunities exist for progression, players may stay within one stage or return to a prior stage. For instance, a player may be identified for the Service Area Player Development Centre as an Under 13 and remain in the centre throughout his youth rugby (Under 13–Under 16) and not progress any further. However, another player may progress to the Regional Player Development Centre at Under 14 and be selected by a professional club to join their scholarship programme at Under 15.

The pathway is designed to improve the development of quality players in rugby league; all clubs must build a clearly defined pathway for players from the school playground to the Super League and international success. Increasing the number and quality of players that have access to talent development opportunities and can progress to Super League and Championship clubs is a key aim, enabling players to access the pathway regardless of age, ability and location. Significant changes to the talent development phase of the pathway include the Service Area moving from a playing opportunity to a development environment with 10–15 per cent of the

TABLE 9.1 The RFL Player Development Pathway (Professional Player Pathway; RFL Talented Player Development Pathway (2010–16))

Phase	Where	Stage	Environment	Purpose	Competition	Volume/Intensity
1	School and Club	6–8 years	School	Developing fundamental movement skills	No formal competition	Mini Rugby Festivals
2	School and Club	8–12 years	Club (PESSYP[1] and Sustain)	Developing fundamental sport skills and core Rugby League skills	Youth and Junior Leagues Champion Schools	U11 Modified games U12 Full
3	Service Area and Regions	13–16 years	Talent Development Groups	Developing the athlete and position specific skills and Talent Identification	Youth and Junior Leagues Champion Schools FE Colleges	League and cup
4	Professional Club	15–16 years	Scholarship	Preparation for elite competition and Talent Confirmation (6–8 years from elite)	National Youth League FE Colleges Scholarship Games	6 Games
5	Professional Club	17–20 years	Academy	Individual specialisation and enhancement for maximal performance at elite level (3–6 years from elite)	National Youth League Super 6 University U18 Academy Games U20 Valvoline Cup	U18 16 Games 20 Rounds + Grand Final
6	Professional Club	18–30 years	1st Grade	Delivering and sustaining elite performance	Championship Super league	27 Rounds + Grand Final Northern Rail Cup 27 Rounds + Grand Final Challenge Cup
7	International	15–30 years	Elite Training Squads	Individualised preparation for elite performance at a world class level	U16 England Youth U18 England Academy U20 England Knights	Full International International Fixtures European Nations Cup 4 Nations World Cup

[1]Physical Education School Sport and Young People, Youth Sport Trust

playing population invited to attend the sessions. Regional Player Development Centres will be established at Under 14 through to Under 16 and whilst there will be playing opportunities these are reduced and are seen as talent confirmation during the centre's programme. Professional clubs will operate scholarship schemes at Under 15 and Under 16 age groups, including five playing opportunities during the year, which will be increased over the next four years to become the primary playing environment for players. A player will only operate in two playing stages at any one time, which reduces the previous over-playing of players where a pathway player would be expected to play upwards of an additional 12 games. This reduces the 'pressure' placed upon a player and replaces the traditional pyramid structure with an environment-based player development pathway.

In relation to the key issues identified through research, the new pathway aims to provide more development and coaching opportunities to a greater number of players with a reduction in player identification and selection. Providing opportunities to players irrespective of relative age, maturational status, physical size and performance is an important element of the new development structure. This would hopefully result in a greater number of quality Rugby League players in future years as more opportunities are available for players to receive advanced coaching. Examples of this include professional clubs' scholarship schemes increasing opportunities from 12 to 24 players at Under 15 and 16 age categories. This reduces the competition for places meaning relatively younger, later maturing and less physically developed players have a greater chance of being selected. The focus on development instead of playing ability and reduction in competition means coaches and clubs can focus on developing players considered to have potential and the key rugby league skills regardless of size and development. An example of the reduction in competition is the new Under 18s competition, which has 16 games throughout the year, however there is no league- or cup-based competition. Elite international squads still exist at under 16s, 18s and 20s levels to provide the players classed as elite an increased level of competition. Although this structure is in its infancy, the changes made to reduce biases in selection and focus on development across the game is a step in the right direction.

Future research

Future research is certainly needed to fully understand and inform talent identification and development practices in UK Rugby League. The large data set presently available from the previous Player Performance Pathway can be used in future research, especially in relation to tracking players longitudinally. Differentiating between adolescent performance and potential for progression is essential in talent identification and development models (Vaeyens, Lenoir, Williams, & Philippaerts, 2008). The current data set from the Player Performance Pathway tracks a number of athletes over three consecutive years, enabling research to not only examine changes in performance over time but also to examine the selection of players to the pathway over consecutive years. Moreover, new research ideas, such as investigating the technical, tactical, psychological and social factors associated with player identification and development and continued evaluation of the new pathway will provide useful information and support talent identification and development within Rugby League in the future.

Advice for coaches, administrators, parents and athletes

Research to date emphasises the physical demands of Rugby League with selection favouring the relatively older, earlier maturing, larger junior players. Although the physical aspect of Rugby League is a dominant feature of the game, it is also important that coaches, parents and administrators promote the technical and tactical aspects of the sport. Detailed below are a number of recommendations for coaches, administrators, parents and athletes that should help ensure the key issues identified within the research and experience of the RFL Player Performance Pathway are considered appropriately for all aspiring young rugby league players.

Player relative age

It is important for coaches, administrators, parents and players to be aware of the participation and selection biases that occur within and across all junior age categories. The consequences of the RAE is that the relatively older players who are born earlier in the selection year (i.e. September–November) have greater participation and selection opportunities compared to relatively younger players (i.e. June–August). Being aware of a player's relative age is therefore important for everyone involved in the game to allow equal opportunities and increase participation numbers across the game. Coaches should aim to provide equal access and opportunities to all players with regard to participation, training and competition including equal playing time and number of involvements within a game. Providing equal opportunities would help increase and maintain participation numbers and ensure all players have access to development opportunities. Administrators should consider relative age in both the assessment of a player's performance within annual-age categories and within any testing that is undertaken as part of a player's development programme. Administrators could also consider a method of selection within annual-age groups by selecting players on three or six monthly age categories instead of yearly ones (e.g. scholarships/development squads – same per cent of players from each quartile or half of year) in an attempt to reduce the size of the relative age effect discrepancies and associated bias in player selection. Both parents and athletes should be aware of the relative age within annual-age categories and the advantages/disadvantages associated with relative age, which may help players understand where they are in relation to development compared to their age grouped peers.

Body size and maturation

As with relative age, coaches, administrators, parents and athletes should all be aware that maturation occurs at different times and rates during adolescence (12–16 years). Early maturation can lead to physical advantages such as increased body size and physical performance, and as a result, coaches and administrators should be aware of the effect of maturation on performance and consider this in their assessments of both players' performance within annual age-categories and within any testing that is undertaken as part of a player's development programme. Where possible, administrators should assess and monitor maturation (e.g., age at PHV) and parents and athletes should be aware of maturation and the advantages and disadvantages that are commonly associated with early and late maturation.

Training and competition

Training and competition should provide developmental opportunities for all players regardless of relative age and maturational status. For younger ages (6 to 12 years) training should be fun and varied with a focus on skills development. Competitions within training should be based around skill and not physical attributes. As age progresses to the junior level (13+ years), skill development should continue to be emphasised alongside fitness development. The focus for competition for all junior ages (up to 18 years) should be on participation, personal and team improvement and not winning. This is supported by the RFL in their new pathway whereby Under 18s age categories play games but have no direct competition (i.e. results do not matter). For junior ages (6 to 12 years) focus should be on enjoyment, promoting the quality of the experience of training and playing. For older juniors (13+ years) the focus should still be on enjoyment; however increased emphasis should be placed on skill development and preparation for higher levels of competition (see Table 9.1). Players should be assigned playing positions based on skill and not physical qualities and size during adolescence. Post-adolescence players should be assigned positions based on skill and physical development, however all players should continue to experience a variety of playing positions within training.

Working together

Coaches, administrators and parents should work together to support player development. Coaches, administrators and parents can educate each other on the impact relative age and maturation has on development and performance. Coaches should explain key decisions within a team, as it is important for parents to under-stand the effect they have on their child. Administrators should provide support to coaches to ensure they are aware of factors relating to identification, selection and development of players. Parents of established players can work with coaches and administrators to ensure an ethos of equal opportunities, and educate new parents who may be unaware of key issues relating to appropriate player development, in order to support coaches who aim to provide equal opportunities regardless of age and maturational status. Parents should also support and educate their child to help understand the key issues surrounding selection and development within rugby league. Continual skill development, hard work and the right attitude are essential to gain selection and develop into a professional rugby league player.

Creation, understanding and re-enforcement of such an inclusive ethos amongst administrators, coaches, players and parents will assist in providing an appropriate environment and inclusive programme of player development, regardless of confounding factors such as age and maturational status.

References

Coutts, A., Reaburn, P., & Abt, G. (2003). Heart rate, blood lactate concentration and estimated energy expenditure in a semi professional rugby league team during a match: A case study. *Journal of Sports Sciences, 21*, 97–103.

Freeman, J. V., Cole, T. J., Chinn, S., Jones, P. R., White, E. M., & Preece, M. A. (1995). Cross sectional stature and weight reference curves for the UK, 1990. *Archives of Disease in Children, 73*, 17–24.

Gabbett, T. J., Kelly, J., Ralph, S., & Driscoll, D. (2007). Physiological and anthropometric characteristics of junior elite and sub-elite rugby league players, with special reference to starters and non starters. *Journal of Science and Medicine in Sport, 21*, 1126–33.

Gabbett, T. J., King, T., & Jenkins, D. (2008). Applied Physiology of Rugby League. *Sports Medicine, 38*, 119–38.

Malina, R. M., Bouchard, C., & Bar-Or, O. (2004). *Growth, maturation, and physical activity.* (2nd ed.). Champaign, IL: Human Kinetics.

Meir, R., Newton, R., Curtis, E., Fardell, M., & Butler, B. (2001). Physical fitness qualities of professional football players: Determination of positional difference. *Journal of Strength and Conditioning Research, 15,* 450–58.

Mohamed, H., Vaeyens, R., Matthys, S., Multael, M., Lefevre, J., Lenoir, M., & Philippaerts, R. M. (2009). Anthropometric and performance measures for the development of a talent detection and identification model in youth handball. *Journal of Sports Sciences, 27*, 257–66.

Sykes, D., Twist, C., Hall, S., & Lamb, K. (2009). Semi-automated time-motion analysis of senior elite rugby league. *International Journal of Performance Analysis in Sport, 9*, 47–59.

Till, K., Cobley, S., O'Hara, J., Chapman, C., & Cooke, C. (2010) Anthropometric, physiological and selection characteristics in high performance UK junior Rugby League players. *Talent Development & Excellence, 2*, 193–207.

Till, K., Cobley, S., O'Hara, J., Brightmore, A., Cooke, C., & Chapman, C. (2011) Using anthropometric and performance characteristics to predict selection in junior UK rugby league players. *Journal of Science and Medicine in Sport*, 14, pp. 264–9.

Till, K., Cobley, S., Wattie, N., O'Hara, J., Cooke, C., & Chapman, C. (2010). The prevalence, influential factors and mechanisms of relative age effects in UK rugby league. *Scandinavian Journal of Science and Medicine in Sport, 20,* 320–29.

Vaeyens, R., Lenoir, M., Williams, M. A., & Philippaerts, R. M. (2008). Talent identification and development in sport: Current models and future directions. *Sports Medicine, 38,* 703–14.

10

BACK TO THE FUTURE

A case report of the ongoing evaluation of the German handball talent selection and development system

Jörg Schorer, Dirk Büsch, Lennart Fischer, Jan Pabst, Rebecca Rienhoff, Peter Sichelschmidt and Bernd Strauß

In taking a step *back* by evaluating the approach taken by the German Handball Federation to identify and develop talent we hope to improve the system for an even brighter *future* for German handball. This case report gives an overview of what handball is, its importance in Germany and how talented handball players are typically selected. In the second section, the theoretical background of existing player assessment and evaluation is described. Third, the results of the last three years of evaluation are presented and conclusions related to the future of this program are drawn. These sections are highlighted by other findings of our work group, which suggest that changes in the system are necessary. Finally, we give advice for policy makers, coaches, parents and researchers.

Handball is a team sport in which two teams of seven players (six field players and one goalkeeper) pass a ball to throw it into the goal of the other team. The German Handball Federation (GHF) is the largest handball organization in the world, with over 800,000 members participating in sport clubs distributed across the country in local communities like small villages to big cities (www.dhb.de). The Federation has been quite successful. Both female (1993) and male (2007) adult teams have been world champions, and the junior and youth age group teams have won the World Championships (e.g., males: 2009; females: 2008). Despite this success, the national coaches wanted to modify the talent selection system to incorporate the future needs of handball. The coaches anticipated that due to several changes in modern handball, future top athletes will require different or additional skills (cf. Lemmel, Kurrat, Hansel, Armbruster, & Petersen, 2007). For instance, some predict handball will develop into a game of more complex techniques, more sophisticated tactics and more speed. This resulted in several changes to the talent development and selection system, which we review below. First, it is important to summarize the German handball system for identifying talent.

The talent development system

The identification of talent in the GHF is grounded within the talent development system shown in Figure 10.1. Children usually gain their first experiences of handball in sports clubs or in school between ages five to ten. In Germany, specific sport-oriented schools can be chosen by sporting talents where the academic schedule is adjusted to reflect the additional sportive requirements. Additionally, extra private lessons from the teachers are available as required. In addition to these sporting schools, the general school system offers a fundamental and broadly conceived provision of education. Later in development (age 15–16), the developmental structure changes into a two-stream system. In the first, promising talents join an academy of first league clubs and get their main training there. In the second, talents have additional national training camps, if they are selected for the youth or junior national team (cf. German Handball Federation, 2009)

As can be seen in Figure 10.1, the talent development structure starts as early as age six. Organized in local communities, mainly structured by the sports club system, children advance their sportive career until their mid-teens. Playing in their clubs, they might be nominated by selection coaches to local and then regional teams at age 10 to 15 (known as the D-squad). Participating in a regional team, athletes compete in a national talent selection camp. This national selection and nomination procedure takes about five days and is described in the next part of this chapter. Selected players constitute the basis of the youth national team (D-/C-squad), which

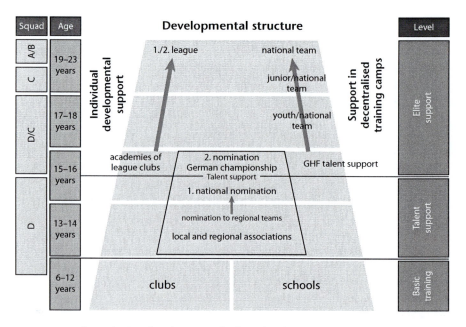

FIGURE 10.1 Organizational and structural talent development in the German handball federation.

is a bi-annual selection. Once selected by the GHF, athletes receive additional support and training within the national talent development system, such as centralized training camps, matches and tournaments against other nations. The second (State Cup) and the third (Rookie Cup) selection and nomination processes, which are performed as the German championship of the regional (selection) teams, are additional chances to be selected for the youth national team for players at the age of 17–18 (U18 national team) and to the junior national team for players at the age of 19–21 (U20/21 national team). With the step to the junior national team the players move from the D-/C-squad to the C-squad, which prepares them for the A- (and B-) squad representing the adult German national team. Late developers also have a chance to be selected. During all stages, athletes not chosen for the national team in the nomination process have the chance to be scouted at tournaments and matches of sports clubs (German youth championships) and schools (Jugend trainiert für Olympia [Youth training for the Olympics]) since these structures are regularly attended by coaches of the German Handball Federation.

Evaluating national talent selection at age 15 to 16 years

Young athletes nominated for regional teams take part in the national talent selection camp at the age of 15 to 16 years. By this time they have participated in different matches and tournaments against other regional teams but this is their first chance to demonstrate their skills on a national level. Selection for the National Team takes place in two different locations: in Kienbaum for the athletes from North and East Germany and in Heidelberg for the athletes from South and West Germany. The camp lasts five days, involving ten regional teams containing 12 athletes each. As girls and boys are scouted separately there are four events with approximately 480 athletes.

The selection program contains several different challenges for the teams that vary in their intentions:

- There are several tests implemented to evaluate whether the regional selections and clubs have followed the guidelines for talent development as set out by the German Handball Federation (GHF). One example would be the inclusion of gymnastic disciplines like floor exercises to test for a broad basic training. Additionally, broad coordinative and technique tests with and without a handball are administered.

There are several tests and matches that are used for selection of the most talented within these homogenous groups of over-achievers. Generally, these include three different parts:

- General motor tests: The endurance and power of the athletes is examined by common motor tests, such as 30m sprints for speed, a shuttle-run test for endurance and several different motor tasks for strength (e.g., chin-ups, jump and reach, etc.). Basically, these are tests administered in several other sports like football or basketball based on a motor ability concept.

•   Handball specific tests: handball specific tests like sprints with a ball, a slalom course as well as duration, speed, and accuracy of ten handball throws are administered (Schorer, Baker, Büsch, Wilhelm, & Pabst, 2009).

•   Match performances: a significant part of the national talent selection camp includes the different matches and competitions between the regional teams. While the members of the regional teams stay together, the number of players differs. There are matches with four against four or five against five field players (the normal amount is six field players). During these matches the coaches of the German National Team observe and analyze the players regarding their sport specific techniques and tactics and register qualitative characteristics. They later discuss these with the regional coaches. Additionally, they observe how the athletes interact with their teammates, how they act in one to one offence and defence situations, what kind of offence and defence systems (e.g., 5:1, 3:2:1) they manage in a small group and in the team among other qualities.

Although the actual nomination is done after the coaches have evaluated all data from matches and the different tests, they inform the regional coaches about trends seen by day three or four of the selection camp, so that the regional coaches can point out other players to them in the event that they disagree with the national coaches' evaluation.

Theoretical background for the modification of the talent selection system

As can be easily concluded, this talent selection is based on a specified ability approach (Hohmann, 2009). In opposition to this approach, one based on the research principles of expertise follows a more retrospective research strategy – researchers infer talent from comparisons of experts and novices on possible variables for talent during their childhood and adolescence in competitive sports (cf. Farrow, Chapter 5). Subsequently, content (e.g., quality and quantity) of training and stages of development that are apparently important factors for high performance in the future are extracted from the data.

Both approaches have relevance for talent selection in competitive sports (cf. Figure 10.2). Nevertheless, two disadvantages need to be mentioned: the ability-orientated approach has to tackle the constant problem of reliable and valid early diagnosis, while the expertise approach only documents the differences of performance between experts and novices, but may not convey the process and the reasons for the differences in performance. Current research suggests that the empirical advantage is in the expert–novice paradigm under ecologically valid conditions especially among the perceptual–cognitive area including technical

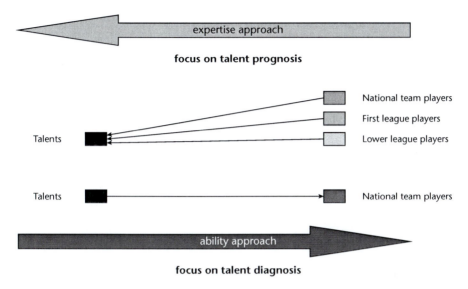

FIGURE 10.2 Talent research on the basis of a combined ability and expertise approach (adapted from Hohmann, 2009).

(Schorer, Baker, Fath, & Jaitner, 2007) and tactical tasks. The advantage for motoric and psychological tests is manifested more likely in the ability approach.

Over the past four years, our research group has been involved with the GHF with the overall aim of developing an empirically valid profile-diagnosis, which optimizes the GHF's talent selection and development system (see a comparable approach for football, Reilly, Williams, Nevill, & Franks, 2000). The catalogue of tests for a revised talent selection system should enable the coaches responsible to conduct the tests and analyse the results without researcher aid. Additional tests to those presented above (which were largely from an 'ability' perspective) were chosen on the basis of studies of expertise, which presented differences between skilled and less-skilled athletes in various sports. Four groups of test batteries were created:

- The first group consisted of anthropometric and motor tests like hand size (Barut, Demirel, & Kiran, 2008; Visnapuu & Jürimäe, 2007, 2008), handgrip strength (Barut *et al.*, 2008; Leyk *et al.*, 2007; Visnapuu & Jürimäe, 2007), maximal feet tapping frequency (Voss, Witt, & Werther, 2006), and handball specific jump tests (Pielbusch, Marschall, Dawo, & Büsch, in press).
- Based on the findings by Elferink-Gemser, Visscher, Lemmink, and Mulder (2004) indicating that tactical tests differentiated elite and sub-elite hockey players, we added a computer-based pattern recognition test (Abernethy, Baker, & Côté, 2005) and a flicker test (Reingold, Charness, Pomplun, & Stampe, 2001) as measures of tactical skills.
- Additionally a technical skill test of the over arm throw was included (cf. Schorer, Baker *et al.*, 2009). For goal keepers both technical and tactical components were

used to create a position-specific goal keeper video test (cf. Schorer, 2007; Schorer & Baker, 2009).

* Last, psychological questionnaires were added. These included questions on achievement motivation (Schorer, Baker, Lotz, & Büsch, 2010), coping strategies (Smith, Schutz, Smoll, & Ptacek, 1995) and motor self-efficacy (Wilhelm & Büsch, 2006).

By adding these tests we hoped to introduce tests that achieved the standards in psychometric qualities, which have been proven in other contexts as potential predictors for the talent selection or differentiation between experts and near-experts.

Results for the evaluation of the talent selection from 2008 to 2010

These additions were introduced in small steps into the handball talent selection system between 2008 and 2010. We can now evaluate whether these test data are able to differentiate between selected and non-selected players for the respective years.

In a first step (2008), systematic interviews with the coaches were conducted. The result was that eight predictive variables were considered for analysis: (1) the speed of the ball, (2) shot precision under time pressure, (3) dribbling a ball in a parcour, (4) 30m sprint, (5) jump and reach, (6) shuttle run, (7) achievement motivation, and (8) body height.

The statistical analysis revealed different talent predictors for both genders and they unfortunately did not present themselves as reliable over the three years of evaluation (cf. Büsch, Schorer, Sichelschmidt, & Strauß, in prep.).

* For the female players in 2008, maximal ball throwing velocity and dribbling time through a parcour were the two tests predicting 68.9 per cent of our cases correctly. In 2009 medicine ball distance throw was the only predictor with only 62.8 per cent of correct classifications. In 2010 maximal hand force, maximal throwing velocity and wide jump length classified 69.7 per cent correctly.
* For the male talents in 2008 dribbling through a parcour classified 64.3 per cent. In 2009 maximal throwing velocity and hand size put 67.7 per cent in the correct clusters. For 2010 dribbling time through a parcour, body mass and maximal throwing velocity predicted 73.4 per cent correct classifications.

To put it in a nutshell, these results showed that at least for the prediction of the first nomination level each year different tests were revealed as 'most predictive'. While the general aim is to find tests that predict long-term success, these changes are reason for concern. If we are not reliably and consistently able to predict at least a certain percentage of players correctly in a short-term forecast, then how can we anticipate having a high percentage of correct selections for long-term success? The talents selected at age 15 to 16 are developed not to perform well during their youth and junior years but when competing in the Olympics.

Therefore, in 2010 we again conducted reliability checks for most tests administered during the talent selection process. The reliability of the tests varied from very good (newly introduced tests) to very poor (some of the old motor tests). One explanation might be that the tests are conducted by different regional coaches per camp measuring in a variety of ways. Additionally, the load of tests needs to be reduced so more time and care can be taken with the ones conducted. Therefore, we currently prepare a test manual and a test carrying case, so that these tests can finally be standardized.

Conclusions drawn for a brighter (and hopefully more predictable) future

So what does our future hold for us? What conclusions can we draw? The first main point is that the national talent selection system and its evaluation need to be ongoing processes. The game of handball changes and therefore, we might have to modify a running system, even if we succeed in a good prediction of talent over the next few years. Therefore, it is essential to have steady scientific feedback from a partner with the same aims as the national coaches. The building of trust on both sides has taken considerable time but has helped to improve the process and strength of the evolving system. An additional issue, which we believe is a consistent limitation of talent identification systems, is the missing distinction between performance and potential. While we might obtain sufficient skill at predicting the nomination with quantitative data from the national talent selection camps, the real aim would be to predict who of these athletes will make it to the adult national team. Longitudinal data are therefore necessary and these studies are rarely conducted, because of their financial and administrative requirements. Better prediction of long-term success for the talent development system should remain a central aim. So far, the best predictor is probably the 'coaches' eye', although no study has tested this. Surprisingly the objectivity of these coaches' decisions has also not been investigated. This is an area where we are currently focusing our efforts.

Taken together, our evaluation shows that there needs to be a lot of work done to find appropriate tests that fulfil the standard psychometric properties *and* have the discriminatory power to predict talent development. Our additional aim as sport scientists is to become obsolete in this process, so that the coaches themselves can conduct a vastly improved talent selection process.

Further research results for consideration

Due to the rich database developed from the talent selection system, additional studies have examined topics considered problematic from talent research (cf. Horton, Chapter 4 and Farrow, Chapter 5), relative age effects (Baker, Schorer, &

Cobley, 2010; Cobley, Baker, Wattie, & McKenna, 2009) and the role of pre-experience in sports (Ford, Ward, Hodges, & Williams, 2009).

In three studies, Schorer, Cobley *et al.* (2009) investigated relative age effects (RAE) in handball by looking at the effect of several moderators like competition level, gender, player nationality, career stage and playing position. In Study 1, birth dates for male and female athletes from the German Handball Federation were analyzed. Data indicated that the RAE is stronger for male than for female athletes and decreases from regional D-squad to the national team (Cobley *et al.*, 2009). Surprisingly, within the A-squad the percentage of relatively younger players from the fourth quartile was higher than the percentage of players from all other quartiles. In Study 2, data from players from the first and second league in German handball for the seasons 1998/99–2005/06 were examined. For all seasons, a stable but small RAE was observed. More interesting was that the RAE was stronger for the international players than the native German players. Looking at their stages of career (from below 21, 21–25, 26–29 and above 30) the RAE remained stable for the international players, but diminished for the German players. Taken together, the results of Study 1 and 2 suggest that relatively younger athletes might turn their disadvantage in early years into an advantage in the later years of their career. Possible explanations might be the necessity to build better technical or tactical skills to be able to compete with relatively older athletes. Additionally, studies (cf. Schorer *et al.*, 2009; 2010) show that while the RAE happens in early years of talent development, in German handball they diminish later in development. The effect is lower with every national selection step, suggesting that solutions need to be implemented in earlier ages and selection levels.

Previous research also suggests pre-experience in sports in general and in handball specifically could play a major role in talent selection (cf. Baker, Schorer, Bagats, Büsch, & Strauß, under review). Using data collected from training histories, we compared training of young athletes who were selected during talent selection camps with athletes from the same camps who were not selected. As expected, selected players had different training profiles than those not-selected, although these effects were restricted to females. More specifically, selected females performed more sport-specific training than their not-selected counterparts and had greater involvement in sports outside their area of expertise (i.e., non-sport-specific training). These results suggest training behaviours can distinguish between skill levels even within a single step along the athlete development pathway, at least in females. Furthermore, they suggest that non-specific training has value during early athlete development. Therefore, an examination of training profiles should be included in talent selection processes.

Advices for coaches, parents, policy makers and researchers

Knowing our own limitations, it feels a little strange to give advice; however, we have learned things from our experiences. *For parents* we would like to remind them that different pathways can lead to expert performance. So even if your child does not get nominated in the first selection there are other pathways open for him or her. As presented above, there are several opportunities for development within the club system and several options to be discovered by the national coaches. So even if your child develops late, elite sport may still be possible. For *policy makers*, we would like to remind them that scientific research is meant as support and not as a negative evaluation. The idea is to improve the current version of the talent selection and development system and not to vilify. This brings us to the *researchers* willing to work in applied settings. As researchers you should aim to develop and maintain a long-term partnership with the sport governing body or development system, even when your project is completed and they need to be able to run the show independently. Finally, our advice *for coaches* is that while data collections are expensive and time-demanding, they build the basis for a better understanding, which helps in the long run. Time invested in evaluations of talent identification and development systems is worthwhile, provided you find the right combination of coaches, administrators and researchers.

Acknowledgments

The authors from the Westfälische Wilhelms-University Münster were funded by the Federal Institute of Sport Science Germany (IIA1–{070704/09}–10). Without these applied research grants, evaluations like the one presented here would not be possible. We would like to express our gratitude for their great cooperation to the German Handball Federation coaches namely Ute Lemmel, Christian Schwarzer, Heike Axmann, Maike Balthazar, Arnold Manz, Martin Heuberger, Klaus-Dieter Petersen, Heiko Karrer and Dr Christoph Armbruster. Additionally, we would like to thank our research assistants, Christina Janning, Sebastian Bagats and Kathrin Thiele, as well as our students who have helped during the talent selections for their interest in the topic and their dedication to help beyond expectations.

References

Abernethy, B., Baker, J., & Côté, J. (2005). Transfer of pattern recall skills may contribute to the development of sport expertise. *Applied Cognitive Psychology, 19*, 705–18.

Baker, J., Schorer, J., & Cobley, S. (2010). Relative Age Effects: An inevitable consequence of elite sport? *The German Journal of Sport Science, 1*, 26–30.

Baker, J., Schorer, J., Bagats, S., Büsch, D., & Strauß, B. (under review). Training differences and selection in a talent identification system. Manuscript under review.

Barut, C., Demirel, P., & Kiran, S. (2008). Evaluation of hand anthropometric measurements and grip strength in basketball, volleyball and handball players. *Anatomy, International Journal of Clinical and Experimental Anatomy, 2*, 55–59.

Büsch, D., Schorer, J., Sichelschmidt, P., & Strauß, B. (in prep.). Methodological aspects of talent diagnosis.

Cobley, S., Baker, J., Wattie, N., & McKenna, J. M. (2009). Annual age-grouping and athlete development: A meta-analytical review of relative age effects in sport. *Sports Medicine, 39*, 235–56.

Elferink-Gemser, M. T., Visscher, C., Lemmink, K. A. P. M., & Mulder, T. (2004). Relation between multidimensional performance characteristics and level of performance in talented youth field hockey players. *Journal of Sports Sciences, 22*, 1053–63.

Federation, G. H. (2009). *Rahmentrainingskonzeption des Deutschen Handballbundes für die Ausbildung und Förderung von Nachwuchsspielern.* Münster: Philippka.

Ford, P. R., Ward, P., Hodges, N. J., & Williams, A. M. (2009). The role of deliberate practice and play in career progression in sport: the early engagement hypothesis. *High Ability Studies, 20*, 65–75.

Hohmann, A. (2009). *Entwicklung sportlicher Talente an sportbetonte Schulen.* Petersberg: Michael Imhof.

Lemmel, U., Kurrat, H., Hansel, F., Armbruster, C., & Petersen, K.-D. (2007). Die neue DHB-Leistungssport-Sichtung „LEBEM", Teil 1. Gemeinsam neue Wege gehen – die Inhaltsbausteine der neuen Sichtung von DHB und Landesverbänden im männlichen und weiblichen Bereich, Teil 1: Sichtungskonzept, Athletik-Überprüfung. *Handballtraining, 29*, 12–19.

Leyk, D., Gorges, W., Ridder, D., Wunderlich, M., Rüther, T., & Sievert, A. (2007). Handgrip strength of young men, women and highly trained female athletes. *European Journal of Applied Physiology, 99*, 415–21.

Pielbusch, S., Marschall, F., Dawo, O., & Büsch, D. (in press). Handballspezifische Sprungkrafts diagnostik. *Leistungssport.*

Reilly, T., Williams, A. M., Nevill, A., & Franks, A. (2000). A multidisciplinary approach to talent identification in soccer. *Journal of Sports Sciences, 18*, 695–702.

Reingold, E. M., Charness, N., Pomplun, M., & Stampe, D. M. (2001). Visual span in expert chess players: Evidence from eye movements. *Psychological Science, 12*, 48–55.

Schorer, J. (2007). Höchstleistung im Handballtor – Eine Studie zur Identifikation, den Mechanismen und der Entwicklung senso-motorischer Expertise. Dissertationsschrift an der Ruprecht-Karls-Universität Heidelberg. www.ub.uni-heidelberg.de/archiv/7310 (accessed 17 March 2011).

Schorer, J., & Baker, J. (2009). An exploratory study of aging and perceptual-motor expertise in handball goalkeepers. *Experimental Aging Research, 35*, 1–19.

Schorer, J., Baker, J., Büsch, D., Wilhelm, A., & Pabst, J. (2009). Relative age, talent identification and youth skill development: Do relatively younger athletes have superior technical skills? *Talent Development and Excellence, 1*, 45–56.

Schorer, J., Baker, J., Fath, F., & Jaitner, T. (2007). Identification of interindividual and intraindividual movement patterns in handball players of varying expertise levels. *Journal of Motor Behavior, 39*, 409–21.

Schorer, J., Baker, J., Lotz, S., & Büsch, D. (2010). Influence of early environmental constraints on achievement motivation in talented young handball players. *International Journal of Sport Psychology, 41*, 42–58.

Schorer, J., Cobley, S., Büsch, D., Bräutigam, H., & Baker, J. (2009). Influences of competition level, gender, player nationality, career stage and playing position on relative age effects. *Scandinavian Journal of Medicine and Science in Sports, 19*, 720–30.

Smith, R. E., Schutz, R. W., Smoll, F. L., & Ptacek, J. T. (1995). Development and validation of a multidimensional measure of sport-specific psychological skills – The athletic coping skills inventory-28. *Journal of Sport & Exercise Psychology, 17*, 379–98.

Visnapuu, M., & Jürimäe, T. (2007). Handgrip strength and hand dimensions in young handball and basketball players. *Journal of Strength and Conditioning Research, 21*, 923–29.

—— (2008). The influence of basic body and hand anthropometry on the results of different throwing tests in young handball and basketball players. *Anthropologischer Anzeiger, 66*, 225–36.

Voss, G., Witt, M., & Werther, R. (2006). *Herausforderung Schnelligkeitstraining.* Aachen: Meyer & Meyer.

Wilhelm, A., & Büsch, D. (2006). Das Motorische Selbstwirksamkeits-Inventar (MOSI) – Eine bereichspezifische Diagnostik der Selbstwirksamkeit im Sport. *Zeitschrift für Sportpsychologie, 13*, 89–97.

11

EXPLAINING AFRICAN DOMINANCE IN RUNNING

Yannis Pitsiladis

The sporting achievements of distance runners from Kenya and Ethiopia and sprinters from Jamaica are impressive; Ethiopia, Kenya, and Jamaica won 36 per cent of all track medals for men and women at the XXIX Olympiad in Beijing. The success of east African athletes at distance running and Jamaican athletes at sprinting will have undoubtedly further enhanced the concept that certain ethnic groups possess some inherent genetic advantage predisposing them to superior athletic performance (e.g., the idea of black athletic supremacy). This idea has emerged from overly simplistic interpretations of performances; combined with the belief that similar skin colour indicates similar genetics (Cooper, 2004). Such stereotyping has been strengthened, sometimes inadvertently, by scientists investigating ethnic differences in sports performance. One approach compared the work capacities of sedentary subjects from different ethnic/racial backgrounds. In a review of performance studies from as early as 1941, it was concluded that there were no differences between racial groups in maximal aerobic power, while small differences reported in sub-maximal work efficiency and endurance performance were attributed to differences in mechanical efficiency owing to test mode and/or level of habituation to the ergometers used for testing (Boulay *et al.*, 1988). These authors concluded 'Thus there does not appear to be valid and reliable evidence to support the concept of clear racial differences in work capacities and powers'. This review has been largely ignored and research efforts have continued with increased vigour to find the elusive evidence to explain the African dominance in sports such as running.

A study well cited to support biological differences between ethnic groups compared the skeletal muscle characteristics of sedentary subjects from different ethnic/racial backgrounds and found that African students from Cameroon, Senegal, Zaire, Ivory Coast and Burundi had 8 per cent lower type I and 6.7 per cent higher type IIa fibre proportions than whites (Ama *et al.*, 1986). Furthermore, Africans had

30–40 per cent higher enzyme activities of the phosphagenic (creatine kinase) and glycolytic (hexokinase, phosphofructokinase, lactate dehydrogenase) metabolic pathways. These authors concluded:

> The racial differences observed between Africans and Caucasians in fiber type proportion and enzyme activities of the phosphagenic and glycolytic metabolic pathways may well result from inherited variation. These data suggest that sedentary male black individuals are, in terms of skeletal muscle characteristics, well endowed for sport events of short duration.

Notably, this conclusion was based on small sample sizes; only 23 black and 23 white subjects (Ama et al., 1986) and these data extrapolated to explain the success of black individuals of West African ancestry in sporting events such as sprinting, basketball and American football. Numerous studies have subsequently compared the physiological characteristics of black and white athletes. Studies compared characteristics such as skeletal muscle, maximal aerobic capacity ($\dot{v}O_2$ max), lactate accumulation and running economy between groups of black and white athletes. For example, black South African athletes were found to have lower lactate levels than white athletes for given exercise intensities (Bosch et al. 1990; Coetzer et al., 1993; Weston et al., 1999). Black athletes also had better running economy (Weston et al., 2000) and higher fractional utilisation of $\dot{v}O_2$ max at race pace (Bosch et al. 1990; Coetzer et al., 1993; Weston et al., 2000). It was suggested that 'if the physiological characteristics of sub-elite black African distance runners are present in elite African runners, this may help to explain the success of this racial group in distance running' (Weston et al., 2000). However, this assertion is difficult to reconcile with the earlier studies concluding that their findings were compatible with the idea that 'Black male individuals are well endowed to perform in sport events of short duration' (Ama et al., 1986). This area of science is clearly confusing when studies comparing subjects of different skin colour can conclude on the one hand that the results can explain the success of this racial group in distance running (Weston et al., 2000), and on the other hand that results are compatible with black athletes being suited to events of short duration (Ama et al., 1986). Such contradictions highlight the problem associated with grouping athletes based on skin colour and making conclusions about racial/ethnic characteristics on the basis of such small subject numbers and not differentiating between Africans of west and east African origin.

The fact that many of the world's best distance runners originate from distinct regions of Ethiopia and Kenya, rather than being evenly distributed throughout their respective countries (Scott et al., 2003; Onywera et al., 2006), appears to further sustain the idea that certain ethnic groups possess some inherent genetic advantage predisposing them to superior athletic performance; a typical explanation for the success of Ethiopian and Kenyan distance runners. A similar phenomenon is also observed in Jamaica where the majority of successful sprinters trace their origins to the north-west region of Jamaica in the parish of Trelawny (Robinson, 2007).

Geographical disparities in athlete production have been proposed to reflect a genetic similarity among those populating these regions for an athletic genotype and phenotype as a consequence of selection for a particular phenotype such as endurance or sprinting, if it offers a selective advantage in that environment. Indeed, some believe that the Nandi tribe in Kenya has been self-selected over centuries for endurance performance through cultural practices such as cattle raiding (Manners, 1997). It is not surprising, therefore, that there are assertions in the literature that Kenyans have the 'proper genes' for distance running (Larsen, 2003). Similarly, others have suggested that the superior sprint performances of African Americans of primarily West African origin were due to a favourable biology (e.g., muscle-fibre characteristics, metabolic pathways, and pulmonary physiology) hypothesized to have been concentrated by natural selection over three centuries in the Afrocentric peoples displaced from West Africa to the New World during the slave trade (Cooper, 2004; Morrison & Cooper, 2006). For example, Morrison and Cooper (2006) proposed that biochemical differences between West African and West African-descended populations and all other groups, including other Africans, began but did not end with the sickling of red blood cells; red blood cells that assume an abnormal, rigid, sickle shape. The authors advocate that individuals with the sickle cell trait possessed a significant selective advantage in the uniquely lethal West African malarial environment that triggered a series of physiological adjustments and compensatory mechanisms, which had favourable consequences for sprinting (Morrison & Cooper, 2006). While this hypothesis remains to be tested, another untested hypothesis that also warrants investigation is that the favourable West African biology, referred to by Morrison and Cooper (2006) and others, may have been concentrated as a consequence of the displacement process and the harsh living conditions where mainly the 'fittest' slaves survived. The transportation across the Atlantic was extremely brutal, lasting many weeks, and at least one in four people who were transported from Africa died before reaching their destination. Despite these untested hypotheses having potential theoretical underpinnings, it is unjustified at present to regard the phenomenal athletic success of Jamaicans, or indeed east Africans, as genetically mediated; to justify doing so one must identify the genes that are responsible for that success. However, it is a justified hypothesis, and being falsifiable is eminently susceptible to experimental verification or disproof. Scientists advocating a biological/genetic explanation typically ignore the socio-economic and cultural factors that appear to better explain ethnic differences in performance (Scott & Pitsiladis, 2007). This chapter aims to address these factors and other beliefs in the context of the ever-increasing scientific evidence.

Genetic explanations for ethnic differences in sports performance

The idea of athletic superiority of certain racial or ethnic groups is based on a preconception that each race or indeed ethnic group constitutes a genetically homogeneous group defined by skin colour. This belief is contrary to the finding that there is more genetic variation among Africans than between Africans and Eurasians (Yu *et al.*, 2002), especially bearing in mind that Eurasians are descended from Africans. Nevertheless, the genetics of race is controversial and gives rise to a number of contrasting viewpoints, with particular emphasis on the use of race as a tool in the diagnosis and treatment of disease. Some argue that there is a role for the consideration of race in biomedical research and that the potential benefits to be gained in terms of diagnosis and treatment of disease outweigh the potential social costs of linking race or ethnicity with genetics (Burchard *et al.*, 2003). Others, however, advocate that race should be abandoned as a tool for assessing the prevalence of disease genotypes and that race is not an acceptable surrogate for genetics in assessing the risk of disease and efficacy of treatment (Cooper *et al.*, 2003). Arguments for the inclusion of race in biomedical research often focus on its use to identify single gene disorders and their medical outcome. The genetic basis of complex phenotypes such as sporting performance is poorly understood and more difficult to study. It is estimated that most human genetic variation is shared by all humans and that a marginal proportion (normally less than 10 per cent) is specific to major continental groups (Cavalli-Sforza & Feldman, 2003). Estimates from the human genome project and analysis of haplotype frequencies show that most haplotypes (i.e., linked segments of genetic variation, rarely subject to re-assortment by recombination) are shared between two of the three major geographic populations: Europe, Asia, and Africa (International HapMap Consortium, 2005). It is estimated that the level of genetic diversity between human populations is not large enough to justify the use of the term race (Jobling *et al.*, 2004). Consequently, any differences in physiology, biochemistry, and/or anatomy between groups defined solely by skin colour are not directly applicable to their source populations, even if the differences found are indeed genetically determined. This point is well illustrated using an example from the recent literature that received much media coverage. Bejan *et al.* (2010) made reference to anthropometric literature that showed that the center of mass in 'blacks' was 3 per cent higher above the ground than in 'whites' and extrapolated this to mean that 'blacks' hold a 1.5 per cent speed advantage in running, and whites hold a 1.5 per cent speed advantage in swimming. These authors also stated that 'among athletes of the same height Asians are even more favored than whites in swimming but they are not setting records because they are not as tall.'

The approach of comparing physiological characteristics between groups defined solely by skin colour does not offer much insight into why some groups are more successful than others in certain sports. Even within groups of individuals with similar skin colour, many ethnic and tribal groups exist. Over 70 languages are in everyday use in Ethiopia, while in Kenya, over 50 distinct ethnic communities speak close to 80 different dialects. Similarly, the Jamaican population, currently estimated to be ~2.8 million, trace their origins primarily to West Africa as a result of the transatlantic slave trade that began during the early sixteenth century and persisted until the passing of the Abolition of the Slave Trade Act in 1807. During this period, slaves were captured from a large number of geographical areas. In particular, slaves were captured from Senegal, The Gambia, Guinea, Sierra Leone, Ivory Coast, Ghana, Benin (Dahamey), Nigeria, Cameroon, and Angola. The ethnic make-up of the slaves transported to the Caribbean was therefore extremely diverse, comprising many main ethnic groups (e.g., Mandinka, Fulani, Wolof, Dyula [Jola], Mande, Dan, Kru, Asante [Cromanti], Fante, Ewe, Ga [dialect of Ewe], Yoruba, Igbo, Nziani, Agni, Fula, and Bantu). Furthermore, it was often the case during the slave trade period that the primarily white European slave owners would father children of their slaves, thus further influencing the resulting gene pool. This admixture is fittingly reflected in the motto of Jamaica 'Out of many, one people'. Consequently, the inadequate classification in the scientific literature of subjects into groups based on characteristics such as skin colour will undoubtedly lead to equivocal results, and serve only to augment existing stereotypes of genetically advantaged black athletes. Studies comparing black and white athletes offer some insight into the physiological determinants of elite performance but provide little if any insight into genetic influences on the disproportionate success of various ethnic groups in sport.

The capacity of Homo sapiens for endurance running is unique among the primates. This has led to the belief that endurance capabilities have been central to the recent evolutionary history of modern humans (Bramble & Lieberman, 2004). The unique endurance capacity of humans relative to the other primates is purported to be due to a number of traceable adaptations beneficial to endurance running in the *Homo* genus (Bramble & Lieberman, 2004). Although anatomically modern humans are young in evolutionary terms (~150,000 years) relative to the age of the *Homo* genus (~2 million years), human populations began to diverge into new environments outside Africa some 70,000 years ago (Macaulay *et al.*, 2005). It is possible, therefore, that divergent human populations (in different continents for a significant portion of the age of the species) have accrued varying degrees of these adaptations due to different selection pressures, further specializing them for an endurance phenotype or otherwise. The varying adaptation to reduced oxygen by geographically isolated high altitude populations represents a well-studied example of this, which may relate to endurance performance. Andean highlanders display higher levels of haemoglobin and saturation than Tibetans at similar altitude, while Ethiopian highlanders maintain oxygen delivery despite having haemoglobin levels and saturation typical of sea level ranges (Beall *et al.*, 2002). There has been much conjecture surrounding such adaptations to altitude and their role in the evolution of human physiological responses (Hochachka *et al.*, 1998). According to the east African origin of modern humans (a higher, drier and cooler environment than our more distant ancestors may have inhabited), the ancestral form of modern humans would have been well adapted for altitude tolerance and, presumably, endurance performance, since the altitude tolerance phenotype is similar to the endurance performance phenotype (Hochachka *et al.*, 1998). If the ancestral form developed in the highlands of east Africa was indeed an altitude/endurance phenotype, east Africans may have further developed an up-regulated, high-capacity version (Hochachka *et al.*, 1998), thus favouring them further for endurance performance.

Other populations may have 'diluted' the ancestral phenotype, or developed down-regulated, low capacity versions through selection for other phenotypes during migration to different environments (e.g., Andean and Tibetan populations) (Hochachka et al., 1998).

The genetic ancestry of elite east African runners was first tested using uni-parentally inherited genetic markers such as mitochondrial DNA (mtDNA). mtDNA provides a unique opportunity to explore the matriline of select groups. mtDNA is passed entirely matrilineally and accumulates mutations along the maternal genealogy, and given the relatively rapid mutation rate of mtDNA compared with the nuclear genome (Atkinson et al., 2009), it is possible to create detailed phylogenies to explore the matrilineal relatedness of people in addition to phenotypes of interest. Grouping particular haplotypes creates easily comparable units of genealogical information with useful levels of predictability. When found in other parts of the world, these haplogroups can be used as indicators of recent migration (Salas et al., 2002). A simplified version of an mtDNA phylogeny is shown in Figure 11.1.

This approach was applied to the unique cohorts of Ethiopian (Scott et al., 2005) and Kenyan (Scott et al., 2009) distance runners. Elite runners from Ethiopia and Kenya were not restricted to one area of the tree but results revealed a wide dis-tribution, similar to their respective general populations and in contrast to the concept that these runners are a genetically distinct group as defined by mtDNA. Therefore, the mtDNA haplogroup diversity found in both Ethiopian and Kenya runners does not support a role for mtDNA polymorphisms in their success. It can be seen from Figure 11.1 that some of the elite athletes share a more recent common mtDNA ancestor with many Europeans. This finding does not support the hypo-thesis that the Ethiopian or indeed Kenyan populations, from which the athletes are drawn, has remained genetically isolated in east Africa but shows that it has undergone migration events and subsequent admixture during the development of the species. This opposes the possibility that these elite athletes have maintained and further developed the ancestral endurance phenotype through having remained isolated in the east African highlands. It is likely that population movements within Africa as recently as a few thousand years ago have contributed to the peopling of east Africa, through the eastern path of the Bantu migrations. However, linguistic data show that Bantu languages are absent in Ethiopia (Scott et al., 2003) but frequent in Kenya (Onywera et al., 2006), indicating that the neighbouring regions may have been subject to widely different patterns of migration. The mtDNA haplogroup data from the Kenyan population and Kenyan runners (Scott et al., 2009) are very different to those found in Ethiopia and show a lower frequency of Eurasian haplogroups M and R; these haplogroups are present at a frequency of 10 per cent in Kenya compared to 45 per cent in Ethiopia (Figure 11.1). It is interesting to note that these two regions that share success in distance running have such different ancestral contributions to their gene pool. In contrast to the Ethiopian cohort where no differences in mtDNA haplogroup distribution were found between athletes and controls, international athletes from Kenya displayed an excess of L0 haplogroups, and a dearth of L3* haplogroups (Figure 11.1). National athletes from Kenya also

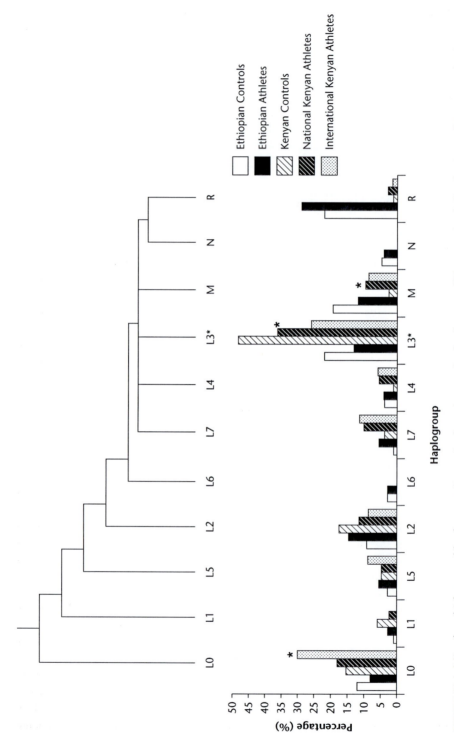

FIGURE 11.1 Mitochondrial tree and haplogroup (i.e. major branches on the family tree of *Homo sapiens*) distributions of Kenyan and Ethiopian athletes and controls. Data redrawn from Scott *et al.* (2009).

showed differences from controls when each haplogroup was compared to the sum of all others, exhibiting an excess of M haplogroups (Figure 11.1). The association of mtDNA haplogroups L0 and M with Kenyan athlete status may suggest that these haplogroups contain polymorphisms, which influence some aspect of endurance performance or its trainability but cannot explain the Kenyan running phenomenon. Higher resolution analysis is now necessary to establish which polymorphisms may be influential in the present association.

Studies have also compared the mtDNA haplogroup profiles of elite sprinters and controls. For example, differences in mtDNA haplogroup profiles of elite sprinters and endurance athletes from Finland have been reported (Niemi & Majamaa, 2005), although no particular haplogroup was over-represented by sprinters when compared to controls (unpublished analysis). Similarly, significant associations were reported between mitochondrial haplogroup G1 and elite endurance athlete status and haplogroup F and elite sprint/power athlete status in Japanese Olympians (Mikami *et al.*, 2010), thus implicating mtDNA haplogroups in determining elite athlete status as suggested in other populations. A more recent study has also investigated the maternal lineage of sprinters from Jamaica and the US (Deason *et al.*, 2011). In this study, highly successful elite sprinters (including world-record holders) from Jamaica and the US were found to derive, in general, from similar source populations (precisely reflecting historical records) although some statistical differences in mtDNA haplotypes were reported. As can be seen from Figure 11.2, the frequency of non Sub-Saharan haplogroups in Jamaican athletes and Jamaican controls were similar (approximately 2 per cent) and lower than African-American athletes and African-American controls (21 per cent and 8 per cent, respectively) suggesting that maternal admixture may play some role in the success of sprinters from the US but once again, these results do not explain the phenomenal success of sprinters from West African ancestry. Instead these associations of mtDNA haplogroups with elite sprint athlete status would suggest that certain lineages contain markers for particular genotypes in both the nuclear and mitochondrial genome that influence some aspect of performance but do not explain the sprint dominance of athletes of West African descent.

The idea that the elite east African runners studied to date do not arise from a limited genetic isolate is further supported by the analysis of the Y chromosome haplogroup distribution of Ethiopian runners (Moran *et al.*, 2004). The Y chromosome can be considered as the male equivalent of mtDNA. Ethiopian runners differ significantly in their Y chromosome distribution from both the general population and that of the Arsi region (Moran *et al.*, 2004), which produces an excess of elite runners (Scott *et al.*, 2003). The finding that Y chromosome haplogroups were associated with athlete status in Ethiopians suggests that either an element of Y chromosome genetics is influencing athletic performance, or that the Y chromosome haplogroup distributions were affected by population stratification (i.e., the population from which the athletes originate has a distinct Y chromosome distribution). However, the haplogroup distribution of the Arsi region did not differ from the rest of Ethiopia, suggesting that the observed associations were less likely

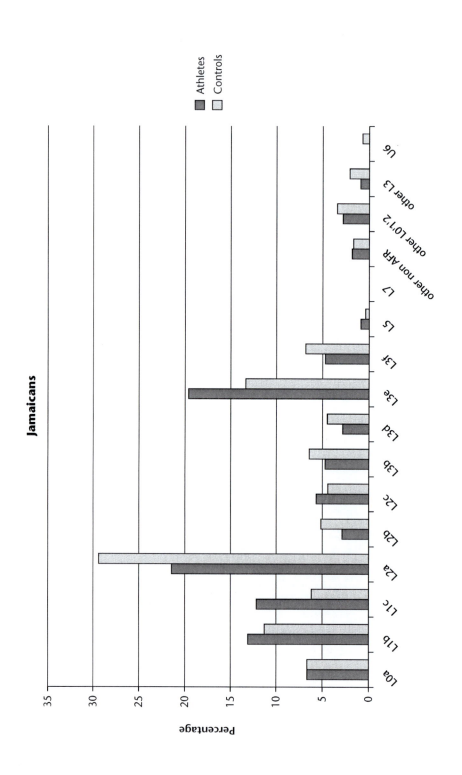

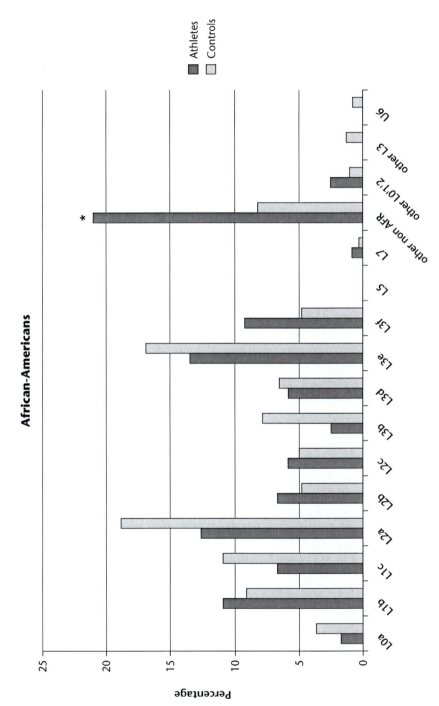

FIGURE 11.2 Mitochondrial tree and haplogroup (i.e. major branches on the family tree of Homo sapiens) distributions of Jamaican and African–American athletes and controls. An asterisk denotes significant overrepresentation of the 'other non AFR' in the African–American athletes. Data redrawn from Deason *et al.* (2011).

to be a result of simple population stratification. Currently, these haplogroup frequencies are being assessed in the larger Kenyan cohort (Onywera *et al.*, 2006). If the same haplogroups are found to be under- or over-represented, this would provide some evidence for a biological effect of the Y chromosome on running performance. However, despite the finding of a potential effect of the Y chromosome on endurance performance, results show similar levels of diversity to those found using mtDNA and reflecting that a significant number of the athletes trace part of their male ancestry to outside Africa at some time during the age of our species. Collectively, the findings from Y chromosome and mtDNA studies do not provide any genetic evidence to support the biology of ethnic differences in sports performance.

Despite the idea being perpetuated that certain ethnic/racial groups are genetically adapted for athletic performance, only two candidate genes for human performance have been investigated in east African athletes (Scott *et al.*, 2005; Yang *et al.*, 2007; Ash *et al.*, 2010) and in sprint athletes from Nigeria (Yang *et al.*, 2007), Jamaica and the US (Scott *et al.*, 2010). The first gene studied in elite east African runners was the Angiotensin converting enzyme (ACE) gene: the most studied of the candidate genes for human performance, where an insertion polymorphism (I) is associated with lower levels of circulating and tissue ACE than the deletion (D) (Danser *et al.*, 1995; see also Chapter 2 in this text). The ACE gene has been associated with a number of aspects of human performance (Jones *et al.*, 2002). In general, the I allele has been associated with endurance performance and the D allele with power performance. The ACE I allele has also been associated with altitude tolerance (Montgomery *et al.*, 1998) making it an ideal candidate gene to investigate in east African runners given the suggestion that the altitude at which these athletes live and train may largely account for their success. As such, ACE I/D genotype frequencies were tested in Kenyan (Scott *et al.*, 2005) and Ethiopian (Ash *et al.*, 2010) runners relative to the general population. Based on previous findings (Jones *et al.*, 2002), it may have been expected that the elite runners would show an excess of the I allele. However, no significant differences were found in I/D genotype frequencies between runners and their respective general populations (Scott *et al.*, 2005; Ash *et al.*, 2010). Different levels of linkage disequilibrium (the non-random association of alleles) in Africans and Caucasians (Zhu *et al.*, 2000) meant that an additional, potentially causal variant (A22982G) was tested. However, no significant differences in A22982G genotype frequencies were found between runners and their respective general populations (Scott *et al.*, 2005; Ash *et al.*, 2010). Indeed 29 per cent of Kenyan controls and only 17 per cent of international Kenyan athletes had the putatively advantageous AA genotype (always found in concert with II in Caucasians) for endurance performance. Although controversy over the influence of ACE genotype on endurance performance continues, these studies did not support a role for ACE gene variation in explaining the east African distance running phenomenon.

The only two genes to have been investigated in elite sprinters are the ACE gene and the alpha-actinin-3 (ACTN3) gene (Yang *et al.*, 2007; Scott *et al.*, 2010). The

ACTN3 has been associated with elite physical performance (Yang *et al.*, 2003) and found at widely differing frequencies in different populations (Mills *et al.*, 2001). In particular, a strong association has been found between the gene variant of ACTN3 called R577X and elite athlete status in Australian Caucasian populations, with the alpha-actinin-3-deficient XX genotype being present at a lower frequency in sprint/power athletes, and at slightly higher frequency in elite female endurance athletes, relative to controls (Yang *et al.*, 2003). This negative association of the XX genotype with sprint performance has subsequently been replicated in a cohort of elite Finnish track and field athletes (Niemi & Majamaa, 2005). Such data have helped established the link between R577X and muscle strength and sprint performance. It was therefore of interest that the alpha-actinin-3 deficient XX genotype was found to be almost absent in controls and sprinters from Nigeria (Yang *et al.*, 2007) and sprinters from the US and Jamaican (Scott *et al.*, 2010), while there was no evidence for an association between the R577X polymorphism and endurance performance in east African runners (Yang *et al.*, 2007), suggesting that ACTN3 deficiency is not a major determinant of east African running success. As for the ACE gene, neither Jamaican sprinters nor sprinters from the US differed from controls. Sprinters from Jamaica did not differ from controls for A22982G genotype, although US sprinters did, displaying an excess of heterozygotes relative to controls, but no excess of GG homozygotes. However, the finding of no excess in ACE DD or GG genotypes in these elite sprint athletes relative to controls suggests that ACE genotype is not a determinant of elite sprint athlete status. In summary, genotyping two of the key candidate genes for human performance in a cohort of the world's most successful endurance athletes and sprinters finds these genes not to be a significant determinant of their success. Whether other nuclear variants can help explain such phenomena remains to be determined. However, the extraordinary achievements of certain populations in sporting success must rely upon the successful integration of a number of physiological, biochemical, and biomechanical systems, which themselves are the product of a multitude of contributors. The success of these athletes is unlikely, therefore, to be the result of a single gene polymorphism; rather it is likely that elite athletes rely on the presence of a combination of advantageous genotypes. Currently, studies are underway to investigate the frequency of other candidate genes in these unique cohorts of world-class athletes.

Non-genetic explanations for ethnic differences in sports performance

Non-genetic explanations for the success of east African distance running include the suggestion that the distances east Africans run to school as children serve them well for subsequent athletic success. A study by Scott *et al.*, (2003) found that Ethiopian distance runners had travelled further to school as children, and more had done so by running. Many of the distances travelled were phenomenal with some children travelling upwards of 20km each day by running to and from school. A previous study by Saltin *et al.* (1995) has shown that east African children who had used running as a means of transport had a $\dot{v}O_2$ max some 30 per cent higher than those who did not, therefore implicating distance travelled to school as a determinant of east African running success. Interestingly, a recent study investigated how and why humans can and did run comfortably without modern running shoes (Lieberman *et al.*, 2010), and found that habitually barefoot runners avoid landing on the heel and instead land with a forefoot or midfoot strike. In doing so they do not generate the sudden, large impact transients that occurs with a heel strike; if impact transient forces contribute to some forms of injury, then barefoot running might have some benefits. Intriguingly, therefore, barefoot running from a young age and not simply running long distances may be a key factor contributing to the success of the east Africans by allowing them to train intensely and for many hours with reduced risk of injury, but that hypothesis remains to be tested. Other studies have shown regional disparities in the production of Ethiopian and Kenyan distance runners (Scott *et al.*, 2003; Onywera *et al.*, 2006). In a study of the demographic characteristics of Ethiopian runners, 38 per cent of marathon athletes were from the region of Arsi, which accounts for less than 5 per cent of the Ethiopian population (Scott *et al.*, 2003). These findings were mirrored in Kenya, where 81 per cent of international Kenyan athletes originated from the Rift-Valley province, which accounts for less than 25 per cent of the Kenyan population (Onywera *et al.*, 2006). Although some believe that this geographical disparity is mediated by an underlying genetic phenomenon (Manners, 1997), it is worth considering that both of these regions are altitudinous (Scott *et al.*, 2003; Onywera *et al.*, 2006) and that athletes have long used altitude training to induce further adaptations. Organized talent identification is rudimentary or even non-existent in both east African countries, as new talents emerge daily as a consequence of the many factors described in this chapter, but particularly the wide training base; modern-day running is a cultural obsession and economic necessity. Consequently, in east Africa, there is far less attention by managers, agents or coaches in identifying and nurturing talented athletes compared to the likes of Great Britain, the US and other sporting nations in the developed world given there is a continuous supply of new talent (like a factory 'conveyor belt') in these east African countries. In other words, the emphasis in Kenya and Ethiopia is more on 'harvesting' young talent than 'sowing' for future stars.

The phenomenal success of Jamaicans in sprinting has also been attributed to non-genetic factors. In Jamaica there exists an excellent and unique model that focuses on identifying and nurturing athletic talent from junior to senior level (Robinson, 2007). It is argued that 'the real explanation of the outstanding achievements of the system is that all of its actors are moved by a spirit that unifies them to work to ensure that Jamaican athletics lives up to its rich history and tradition of excellence' (Robinson, 2007). A theme that echoes what is found in Ethiopia and Kenya (Scott *et al.*, 2003; Onywera *et al.*, 2006).

Others have suggested that African or black athletes enjoy a psychological advantage, mediated through stereotype threat (Baker & Horton, 2003). A consequence of strengthening the stereotypical view of the superior black or African athlete is the development of a self-fulfilling prophecy of white athletes avoiding sporting events typically considered as favouring African or black athletes. This self-selection has resulted in a vicious cycle where the avoidance of these athletic events by whites has further strengthened the aforementioned stereotype to the extent that the unsubstantiated idea of the biological superiority of the African or black athlete becomes dogma. The reverse of this is also observed as black or African athletes tend to avoid sports such as swimming and skiing. This form of self-selection for sport is surprising given the lack of scientific evidence to support this stereotype.

Conclusions

The results of the Beijing Olympics have sparked even greater interest from scientists, the media, and the general public to identify the putative biological mechanisms responsible for the selective dominance of various ethnic groups on the running track. The limited studies reviewed in this chapter would constitute the only available studies on the genetics of the sprint and endurance running phenomena and demonstrate that these athletes, although arising from distinct regions of east Africa or Jamaica (the latter with earlier ancestry from West Africa), do not arise from a limited genetic isolate. Ethiopians and Kenyans do not share similar genetic ancestry but they do share a similar environment: namely moderate altitude as well as high levels of relevant physical activity. Furthermore, the implications of the Jamaican motto 'out of many, one people' that is seemingly overlooked by those arguing a genetic explanation for the Jamaican sprint success, is that these islanders are potentially of even greater genetic diversity than either Kenyans or Ethiopians. It is unlikely, therefore, that these remarkable athletes from east Africa or Jamaica possess unique genotypes that cannot be matched in other areas of the world, but more likely that athletes from these areas with an advantageous genotype realize their biological/genetic potential.

Acknowledgements

I acknowledge the important contribution of all my co-investigators in the studies on which I have based this review (especially my doctoral student Dr Robert Scott) and Professor Craig Sharp for proof-reading this chapter. I also acknowledge the invaluable assistance of the Ethiopian Olympic Committee, the Ethiopian Athletics Federation, Athletics Kenya, the Jamaica Amateur Athletic Association (JAAA), the Jamaica Olympic Association (JOA), the Olympians Association of Jamaica, the United States Olympic Committee (USOC), and United States of America Track and Field (USATF). The cooperation of all the athletics coaches, agents and managers is also greatly appreciated. Most of all, however, I would like to thank the national and elite (i.e., the 'living legends') athletes and controls who volunteered to take part in the genetic studies reviewed here for very little, if anything, in return other than sheer intrinsic interest in their sport.

References

Ama, P. F., Simoneau, J. A., Boulay, M. R., Serresse, O., Thériault, G. & Bouchard, C. (1986). Skeletal muscle characteristics in sedentary black and caucasian males. *Journal of Applied Physiology, 61*, 1758–61.

Ash, G. I., Scott, R. A., Dawson, T. A., Wolde, B., Bekele, Z., Teka, S., & Pitsiladis, Y. P. (2010). No association between ACE gene variation and endurance athlete status in Ethiopians. *Medicine & Science in Sports & Exercise*, 23 August (Epub ahead of print).

Atkinson, Q. D., Gray, R. D., & Drummond, A. J. (2009). Bayesian coalescent inference of major human mitochondrial DNA haplogroup expansions in Africa. *Proceedings of the Royal Society B: Biological Sciences, 276*(1655), 367–73.

Baker, J. & Horton, S. (2003). East African running dominance revisited: A role for stereotype Threat? *British Journal of Sports Medicine, 37*, 553–55.

Beall, C. M., Decker, M. J., Brittenham, G. M., Kushner, I., Gebremedhin, A. & Strohl, K. P. (2002). An Ethiopian pattern of human adaptation to high-altitude hypoxia. *The Proceedings of the National Academy of Sciences of the United States of America, 99*, 17215–18.

Bejan, A., Jones, E. C. & Charles, J. D. (2010). The evolution of speed in athletics: Why the fastest runners are black and swimmers white. *International Journal of Design and Nature, 5*, 1–13.

Bosch, A. N., Goslin, B. R., Noakes, T. D., & Dennis, S. C. (1990). Physiological differences between black and white runners during a treadmill marathon. *European Journal of Applied Physiology, 61*, 68–72.

Boulay, M. R., Ama, P. F., & Bouchard, C. (1988). Racial variation in work capacities and powers. *Canadian Journal of Sport Sciences, 13*, 127–35.

Bramble, D. M., & Lieberman, D. E. (2004). Endurance running and the evolution of Homo. *Nature, 432* (7015), 345–52.

Burchard, E. G., Ziv, E., Coyle, N., Gomez, S. L., Tang, H., Karter, A. J., Mountain, J. L., Pérez-Stable, E. J., Sheppard, D., & Risch, N. (2003). The importance of race and ethnic background in biomedical research and clinical practice. *New England Journal of Medicine, 348*, 1170–75.

Cavalli-Sforza, L. L., & Feldman, M. W. (2003). The application of molecular genetic approaches to the study of human evolution. *Nature Genetics, Suppl 33*, 266–75.

Coetzer, P., Noakes, T. D., Sanders, B., Lambert, M. I., Bosch, A. N., Wiggins, T., & Dennis, S. C. (1993). Superior fatigue resistance of elite black South African distance runners. *Journal of Applied Physiology, 75*, 1822–27.

Cooper, P. D. (2004). *Black Superman: A cultural and biological history of the people who became the world's greatest athletes*. Austin, TX: First Sahara Enterprises.

Cooper, R. S., Kaufman, J. S., & Ward, R. (2003). Race and genomics. *New England Journal of Medicine, 348*, 1166–70.

Danser, A. H., Schalekamp, M. A., Bax, W. A., van den Brink, A. M., Saxena, P. R., Riegger, G. A., & Schunkert, H. (1995). Angiotensin-converting enzyme in the human heart. Effect of the deletion/insertion polymorphism. *Circulation, 92*, 1387–88.

Deason, M. L., Scott, R. A., Irwin, L. E., Macaulay, V., Fuku, N., Tanaka, M., Irving, R., Charlton, V., Morrison, E., Austin, K. G., & Pitsiladis, Y. P. (2011). Importance of mitochondrial haplotypes and maternal lineage in sprint performance amongst individuals of west African ancestry. *Scandinavian Journal of Medicine and Science in Sports*, Mar 16. doi:10.1111/j.1600-0838.2010.01289.x.

Hochachka, P. W., Gunga, H. C., & Kirsch, K. (1998). Our ancestral physiological phenotype: an adaptation for hypoxia tolerance and for endurance performance? *The Proceedings of the National Academy of Sciences of the United States of America, 95*, 1915–20.

International HapMap Consortium (2005). A haplotype map of the human genome. *Nature, 437* (7063), 1299–1320.

Jobling, M. A, Hurles, M. E, & Tyler-Smith, C. (2004) *Human evolutionary genetics.* London: Garland Publishing.

Jones, A., Montgomery, H. E., & Woods, D. R. (2002). Human performance: A role for the ACE genotype? *Exercise and Sport Sciences Reviews, 30,* 184–90.

Larsen, H. B. (2003). Kenyan dominance in distance running. *Comparative Biochemistry and Physiology, 136,* 161–70.

Lieberman, D. E, Werbel, W. A., Daoud, A. I., Venkadesan, M., D'Andrea, S., Ojiambo Mang'Eni, R., Pitsiladis, Y. P. (2010). Foot strike patterns and collision forces in habitually barefoot versus shod runners. *Nature, 463* (7280), 531–35.

Macaulay, V., Hill, C., Achilli, A., Rengo, C., Clarke, D., Meehan, W., Blackburn, J., Semino, O., Scozzari, R., Cruciani, F., Taha, A., Shaari, N. K., Raja, J. M., Ismail, P., Zainuddin, Z., Goodwin, W., Bulbeck, D., Bandelt, H. J., Oppenheimer, S., Torroni, A., & Richards, M. (2005). Single, rapid coastal settlement of Asia revealed by analysis of complete mitochondrial genomes. *Science, 308* (5724), 1034–36.

Manners, J. (1997) Kenya's running tribe. *The Sports Historian, 17* (2), 14–27.

Mikami, E., Fuku, N., Takahashi, H., Ohiwa, N., Scott, R. A., Pitsiladis, Y. P., Higuchi, M., Kawahara. T., & Tanaka, M. (2010) Mitochondrial haplogroups associated with elite Japanese athlete status. *British Journal of Sports Medicine* 15 June (Epub ahead of print).

Mills, M., Yang, N., Weinberger, R., Vander Woude, D. L., Beggs, A. H., Easteal, S., & North K. (2001). Differential expression of the actin-binding proteins, alpha-actinin-2 and -3, in different species: Implications for the evolution of functional redundancy. *Human Molecular Genetics, 10,* 1335–46.

Montgomery, H. E., Marshall, R., Hemingway, H., Myerson, S., Clarkson, P., Dollery, C., Hayward, M., Holliman, D. E., Jubb, M., World, M., Thomas, E. L., Brynes, A. E., Saeed, N., Barnard, M., Bell, J. D., Prasad, K., Rayson, M., Talmud, P. J., & Humphries, S. E. (1998). Human gene for physical performance. *Nature, 393* (6682), 221–22.

Moran, C. N., Scott, R. A., Adams, S. M., Warrington, S. J., Jobling, M. A., Wilson, R. H., Goodwin, W. H., Georgiades, E., Wolde, B., & Pitsiladis, Y. P. (2004). Y chromosome haplogroups of elite Ethiopian endurance runners. *Human Genetics, 115,* 492–97.

Morrison, E. Y., & Cooper, P. D. (2006). Some bio-medical mechanisms in athletic prowess. *West Indian Medical Journal, 55,* 205–09.

Niemi, A-K., & Majamaa, K. (2005). Mitochondrial DNA and ACTN3 genotypes in Finnish elite endurance and sprint athletes. *European Journal of Human Genetics, 13,* 965–69.

Onywera, V. O., Scott, R. A., Boit, M. K., & Pitsiladis, Y. P. (2006). Demographic characteristics of elite Kenyan endurance runners. *Journal of Sports Sciences, 24,* 415–22.

Robinson, P. (2007). *Jamaican athletics: A model for the world.* Kingston: Marco Printers Ltd.

Salas, A., Richards, M., De la Fe, T., Lareu, M. V., Sobrino, B., Sánchez-Diz, P., Macaulay, V., & Carracedo, A. (2002). The making of the African MtDNA landscape. *American Journal of Human Genetics, 71,* 1082–111.

Saltin, B., Larsen, H., Terrados, N., Bangsbo, J., Bak, T., Kim, C. K., Svedenhag, J., & Rolf, C. J. (1995). Aerobic exercise capacity at sea level and at altitude in Kenyan boys, junior and senior runners compared with Scandinavian runners. *Scandinavian Journal of Medicine and Science in Sports, 5,* 209–21.

Scott, R. A., Georgiades, E., Wilson, R. H., Goodwin, W. H., Wolde, B., & Pitsiladis, Y. P. (2003). Demographic characteristics of elite Ethiopian endurance runners. *Medicine and Science in Sports and Exercise, 35,* 1727–32.

Scott, R. A., & Pitsiladis, Y. P. (2007). Genotypes and distance running: Clues from Africa. *Sports Medicine, 37,* 1–4.

Scott, R. A., Fuku, N., Onywera, V. O., Boit, M., Wilson, R. H., Tanaka, M., Goodwin,

W., & Pitsiladis, Y. P. (2009). Mitochondrial haplogroups associated with elite Kenyan athlete status. *Medicine & Science in Sports & Exercise, 41*, 123–28.

Scott, R. A., Irving, R., Irwin, L., Morrison, E., Charlton, V., Austin, K., Tladi, D., Headley, S. A., Kolkhorst, F. W., Yang, N., North, K., & Pitsiladis, Y. P. (2010). ACTN3 and ACE genotypes in elite Jamaican and US sprinters. *Medicine and Science in Sports and Exercise, 42*, 107–12.

Scott, R. A., Moran. C., Wilson, R. H., Onywera, V., Boit, M. K., Goodwin, W. H., Gohlke, P., Payne, J., Montgomery, H., & Pitsiladis, Y. P. (2005). No association between angiotensin converting enzyme (ACE) gene variation and endurance athlete status in Kenyans. *Comparative Biochemistry and Physiology, 141*, 169–75.

Scott, R. A., Wilson, R. H., Goodwin, W. H., Moran, C. N., Georgiades, E., Wolde, B., & Pitsiladis, Y. P. (2005). Mitochondrial DNA lineages of elite Ethiopian athletes. *Comparative Biochemistry and Physiology, 140*, 497–503.

Weston, A. R., Karamizrak, O., Smith, A., Noakes, T. D., & Myburgh, K. H. (1999). African runners exhibit greater fatigue resistance, lower lactate accumulation, and higher oxidative enzyme activity. *Journal of Applied Physiology, 86*, 915–23.

Weston, A. R., Mbambo, Z., & Myburgh, K. H. (2000). Running economy of African and caucasian distance runners. *Medicine and Science in Sports and Exercise, 32*, 1130–34.

Yang, N., MacArthur, D. G., Gulbin, J. P., Hahn, A. G., Beggs, A. H., Easteal, S., & North, K. (2003) ACTN3 genotype is associated with human elite athletic performance. *American Journal of Human Genetics, 73*, 627–31.

Yang, N., MacArthur, D. G., Wolde, B., Onywera, V. O., Boit, M. K., Lau, S. Y., Wilson, R. H., Scott, R. A, Pitsiladis, Y. P., & North, K. (2007). The ACTN3 R577X polymorphism in East and West African athletes. *Medicine and Science in Sports and Exercise, 39*, 1985–88.

Yu, N., Chen, F.C., Ota, S., Jorde, L. B., Pamilo, P., Patthy, L., Ramsay, M., Jenkins, T., Shyue, S. K., & Li, W. H. (2002). Larger genetic differences within Africans than between Africans and Eurasians. *Genetics, 161*, 269–74.

Zhu, X., McKenzie, C. A., Forrester, T., Nickerson, D. A., Broeckel, U., Schunkert, H., Doering, A., Jacob, H. J., Cooper, R. S., & Rieder, M. J. (2000). Localization of a small genomic region associated with elevated ACE. *American Journal of Human Genetics, 67*, 1144–53.

12

APPLYING TALENT IDENTIFICATION PROGRAMS AT A SYSTEM-WIDE LEVEL

The evolution of Australia's national program

Jason Gulbin

This chapter focuses on the implementation of a national talent identification and development (TID) system. This approach contrasts the single-sport perspectives elegantly provided in the previous chapters by showcasing Australia's nationally funded TID system designed to support and enhance the development pathways of multiple sporting organisations. The information contained within this chapter will attempt to relay the evolution, techniques, and experiences through the lens of an author who has been responsible for implementing national TID programs on behalf of the Australian Government throughout the previous decade.

The chapter will chart a quick course across almost 25 years of the Australian TID timeline, and will follow the *concept, growth, refinement, and maturation phases* of the formative program elements. This evolutionary perspective exposes the failings as well as the successes and is in keeping with the authenticity of creating and launching multiple TID programs. The remaining section of this chapter will then reflect on a framework for any future systems that might be established to capitalise on the progress made thus far and has been presented in a form that is generalisable and applicable to any international system.

This information is shared without reservation. Broadening the understanding of these dynamic and imperfect TID processes will also hopefully improve the collective international comprehension of TID – thus raising the bar for all those interested in this fascinating, but challenging area. From the authors' own experiences and reinforced by others, international sporting systems are becoming more uniform than different (Augestad, Bergsgard, & Hansen, 2006; Oakley & Green, 2001). This suggests that there are few secrets in elite sport, but rather the point of differentiation being a nation's ability to optimally coordinate these common components.

The Australian system and challenges for TID

The national system of TID in Australia has evolved over a period of approximately 25 years. From its early and successful forays instigated by the Australian Institute of Sport (AIS) in the late 1980s to the features and approaches of the current program, it has taken time to understand, learn, and develop an approach that suits Australia. Currently, it is far from perfect and there are a number of system challenges that are still being addressed today.

Despite failing to win a single gold medal at the 1976 Montreal Olympic Games, Australia won 17 gold at the 2004 Athens Olympic Games and was ranked fourth nation in the overall medal tally, and second only to the Bahamas for the most medals won per capita. Many outsiders looking into the Australian sports system seem to admire and applaud how it can deliver strong international performances despite having a relatively small population. While it is true that these international performances are impressive, the reason often cited – our laudable sporting system – is not.

The Australian sports system has recently been subjected to a thorough period of review, introspection and debate (Australian Olympic Committee, 2009; Australian Sports Commission, 2008; Commonwealth Department of Health & Ageing, 2009; 2010). Reading these critical documents will expose the areas where Australia has much to do to develop a great sporting system and this is also true of the TID system within it. However, in brief, some of the major concerns included: the absence of a clear national sports policy and vision; declining participation rates in sport; a reduction in the international performances of Australia's elite athletes; a disjointed and fragmented system with perceived areas of duplication; large gaps evident in the coach and athlete talent development pathways; and an overall insufficiency in system resourcing.

There is a degree of imperfection in any sporting system as politics and funding promote or retard its effectiveness (De Bosscher, De Knop, Van Bottenburg, & Shibli, 2006). This can result in TID system solutions impacting in a transitional rather than transformative way, as overall system inertia results in the achievement of compromised, rather than optimised outcomes. In fact, De Bosscher and colleagues (2006) have indicated that more than 50 per cent of a nation's international sporting success can be attributed to macro-level factors such as its political system, population, extent of urbanisation, culture, geography, and climate. These elements provide the context and constraints as to the type of policies or systems (i.e. the meso-level factors) that should or could be implemented to influence an individual or national outcome (micro-level). Thus, a brief summary of the Australian sporting macro-level environment and how this specifically interrelates with the meso-level TID system is provided.

Size, population, and its dispersion

Australia has the sixth largest land mass of 239 countries but one of the lowest population densities, ranking 233rd (Wikipedia, 2010). Coupled with a relatively low total population of approximately 22 million people (ranked 188th), Australians are relatively well spread out and can be far from the critical pathway elements of coaching, support services, and infrastructure. Geographically, Australia is situated a long way from international sporting competitions. Apart from those countries in the immediate Oceanic or south-eastern Asian region, large travel distances (and expenses) are required to participate in the bulk of international competition which remain largely in the northern hemisphere.

The implication of these challenges from a TID perspective is that: (a) overall, the population is relatively small in comparison with Australia's international sporting competitors, which limits the absolute numbers of talented athletes; (b) of the talent that does exist, it is dispersed widely, thus requiring significant logistical challenges to first identify it and then to optimally develop it; (c) the upward pressure from domestic competition can be limited by talent depth; and (d) international competition experiences for developing athletes are somewhat curtailed because of time and travel expenses (e.g. contrast this with those countries in the European Union who can achieve this through daily or weekend experiences!).

Sporting culture

Sport is important to Australians. A survey of 2,382 Australians confirmed that the nation's achievements in sport were the greatest source of national pride than any other field including science, arts and literature, political influence, economic achievements, and history (Kelley & Evans, 1998).

From a participation perspective, Australians typically gravitate towards playing team sports, and our most popular are in fact non-Olympic team events. Of all the organised activities undertaken by 15 to 24 year olds, team sports such as cricket, rugby league, AFL (Australian Rules Football), and netball account for more than 25 per cent of the entire activity profile of this future talent cohort (Standing Committee on Recreation and Sport, 2009). This proportional activity is more than the combined participation of any of the Olympic sports inside the top ten (e.g. basketball, football, tennis). If you also add in other popular non-Olympic sports such as rugby union and surf lifesaving, there is a significant pool of athletic talent that does not currently have an Olympic event focus (although a modified seven-a-side rugby game will make its debut at the 2016 Olympic Games).

While this team sport participation profile yields many benefits of its own relating to cultural identity, national pride, and general health of the nation, there is a strong public expectation that Australians do well at the Olympic Games and often government funding has been specifically provided to meet this desire. Due to the popularity and patronage of our non-Olympic sports, many Olympic sports have to rely on the 'leftover' talent. Contrast this delicate sporting equilibrium with more aggressive, competitive, and better funded recruitment and identification practices by the professional sports and there will almost certainly be a time when Australia's international success across a broad range of sports will be compromised.

The implication of these challenges from a TID perspective is that (a) excellence in sport is highly valued by Australians and TID is well positioned to play a pivotal role in this endeavour and (b) greater talent sharing strategies between sports will be required to maximise the finite talent resource and this becomes more critical for the success of Olympic sports.

Politics and funding

Australia is a federated nation comprised of six states and two territories. This structure creates a number of tiers of government at the national, state/territory, and local levels and results in multiple partnerships and relationships that require careful nurturing to align sporting pathways and outcomes. Any intergovernmental differences can affect the cohesiveness, effectiveness, and efficiency of the national sports system – that is, one which is designed to achieve an outcome for the 'green and gold' (i.e. Australia), versus the preferred needs of a state or a local government. These tensions between the federal and state governments have been well documented in the Australian Government's Crawford Review into sport (Commonwealth Department of Health & Ageing, 2009), and in particular highlight the challenges that exist within Australia's high performance system.

At the state government level, the State Departments of Sport and Recreation fund their respective high performance state sporting institutes and academies (SIS/SAS), which form part of the backbone of the coach and athlete high performance development pathways. Together with the federally funded and pre-eminent Australian Institute of Sport (AIS), these institutes and academies represent the National Institutes Network (NIN). The relationships within the NIN, have been far from being fully functional (Sotiriadou & Shilbury, 2009) and resulted in Crawford's recommendation to abolish the fragmented state and national high performance system and replace it with a single national institutes model (Commonwealth Department of Health & Ageing, 2009).

Apart from the major professional sports such as AFL and cricket who are capable of achieving annual revenues of $303 million and $115 million respectively (AFL, 2009; Cricket Australia, 2009), most other national sporting organisations (NSOs) in Australia are heavily reliant on government revenue and are limited in their capacities to generate it. This means that the capacity for financial independence is limited, which translates to NSOs being beholden to government policy and their priorities. For example, sport is a relatively low priority with federal government spending on sport remaining stable at around 0.30 to 0.36 per cent of the total government budget between 2003/04 and 2008/09 (Hoye & Nicholson, 2009). Given Australia's relatively smaller overall economy in comparison with its international competitors such as China, Russia, the US, Great Britain, and Germany, sports funding limitations will necessitate targeted approaches to remain internationally competitive.

The priority that is given to sport by the elected government of the day also varies. For instance, the sport portfolio has not resided within a department with the term 'sport' in the title since 1996 (Environment, Sport and Territories, 1993–96) (Hoye & Nicholson, 2009). Since that time, the elected governments have created at least five departmental name changes with sport concealed in departments such as Environment (1996–98), Industry, Science & Resources (1998–2001), Communications, Information Technology and the Arts (2001–07), Health and Ageing (2007–10), as well as Prime Minister and Cabinet (beginning in 2010). Furthermore, since 1996, there have been a total of eight different ministers of sport and four elected governments reinforcing that sport and stability are very uncomfortable bedfellows.

The implication of these challenges from a TID perspective is that: (a) the fragmented nature of Australia's administrative sporting structures can mean that national level priorities (such as the 'green and gold' outcomes) require different delivery partnerships and models rather than a one-size fits all solution; (b) the significant reliance on government funding and the immersion of sport within the ever changing political environment necessitates regular system, program, or project modifications; (c) constant changes in government policy can make long-term planning vulnerable; and (d) the ongoing changes to key decision makers within the sporting environment (e.g. governments, Ministers, CEOs) necessitates a method of information exchange to ensure that corporate knowledge is not lost, and that strategic visions and decisions related to TID are well informed and evidence based.

These TID challenges may not be totally germane to Australia. Perhaps some readers from other countries might even feel that Australia's TID challenges are actually no different to their own national sporting landscapes. However, context and culture are critical to the understanding and application of TID systems.

What was – the evolution of TID (1987–2005)

Within this almost two-decade period, there were three distinct phases that were responsible for providing a tremendous amount of insights into TID. These phases and approximate time periods could be summarised as follows:

- The Concept Phase – Talent Detection Experimentation (1987 to 1993)
- The Growth Phase – National Talent Detection and Mass Screening (1994 to 2000)
- The Refinement and Maturation Phase – Targeted Talent Detection and Development (2001 to 2005).

The Concept Phase – Talent Detection Experimentation (1987 to 1993)

There were two early TID adopters in Australian sport. These were the sports of rowing and cycling. Both sports had seen the arrival of successful Eastern European coaches throughout the mid-1980s, and their qualifications and experiences within their former countries of origin promoted the importance of systematic testing as a method of detecting future talent.

At the time, talent selection was the only method of talent identification and those athletes performing well in competition within their own sport received the most support. However, to support completely untried and inexperienced athletes based on laboratory test results was a complete paradigm shift at the time.

Allan Hahn, who was working as a physiologist at the AIS, pioneered Australia's first true talent detection programs throughout 1987 and 1988 (Hahn, 1990). In a seminal case study in the sport of rowing, Hahn tested about 500 students aged 14 to 16 years from the local secondary schools near to the AIS. Field tests included anthropometric measures, a 15 second all out effort on a modified arm-leg cycle ergometer and a progressive test to volitional exhaustion using the same apparatus. Approximately 10 per cent of the students ($n = 47$) were then invited for additional laboratory testing, and then approximately half again ($n = 24$) were immersed into an AIS supported rowing environment. This level of AIS support included access to quality coaching, competition, and equipment, as well as key services from a range of professional sport scientists specialising in physiology, nutrition, strength and conditioning, biomechanics, and psychology. The provision of such a high quality talent development environment for these novices was highly controversial within the rowing communities. Existing club rowers had a far greater sense of entitlement to AIS support than their novice counterparts who actually couldn't row! However, the observation that successful elite rowers were large, muscular people with long limbs and excellent aerobic and anaerobic capabilities necessitated a talent intake that was representative of a performance-based model rather than an experience-based model.

Finally, Hahn's vision was spectacularly vindicated when one of the TID athletes (Megan Still) partnered a non-TID rower (Kate Slatter) to win a gold medal in the women's pairs at the 1996 Atlanta Olympic Games. This approach reinforced to NSOs that it was possible for two diverse development pathways (i.e. talent selection and talent detection) to intersect and achieve identical outcomes.

Hahn's work and the promising results achieved in these timeframes generated significant interest in the sport and scientific communities. Other sports such as cycling, athletics, and canoeing were also inspired to experiment with TID. In 1993, Cycling Australia in partnership with the South Australian Sports Institute was keen to increase the depth of talent in women's cycling. Using a similar method of secondary school talent recruitment, novice cyclists were initially identified using general field tests of muscular speed and endurance, followed by more specific cycle ergometer testing with a smaller cohort. A final squad was then selected following some basic cycling exposure and skill development. Thereafter, selected athletes commenced an intensive development program, which was overseen by experienced high performance coaches as well as sports science and sports medicine staff. By 1996, the first of three Junior World Championship medals had been won with one of the athletes, track endurance specialist Alayna Burns, eventually claiming a Commonwealth Games gold medal in 1998, and two top ten finishes at the 2000 Olympic Games.

These case studies were incredibly important in demonstrating proof of concept. That is, TID was a credible and legitimate tool to increase an NSOs talent pool, but it could also deliver the outcome they were looking for – international success. It cannot be underestimated how critical Hahn's experiment was for Australian sport. This period became the foundation years for TID and blazed a trail for others to follow. Importantly, the successes silenced many of the sceptics, and opened up the opportunity for a new phase within TID.

The Growth Phase – National Talent Detection and Mass Screening (1994 to 2000)

By the end of this TID experimentation period, it became clear that a greater level of coordination and efficiency could be achieved. The enthusiasm by NSOs for unearthing talent within schools was significant, and physical education teachers were being bombarded with many requests to access their students. In many instances, a number of sports conducted similar field tests (e.g. vertical jump, 20/40 meter sprint, 20 meter shuttle run) resulting in much duplication and drain on school resources and time. The implementation of the Australian Sports Commission's *Talent Search* program in 1994 alleviated many of these problems as it was the first coordinated, national effort between sports and necessitated testing students only once.

The genesis of *Talent Search* can be traced back to the decision in late September 1993 with Juan Antonio Samaranch, then President of the International Olympic Committee, awarding the 2000 Summer Olympic Games to Sydney, Australia. With this came the creation of the federal government's new $135 million Olympic Athlete Program (OAP), which was launched on 1 July 1994 and designed to be spent on the preparation of athletes in the lead up to the 2000 Olympic Games (Bloomfield, 2003). The priority areas of spending included sports science and medicine, research, direct athlete payments, and international competition.

Emanating from the OAP plan were two very different TID initiatives and both pioneered by developmental scientist Deborah Hoare. The first was an interactive sports counselling computer program called *Sports Search* (Australian Sports Commission, 1993). This program was designed to increase the sports participation of 11 to 17 year olds by matching their interests and abilities with local opportunities. Basic anthropometric and field testing data were entered into the computer along with their sport related preferences (e.g. indoor/outdoor sports, aquatic/non-aquatic sports, team/individual sports). The computer would then generate a list of potentially suitable sports with key local contact information provided. While this was a non-elite approach to TID because the focus was on participation only, the desire for high performance success at the Sydney Olympics elevated the interest in high performance TID. Thus, *Sports Search* became the conceptual framework for a more sophisticated system of TID – *Talent Search*. While alike in foundation (both programs used similar anthropometric and physiological field based tests), these programs were designed for entirely different performance outcomes although both have erroneously been reviewed as being the same (Abbott & Collins, 2002).

Summaries and reflections regarding the operational details of this period of *Talent Search* can be found elsewhere (Hoare, 1995, 1998). However, in brief:

- Eight sports were chosen for involvement in the mainstream talent identification program. These were the sports of athletics, cycling, canoeing, swimming, rowing, triathlon, water polo, and weightlifting. A major focus of the funding was an ambitious attempt to identify talent and fast-track athletes for the 2000 Olympic Games. The age range for testing was 14 to 16 years which meant that athletes would be 20–22 years old by the time of the 2000 Sydney Olympics. Targeting older athletes (e.g. 16 years +) was deemed to be too disruptive to school studies and thought to receive modest support by educators.
- *Talent Search* was established and coordinated nationally with state *Talent Search* coordinators employed and based at each SIS/SAS facility.
- Three key phases were identified for the operational framework of the *Talent Search* program. These included secondary school screening at Phase 1, sports specific testing at Phase 2, and talent development at Phase 3.
- Phase 1 included a battery of eight physical and physiological tests (height, weight, arm span, vertical jump, basketball throw, 40 meter sprint, cricket ball throw, and the 20 meter shuttle run test). In most cases, physical education teachers conducted the tests with the assistance of the state coordinators. Results were compared with a national database and selected students were then invited to participate in Phase 2 testing. In general, students needed to be in the top 2 per cent on any one of the eight tests to be eligible to participate in Phase 2.
- Phase 2 testing refined the accuracy of some Phase 1 tests and incorporated sport-specific testing, including some laboratory tests. For example, in the sport of cycling, the basic field test of muscular endurance (20 meter shuttle run test) was replaced with a progressive, maximal test on the cycle ergometer.
- Following Phase 2, students identified with talent for a specific sport were invited to join a talented athlete program organised by the state and/or national sporting organisation (Phase 3). Funding for the talent development component of *Talent Search* was the responsibility of these organisations.

The key *Talent Search* years (1994 to 2000) were a particularly fertile phase for TID and could be described as a significant growth and legacy period for Australian sport. The legacies that were created during this time and have remained to this day include: (a) the development of a system and a methodology for TID – especially standardising procedures related to testing and selection; (b) the detection of new high performance athletes which significantly deepened the NSOs' talent pool; (c) an understanding of the strengths and weaknesses of a systematic TID program; (d) building the national capability and capacity of staffing expertise within TID; and (e) the establishment of a well-regarded international reputation in the area of TID.

While this growth and legacy period was extremely positive, the original format of the *Talent Search* program was not sustainable in its current form. The major issues and challenges included:

- A relatively poorly funded program (an average federal contribution of less than $350,000 AUD), which significantly limited expansion possibilities.
- Variable support by the SIS/SAS network, which meant that talent detection activities were completely absent in some states.
- The detection process was mostly one dimensional and relied heavily on the physical education teachers to test, collate, and forward results. Teachers unwilling to conduct the testing or philosophically opposed to the program nullified any opportunities for their talented students to be recognised.
- The increase in concerns about information privacy by the state education departments meant that it was far more difficult to identify and contact students directly as opposed to identifying students by their ID numbers. This latter approach definitely increased the administrative requirements of the program at all levels.
- The age-range of detection meant that there were going to be long waiting periods to capitalise on the talent, when many NSOs needed talent immediately.
- The number of sports accessing the national system of talent detection was low.
- Athlete development environments were highly variable across sports and states.
- Competing and sometimes conflicting performance outcomes from a state and national perspective made consensus on program elements challenging.
- The recognition and status of staff working in the discipline of TID was relatively poor as evident by lower rates of pay in comparison with other areas of sports science (e.g. physiology, biomechanics etc.) and a preference by SIS/SAS to employ junior staff in their *Talent Search* coordinator positions.

The Refinement and Maturation Phase – Targeted Talent Detection and Development (2001 to 2005)

The development of the Australian national TID system shifted gears again in the period 2001 to 2005 in order to address the previously cited challenges. This period could be summarised as a significant period of maturation as refinement and diversification in program elements were undertaken. An element of the 'old' *Talent Search* methodology was retained but this was supplemented with diversified recruitment approaches with new sports, targeted disciplines, engagement with a broader age range of athletes, centralised development coordination, and new high performance partners.

While modifications to the original *Talent Search* program had begun to emerge in the lead up to the 2000 Olympics, with variations trialled in sports and recruitment methods (Gulbin, 2001; Hoare & Warr, 2000), the post Sydney Olympics period provided a good opportunity to review and refocus the operational framework of the *Talent Search* program. A significant milestone in Australian sport had now been achieved, and the sobering reality of preparing for the 2004 Athens Olympics quickly captured the sports system's attention. During this period, a number of NSOs lamented about a shortfall in talent (perhaps due to post Olympics retirement or pathway inattention – or both). Similarly, the AIS sport programs had difficulty in filling vacant scholarship positions, reinforcing that the 'trickle up' effect of the sport development pyramid was clearly an oversimplification of the talent supply chain (Sotiriadou, Shilbury, & Quick, 2008). Therefore, the mood was one of impatience and new approaches were needed to plug pathway gaps by identifying and developing talent quickly.

Moving forward necessitated a far more targeted approach to meet the specific needs of individual sports and would require broadening recruitment efforts beyond the secondary school system. Newer recruitment methods were required to be established and included a focus on older athletes, media drives, sport specific talent transfer, and even the profiling of elite athlete siblings (Gulbin, 2001). Some of these documented examples included specific searches for female sprint cyclists (Gardner *et al.*, 2002; Gulbin & Ackland, 2008; Halson, Martin, Gardner, Fallon, & Gulbin, 2006), rowers specifically suited to lightweight sculling (Slater, Rice, Jenkins, Gulbin, & Hahn, 2006), and women able to transfer to the winter Olympic sliding sport of skeleton (Bullock, Gulbin, Martin, Ross, Holland, & Marino, 2009).

Extending the talent detection age range to older athletes became a major focus in order to shorten the time needed to boost the talent pool at the senior national level. The essence of this approach was to use a 'talent transfer' or a 'talent recycling' model whereby mature and well credentialed athletes were provided with the opportunity to switch sports relatively late in their athletic careers. The rationale and the efficacy of such an approach has been detailed elsewhere (Gulbin, 2008; Gulbin & Ackland, 2008) but in brief, targeting the previously ignored mature age talent pool allowed Australia's TID system to: (a) access more of its limited talent pool; (b) achieve quicker performance gains at the senior international level; (c) maximise government investments already made into some athletes; (d) avoid the maturational issues inherent with younger developing athletes and improve the capacity to predict talented performers; (e) engage with more independent and autonomous athletes; (f) catalogue more of the developmental histories and sports experiences to capture greater insights into an athlete's 'coachability', 'self-management', and commitment potential; and (g) establish donor/recipient type relationships between sports to more positively support athlete exit/transition pathways. Interestingly, this approach now appears to have gained mainstream interest, with UK Sport successfully adopting the approach within their national TID system (Vaeyens, Gullich, Warr, & Philippaerts, 2009).

In the latter half of this period additional recognition was bestowed upon the program as a result of some of the new and continuing successes in the now hybrid *Talent Search* program. The increase in program success and its change in direction resulted in a doubling of the budget (an additional $390K indexed each year) to specifically pilot central coordination of TID initiatives on behalf of targeted NSOs in the sports of cycling, canoeing, and rowing. Furthermore, the introduction of a special initiatives grant program was another intervention that broadened the involvement of more sports into the mainstream TID system. Resources were made available for NSOs to conduct some of their own specialised TID projects. The intent of this grants program was to encourage innovation within discrete components of the NSO's talent development pathways. The hallmarks of well-regarded projects included those that were high NSO priorities, had matching funding or resources, and that the development pathway was clearly defined. These key criteria assisted an independent panel to assess and prioritise applications when demand consistently outstripped the funding supply.

Finally, a small number of local government supported Regional Academies of Sport (RAS) were also selectively brought into the *Talent Search* delivery system in order to supplement the reach of the program into more localised communities. Thus, the high performance TID network now extended to more centres of excellence through a flexible and extended NIN framework.

Towards the end of this period, the impact of the national *Talent Search* program on national and international U23 success was summarised (Table 12.1). Despite the modest national budget the *Talent Search* program was not only able to achieve podium performances, but it substantially increased the depth of the talent pool in many sports (especially those with a large anthropometric/physiological component) creating upward pressure on the existing talent selection athletes.

One aspect of this refinement/maturation period that doesn't appear in the impact tables is the effect that new or novel projects had among NSOs, coaches, administrators, and/or sports scientists. TID programs can be very stimulating in terms of interaction. A new approach in sport can create significant levels of enthusiasm across a broad section of high performance staff and provides a focus point for people to debate, discuss, challenge, think, and motivate. Attempting a new project or technique within sport galvanises interest, not necessarily consensus, and has the opportunity to challenge 'traditional' ways of developing athletes. Arguments surrounding talent selection versus talent detection can be divisive enough; however, add to this an entirely new talent demographic, a preferred method of high performance development termed 'deliberate programming' (Bullock *et al.*, 2009), and a philosophy of accelerated skill acquisition, then much healthy and productive discussions are guaranteed!

TABLE 12.1 Summary of national U23 *Talent Search* program achievements (1994 to 2005)

Achievement	2001[a]	2005[b]
World Age Championships – Medals	28	56
World Age Championships Representation	100	170
National Age Championships	403	609
National Age Championships – Placing (1st – 3rd)	1075	1690
National Age Championships – Top 10 Placing	2074	3402

The Investment Phase – What is (2006 to 2010)

Prior to 2006, Australia's TID system was shaped by the historical elements of the concept, growth, and refinement/maturation phases of the previous 20 years. There had been an important and strategic shift during the maturation phase (2001 to 2005) that reinforced the critical importance of combining simultaneous identification and development emphases.

In the federal government budget announcement in May 2006, an unprecedented commitment of $20.8 million over a four-year period enabled the existing *Talent Search* program to be restructured to form the *National Talent Identification and Development program* (NTID). The program was established to enhance the identification and development of Australia's next generation of high performance athletes as well as improve social inclusivity through the establishment of a broader national system to improve the identification of talent, enhancing the identification and development of indigenous athletes and targeting Asian-centric sports (such as judo, badminton, taekwondo).

Broadly, the significant increase in resources allowed a far greater depth of support to be provided to NSOs in their development pathways and for new concepts in pathway support to be trialled and implemented. Specifically, it was now possible to substantially increase system-wide support to the next generation of athletes that were currently outside of the mainstream NIN. This was possible through an increase in the quality and quantity of coaching, the amount of international competition, access to mostly unattainable athlete services in sports science and sports medicine, the establishment of new regional centres of excellence, and enhanced individual case-management of athletes and coaches.

Staffing had increased from a total of four staff in 2005 to 14 throughout the 2006/10 period, and was an important step forward in establishing a succession plan for a critical mass of skilled practitioners in the field of TID. This was necessary to develop a central resource in the area of TID for the sports system but to also have enough personnel and accompanying expertise to maximise the outcomes for targeted NSOs. This model also allowed each targeted NSO to have its own TID case manager as a part of the succession planning to enhance the NSO's future capability and capacity.

An electronic, free online talent identification platform called eTID (www.ausport.gov.au/etid) was established to enable far more of the talent pool to be assessed through their own proactivity. This platform has both general and sports specific self-identification components that cater to all Australians within a targeted age range (12 to 29 years) who are able to access an internet connection. The website allows users to enter their results for a series of self-initiated performance tests and measurements, and receive a report assessing their non-sport specific potential by comparing their results with normative data. The tests are similar to the *Talent Search* tests, with some 'home-based' alternatives to minimise equipment requirements and promote inclusivity (e.g. the 1.6 kilometer run would replace the 20 meter shuttle run for the endurance component). These self-collected data are not needed for selection purposes but are utilised to encourage users to progress to a more sophisticated and accurate screening session at a designated Talent Assessment Centre. The website also acts as an independent and confidential counselling service for current and former elite athletes interested in talent transfer opportunities.

A three-year evaluation of the operation and impact of the NTID program during this *investment phase* has been published (Australian Sports Commission, 2009), with detailed program information, facts, and figures provided. Rather than repeat these data, it is perhaps worth contrasting what the major points of difference were with the current and previous programs to emphasise the evolution of the TID system. Table 12.2 highlights the current approach that Australia has taken with its national TID program.

Assessing the effectiveness of this current phase involved a five-month independent review into the performance and impact of the NTID program. In keeping with the critical importance of canvassing the perspectives of the 'end-users' of the program (Chelladurai & Chang, 2000; Papadimitriou, 2001) the review concluded that 'the program is well regarded by the national sporting organisations, and athletes and coaches in the program (378 anonymous survey respondents) reported an impressive 96 per cent satisfaction with the overall program delivery and impact' (Muldoon, 2009, p. 5). The findings also reinforced the successful impact of the program with one in four of the 573 athletes who had initially developed outside of the NIN, achieving national selection in either a junior or senior team. The areas of the NTID program that required the most improvement were those activities that had received the least resourcing and attention. These included alignment with a relevant mentor, career and education support, and sport psychology assistance.

To the future and beyond

The immersion phase – what could be (2011 and beyond)

The period 2006 to 2010 was a notable investment period into Australia's TID system through the establishment of the NTID program. Beyond 2010, the specific direction for TID is largely unknown as the details for NTID version 2.0 will be determined by the meso-level elements of policy, planning, and resourcing. However, a glimpse of the future has been framed by a recent Australian Government announcement that has recognised that Australian sport is at a critical junction and a new sporting pathway approach is needed (Commonwealth Department of Health & Ageing, 2010).

In particular, the Australian Government has at least addressed the concern raised in the Crawford Report (Commonwealth Department of Health & Ageing, 2009) regarding the poor planning, resourcing, and management of the coaches and athletes residing in the development pathway gap between junior participation and senior elite. When the Australian Government announced its blueprint for the future of Australian sport in May 2010, it declared:

> A way forward that not only delivers on the Australian Government's commitment to boost funding to both the community and high performance

TABLE 12.2 A summary of the evolution of the key areas of the TID system within Australia

	Concept (1987 to 1993)	Growth (1994 to 2000)	Refinement Maturation (2001 to 2005)	Investment (2006 to 2010)
Period (years)	7	7	5	5
Federal Funding (approx. $ '000's)	< 50	300 to 350	350 to 690	5,800 to 6,000
No. of national staff	0	1	4	14
Athlete age focus (%)				
Under 16 years	100[a]	90[a]	75[a]	36[b]
16 to 18 years	0	10	15	36
Over 18 years	0	0	10	28
Identification method (%)				
Detection	100[a]	100[a]	90[a]	33[b]
Selection	0	0	10	67
Breadth and Focus of Identification	Narrow focus on targeted local secondary schools	Initial broad focus on all Australian secondary schools, switching to mainly metropolitan schools	Reduced emphasis on secondary schools; large growth in community TID campaigns and older athletes	Minimal secondary school emphasis; some community campaigns; large NSO recruitment; and self-ID via the internet
Defining Legacy	Proof of concept	Creation of a national approach	Diversification of national elements	Large scale impact of TID on NSO pathways

a = estimation
b = (ASC, 2009)

sport, but also for the first time, one that delivers a significant investment to the development pathway, the vital link that connect grassroots and high performance sport.

(Commonwealth Department of Health & Ageing, 2010, p. 1)

The government went further to state that TID was the key vehicle for this new way forward:

(TID) . . . is the all important bridge that fills the gap between grassroots sport and the development pathway.

(Commonwealth Department of Health and Ageing, 2010, p. 7)

Therefore, in thinking about how the TID system might operate in the future, it might well evolve as an *Immersion Phase*. That is, NSOs have TID programs entirely immersed within their high performance plans as a core business element and are responsible for fostering the connectivity between the *Elite* and *Non-elite* components of the pathway.

Thus, as a concept for the future, a national TID system might be viewed as a *Pre-Elite* specialisation that shares a common language and positioning within the athlete development pathway of every NSO. Such a view might cease the unhelpful dichotomous language of 'grass roots' and 'elite' and acknowledge a new 'trichotomy' – with the *Pre-Elite* underclass bookended by the *Non-Elite* and *Elite*. The term *Pre-Elite* would be defined as having the potential to be *Elite* (i.e. senior international representation) and isn't necessarily limited by age or competition level. Collectively the high performance pathway is represented by the amalgam of the *Pre-Elite* and *Elite* components.

Figure 12.1 provides a conceptual model for the fully immersed and integrated role of a future TID system. The key features include: (a) TID specialising at the *Pre-Elite* level of the pathway; (b) NSOs planning their high performance programs around an integrated *Elite* and *Pre-Elite* talent pathway; (c) continued development of broader system elements that provide distinct support to the *Pre-Elite* phase of the talent pathway; (d) dedicated strategies at three distinct levels of the athlete development pathway (*Non-Elite, Pre-Elite, Elite*); (e) integrated and transitional elements at each of the phases; and (f) monitoring and evaluating elements of talent flow.

Conclusion

Australia's national system of TID has been developed as a result of almost 25 years of continuous modification and growth through experience, trial and error, risk-taking and attempts at being creative and innovative. Implementing a national TID system in Australia has been a steady evolution. It takes time to set up different types of projects or programs and to achieve performance outcomes and catalogue the lessons learnt. The reality of implementing a total system within a national sporting

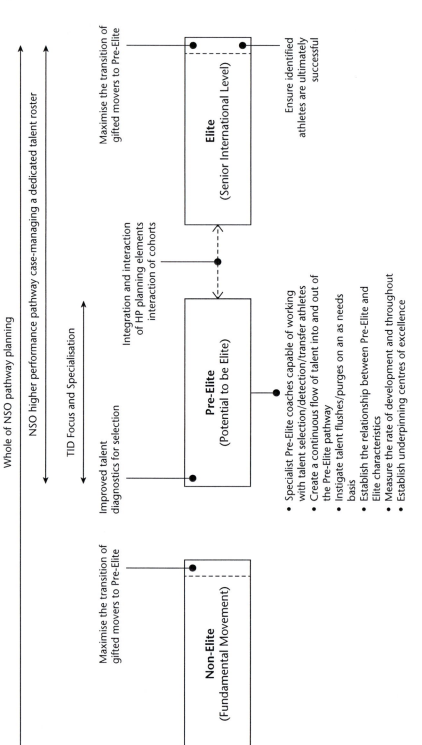

FIGURE 12.1 A conceptual model for the fully immersed and integrated role of a future TID system.

framework is as much about 'early adopters' versus 'late adopters'. That is, the concept of TID is still very much underpinned by personal and academic philosophies about the genesis of talent and the process of development. Successful TID system implementation will continue to be an iterative process, with the next quarter of a century undoubtedly producing new techniques, partnerships, enhanced prognostics, and more efficient development processes to meet Australia's cultural and contextual challenges.

Systems of TID are not a panacea for poor international sporting performances, but rather a key catalyst that plays its integrated role in maximising outcomes within a comprehensive national sports system. By themselves, TID systems are certainly effective, yet maximum impact can be achieved within a fully supportive and embracing national system of sport that recognises TID as core business.

Finally, a national purview does not always adequately pick up the outstanding pockets of TID related activities that can and will occur outside of any formalised system. These sweet spots of activity have contributed substantially to Australia's sporting successes, yet it is recognised that these can often be overlooked in any system audit.

Acknowledgements

There have been a number of staff who have made a tremendous contribution to the evolution of the Australian TID system. Broadly, I would like to recognise the contribution of all staff who have worked tirelessly in the Talent Search and/or the NTID programs. Specifically, there have been some very clever, passionate, and talented individuals that have made a major impact on the outcomes in the Australian TID system. The scope of this paper provides an opportunity to acknowledge Professor Allan Hahn, Dr Deborah Hoare, Dr David T. Martin, Morag Croser, Elissa Morley, Dr Tammie Ebert, Dr Juanita Weissensteiner, Warren McDonald, David Foureur, Peter Petho, Don Abnett, and Chris Muldoon.

References

Abbott, A., & Collins, D. (2002). A theoretical and empirical analysis of a 'state of the art' talent identification model. *High Ability Studies, 13,* 157–78.

Augestad, P., Bergsgard, N. A., & Hansen, A. (2006). The institutionalization of an elite sport organization in Norway: the case of 'Olympiatoppen'. *Sociology of Sport Journal, 23,* 293–313.

Australian Football League (AFL) (2009). *Annual Report 2009.* Melbourne: Australian Football League.

Australian Olympic Committee (2009). *The Australian Olympic Committee's (AOC's) response to the Crawford report.* Sydney: Australian Olympic Committee.

Australian Sports Commission (ASC) (1993). *Sports search – the search is over.* Canberra: Australian Sports Commission.

—— (2008). *Submission to the Commonwealth Government's independent review of sport in Australia.* Canberra: Australian Sports Commission.

—— (2009). *National talent identification in three*. Canberra: Australian Sports Commission.

Bloomfield, J. (2003). *Australia's sporting success: The inside story*. Sydney: University of New South Wales Press Ltd.

Bullock, N., Gulbin, J. P., Martin, D. T., Ross, A., Holland, T., & Marino, F. E. (2009). Talent identification and deliberate programming in skeleton: ice novice to winter Olympian in 14 months. *Journal of Sports Sciences, 27*, 397–404.

Chelladurai, P., & Chang, K. (2000). Target and standards of quality in sport services. *Sport Management Review, 3*, 1–22.

Commonwealth Department of Health & Ageing (2009). *The future of sport in Australia*. Canberra: Australian Government.

—— (2010). *Australian Sport: The pathway to success*. Canberra: Australian Government.

Cricket Australia (2009). *Annual Report 2008/09*. Melbourne: Cricket Australia.

De Bosscher, V., De Knop, P., Van Bottenburg, M., & Shibli, S. (2006). A conceptual framework for analysing sports policy factors leading to international sporting success. *European Sport Management Quarterly, 6*, 185–215.

Gardner, A. S., Martin, D. T., Gulbin, J., Doney, G. E., Jenkins, D. G., & Hahn, A. G. (2002). Laboratory and velodrome sprint cycling power in female cyclists in response to 6 weeks of training. *Medicine and Science in Sports and Exercise, 35*, S337.

Gulbin, J. (2001). From novice to national champion. *Sports Coach, 24*, 24–26.

—— (2008). Identifying and developing sporting experts. In D. Farrow, J. Baker, & C. MacMahon (Eds). *Developing sport expertise: researchers and coaches put theory into practice* (pp 60–72). London: Routledge.

Gulbin, J. & Ackland, T. (2008). Talent identification and profiling. In T. Ackland, B. Elliott, & J. Bloomfield (Eds). *Applied anatomy and biomechanics in sport* (pp. 11–26). Champaign IL: Human Kinetics.

Hahn, A. (1990). Identification and selection of talent in Australian rowing. *Excel, 6(3)*, 5–11.

Halson, S., Martin, D. T., Gardner, A. S., Fallon, K. & Gulbin, J. P. (2006). Persistent fatigue in a female sprint cyclist after a talent-transfer initiative. *International Journal of Sports Physiology and Performance, 1*, 65–69.

Hoare, D. (1995). Talent search: The national talent identification and development program. *Sports Coach, 18(3)*, 24–25.

—— (1998). Talent search: A review and update. *Sports Coach, 21(3)*, 32–33.

Hoare, D. G. & Warr, C. R. (2000). Talent identification and women's soccer: An Australian perspective. *Journal of Sport Sciences 18(9)*, 751–58.

Hoye, R., & Nicholson, M. (2009). Australia. *International Journal of Sport Policy, 1*, 229–40.

Kelley, J. & Evans, M. D. R. (1998). Sources of national pride in 24 nations. *Australian Social Monitor 2*, 23–30.

Muldoon, C. (2009). *Strengthening TID: Independent review to evaluate and examine opportunities to strengthen the national talent identification and development program*. Melbourne: Sport Business Partners.

Oakley, B., & Green, M. (2001). The production of Olympic champions: international perspectives on elite sport development system. *European Journal of Sport Management, 8*, 83–105.

Papadimitriou, D. (2001). An exploratory examination of the prime beneficiary approach of organisational effectiveness: the case of elite athletes of Olympic and non-Olympic sports. *European Journal of Sport Management, special issue*, 63–82.

Slater, G. J., Rice, A. J., Jenkins, D., Gulbin, J. P., Hahn, A. G. (2006). Preparation of former heavyweight oarsmen to compete as lightweight rowers over 16 weeks: three case studies. *International Journal of Sport Nutrition & Exercise Metabolism, 16*, 108–21.

Sotiriadou, K., & Shilbury, D. (2009). Australian elite athlete development: An organisational perspective. *Sport Management Review, 12,* 137–48.

Sotiriadou, K., Shilbury, D., & Quick, S. (2008). The attraction, retention/transition, and nurturing process of sport development: some Australian evidence. *Journal of Sport Management, 22,* 247–72.

Standing Committee on Recreation and Sport (2009). *Participation in exercise, recreation and sport. Annual report 2009.* Canberra: Australian Sports Commission.

Vaeyens, R., Gullich, A., Warr, C. R., & Philippaerts, R. (2009). Talent identification and promotion programmes of Olympic athletes. *Journal of Sport Sciences, 27,* 1367–80.

Wikipedia (2010). Wikipedia.http://en.wikipedia.org/wiki/List_of_countries_and_outlying_territories_by_total_area (accessed 30 August 2010).

13

LESSONS LEARNED

The future of research in talent identification and development

Joseph Baker, Jörg Schorer and Steve Cobley

The preceding chapters, particularly those in section two describing the range of international success at identifying and developing talent, have highlighted the limits of our knowledge in this area. In this chapter, we draw attention to the theoretical and practical obstacles that impede our understanding. It is our intent that this chapter will be relevant not only as a plan for future research in this area, but as a summary of the boundaries of current knowledge that is intended to assist coaches, athletes and administrators in developing more effective sport policy.

Generally, we know much more about the essential elements of talent development than talent identification. A recent special issue in the journal *Talent Development and Excellence* (Baker & Schorer, 2010) reflected this discrepancy – although the issue was focused on both talent identification and development in sport, only one article truly dealt with identification issues. This trend reflects the clear need for more research in order to make informed decisions about the efficacy of talent identification processes. This is no simple task, but initiatives such as those described by Jason Gulbin in the previous chapter reflect the possibilities for success in the right circumstances.

What can we learn from previous successful initiatives?

Resources are important

Several of the chapters have highlighted the importance of athletes having access to necessary resources. High quality training facilities, good coaches, and financial and emotional support may be the most obvious resources for the developing performer but others remain undiscovered. The birthplace effect summarized by Horton in Chapter 4 seems to be very robust in North America and Australia, indicating that some characteristic of an athlete's early developmental environment increases their likelihood for future success; however, we currently have no conclusive evidence regarding what this factor is, although several hypotheses have been proposed. What seems clear is that access to these resources allows young athletes to capitalize on developmental 'opportunities'. For instance, supportive parents with financial means to provide sport opportunities to their child likely provide an important resource allowing the young athlete to experience sports at a young age, a critical factor in developing expertise. Later in development, parental resources become less important and access to the best coaches, training partners and competitors become more relevant for continued development.

A long term approach is necessary

Many of the chapters in Section 2 reflect that developing an effective talent identification process coupled with a talent development system is a long-term approach. German handball, Dutch soccer, US Gymnastics and UK Rugby League have all established long-term relationships between researchers, coaches and administrators in an effort to 'create' success. Even Chapter 11 by Pitsiladis in explaining the dominance of African runners highlights that this dominance did not come overnight but was the end result of an interaction between numerous factors.

The same goes for the approach taken with the talented athletes. The aim should not be to win the next championship or match, but to provide the best possible environment to develop. Short-term success should not come at the price of long-term development. One nice example is the excellent German handball player, Steffen Fäth, who would have been eligible to participate in the European U18 tournament, but was taken by his coaches to the U21 World Cup, because he would learn more through this experience. Notably, the coaches were concerned with the best learning opportunity and not with ensuring that they showcased (arguably) the best player in the world at the U18 tournament. Policy makers may wish to consider this by providing benefits not for the current successes but for positive long-term development.

Have an inclusive focus

The initiatives highlighted in this book also reflect that talent identification and development, once largely considered from a physiological perspective, has evolved into a multidisciplinary approach. Integrating the fields of sport psychology, skill acquisition and expertise, and motor learning/development in addition to exercise physiology indicates a superior system with fewer 'gaps' than an approach grounded in a single discipline.

In addition to considering the talent issue from a multidisciplinary scientific perspective, many of the preceding chapters have also reinforced the need to include important stakeholders. The addition of sport policy makers, coaches, trainers, etc. (i.e., the ones who actually put the theory into practice) is an important element of success, one too often ignored by sport scientists working in this area. Given their important role as emotional and financial resources to the developing athlete, it may also be beneficial to consider the manner in which parents and significant others may assist talent development.

Acknowledge developmental dynamics

As the athlete matures and develops along with their peer comparison group it is likely the factors predicting who is seen as talented will vary considerably. As we discussed in Chapter 1, groups become more homogeneous as they move through the talent development system and variables that seem important early in development (such as anthropometric variables like height and weight) no longer have any discriminatory power at later stages of development. During later stages, other variables (e.g., tactical or perceptual expertise) become superior at differentiating between those most suitable to move up to the next level of development and those at the end of their journey. Successful initiatives described in Section 2 acknowledge the limitation of their tests and highlighted the difficulty of identifying talent in younger athletes. It is critical that those involved in talent identification and development initiatives recognize that the factors that may predict talent at a given point in time do not remain fixed across development. Moreover, it is important that coaches and trainers recognize the role that increasing homogeneity has on developmental opportunities. Sometimes providing a more heterogeneous (a more variable and less predictable) environment may help prevent performance or developmental plateaus and prevent negative consequences like relative age effects.

Think creatively

Section 2 also emphasizes the range of creativity used by the various sport systems in developing their talent identification and development systems. All evidence suggests that we are far from 'solving' the talent question and so creative solutions are important. For those interested in developing systems for developing talent, there are lessons to be learned from the Australian approach summarized by Gulbin in Chapter 12. The first is 'start slow'. Given the limits of our understanding of talent identification and development, resources for creating new (or modifying old) systems will likely be limited (unless you are an Olympic host country; see U.K. 2012 initiatives). Australia began with a very small initiative and used that success to build support for their program. While starting slow is necessary due to limits of available forms of support (e.g., finances, personnel), it would also be prudent to 'think big', by planning how the program would develop over time. Being proactive whenever possible would allow anticipation of possible obstacles ahead. In Canada, for example, proactive winter sports have already anticipated ways to manage the reduction in government funding after the 2010 Winter Games without compromising the quality of support offered to the developing athlete. A final lesson underpins the need for regular evaluations of the system. In systems that operate via government funding, often these evaluations are by necessity when governments (and priorities) change; however, it is important that approaches such as the one taken by German handball (i.e., *Looking back to plan ahead*) are repeated on a regular basis to ensure that policy decisions are evidence based.

Evaluating TID initiatives

As mentioned above, there are few studies examining talent identification in general, particularly at early ages, still fewer evaluating the efficacy of talent identification initiatives. One reason for this may lie in the difficulty of determining 'success'. For those actively participating within a talent development program, potential is deemed fulfilled and development complete when specific performance goals are realized and attained (e.g., Olympic or World Championship medals), even though the probability for attaining these ultimate outcomes may be low. Researchers have developed effective statistical methods for determining the amount of variability between individuals accounted for, and for determining whether groups of differentially skilled athletes also differ on variables related to identification and prediction. However, these statistics may not have 'real world' relevance. Consider, for example, a recent study by Koz, Fraser-Thomas and Baker (2010) that examined the drafting system in North American sports (NBA, NHL, NFL and MLB) to determine how well it predicted career potential (measured in games played at the professional level). For those unfamiliar, these drafts typically select athletes during late adolescence/early adulthood to professional sports teams. Their analyses suggested that the scouting (i.e., talent identification) processes that informed draft choice (i.e., who to pick in each round of the draft) accounted for less than 20 per cent of the variation in games played at the professional level. At first, this may seem a paltry amount; however, when contextualized in 'real world' terms where talent identification and development is an immensely complex process with a range of influential variables acting upon it, 20 per cent may reflect an extremely successful process. This can only be determined through additional research.

To complicate things further, criteria for success will vary according to the stage of development of those being tested and the length of time between testing and the actualization of potential. Figure 13.1 presents the hypothetical relationship between time from testing and when potential is actualized. From one training session to the next, it is relatively easy to predict performance but as the distance between performance sessions increases (or between a testing session and anticipated date of future performance) the reliability of the prediction decreases. Determining the evaluative success of talent identification processes must take this into account. Prediction of successful talent identification for athletes tested at ages 7, 14, and 18 should not be expected to be similar in quality. A critical avenue for future research is determining the limits of success of talent identification at different ages.

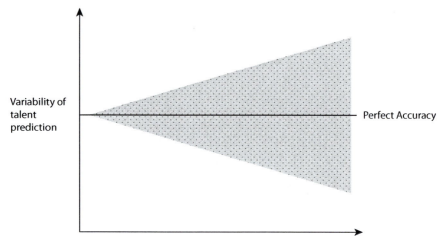

FIGURE 13.1 Relationship between time since talent prediction and actual demonstration of the performance. As time increases, accuracy of talent detection becomes less reliable (i.e., more variable).

The costs of talent identification and development

On the one hand, the process of talent identification and development involves a small number of elite athletes, with the number of athletes decreasing as the levels of competition increase. On the other hand, the process is entrenched in the larger social and political milieu of sport and physical activity. Among industrialized nations there are increasing rates of physical inactivity, sedentary behaviour and obesity, and research indicates that physical activity and exercise is the primary means of preventing morbidity and premature mortality. Moreover, talent identification and development initiatives are often dependent upon government support. These factors reinforce the need to discuss the role of talent identification and development in broader social terms.

Based on our understanding of human motivation and development, the basic philosophy of talent identification selection may actually be detrimental to sport participation. As more intensive detection programs are applied, on the assumption that early identification equals an earlier opportunity to specialize in training and increased likelihood of later success, then the very nature of isolating the few and excluding the many could result in larger proportions of potentially enthusiastic participants terminating their sport involvement. A psychological climate characterized by the values of performance assessment, and externally imposed perceptions of potential and competence, may undermine what should be an enjoyable activity. Moreover, a devalued psychological climate for those deemed to be without potential at early ages may stimulate higher rates of sport termination. Moreover, systems that reward the few at the expense of the many seem contrary to the social functioning and the adoption of healthy lifestyles that sport engagement is meant to promote. The value of current talent selection systems has to be considered against such outcomes.

There is also the possibility that early selection may miss talent that emerges in later years. For instance, early talent identification usually assumes (or at the very least does not control for) that individuals mature at similar rates and that they are at similar rates of development at the time of testing, which is problematic (see Relative Age Effect, Chapter 4). As maturation status impacts performance in sport-related tasks, talent identification and testing protocols conducted within annual age groups, should consider age and maturity related indicators (Chapter 9 describes how rugby league has modified their system with this in mind). Cross-sectional testing, without considering longitudinal influences and the complexity of growth and maturation, will only achieve the outcome of capturing performance differences at the present moment, remaining blind to the numerous physical changes that can occur over time. Moreover, early talent identification efforts have been largely focused on physical differences, ignoring the numerous other factors (e.g. technical, tactical, and psychological skills) which are or will become associated with performance beyond maturation. What appears to be talent right now may not reflect talent in the long-term as players grow, mature, and develop.

Additionally, long-term programmes should consider whether exclusionary practices (i.e., testing, trials, and selection) from early stages of participation affect long-term outcomes. The concentration of resources to the early identified few in present systems may be at the expense of missing (or ignoring) late emerging talent. In response to this possibility, increasingly systems (see Bullock et al., 2009 for an example) are exploring ways to facilitate athletes' maintained engagement, retention, and even late transfer between related sports (e.g., rowing to cycling, as exemplified by Rebecca Romero or cycling to speed skating as exemplified by Clara Hughes). The evaluation of such systems remains to be conducted; yet their significance may be profound, ultimately leading to a reconsideration of how talent identification and development systems are framed in policy and applied in practice.

Developing a theory of Talent Identification and Development

A consistent limitation of much of the work done in this area is the lack of a comprehensive model guiding research. As outlined in Chapter 1, one model that has been used previously is Baker and Horton's (2004) model of primary and secondary influences; another is Newell's (1986) Constraints Model, which is grounded in the notion that the varying influences can be generally organized into three categories of constraints – those pertaining to the Individual, Task or Environment. In Figure 13.2 we modify this model to reflect the varying influences on talent identification and development.

The 'talent' displayed by an individual at a given point in time will be determined by qualities they possess at that moment, as well as the requirements of the task and the facilitative (or debilitative) characteristics of the environment. Let us consider

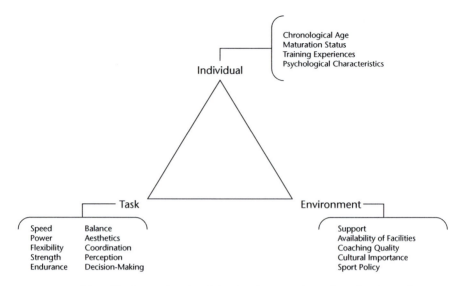

FIGURE 13.2 Newell's Constraints Model as it relates to talent identification and development. At a given point in time, those deemed as 'talented' will be determined by an interaction between individual, task and environmental constraints.

basketball performance as an example. Although the task requirements may remain relatively stable (i.e., scoring through a regulation sized basket), unless modified by coaches to facilitate learning (e.g., younger players may play with a lower basket), the individual and environmental characteristics affecting who is deemed 'talented' will differ significantly. A young basketball player with exceptional height (an individual characteristic) playing against peers who are shorter (an environmental characteristic) may find that this quality is highly effective for demonstrating her 'talent' compared to her peers; however, during late stages of basketball develop-ment, where athletes are much more homogeneous in height, other personal and environmental characteristics determine the talented from the untalented (e.g., decision-making or tactical skills that distinguish them from their peers).

While this model is capable of conceptualizing the varying influences on an individual at a specific point in time, it can also describe the long-term effects of these variables on talent development. If we return to our tall young basketball player described above, being selected as talented will lead to significant changes in the quality of the training environment which facilitates the acquisition of superior skills (physical and psychological) compared to those working on the outside of this environment. Ultimately, Newell's model provides a framework for conceptualizing issues ranging from relative age and birthplace effects to skill acquisition and expertise development.

Concluding remarks

The preceding chapters emphasize the rich potential for research in the field of talent identification and development. This chapter has highlighted some of the research questions, but many others remain. As others in this text have suggested, it is critical that sport scientists, policy makers, coaches, and administrators work together to solve problems that have nagged this field of research for too long. However, this would require greater commitment to program evaluation and basic research from those funding talent identification and development programs. An important step is bringing the necessary stakeholders together as part of an international working group to continue the discussion started in this text. The focus of this group should be to reduce the lag-time between research and implementation and to promote exploration of research questions with the greatest relevance to those in the field.

References

Baker, J. & Horton, S. (2004). A review of primary and secondary influences on sport expertise. *High Ability Studies, 15,* 211–28.

Baker, J. & Schorer, J. (2010). Identification and development of talent in sport (Special Issue). *Talent Development and Excellence, 2* (2).

Bullock, N., Gulbin, J. P., Martin, D. T., Ross, A., Holland, T. and Marino, F. (2009). Talent identification and deliberate programming in skeleton: Ice novice to Winter Olympian in 14 months. *Journal of Sports Sciences, 27,* 397–404.

Koz, D., Fraser-Thomas, J. & Baker, J. (2010). *Professional sports drafts and their ability to predict career potential.* Manuscript under review.

Newell, K. (1986). Constraints on the development of coordination. In M.G. Wade & H.T.A. Whiting (Eds) *Motor development in children: Aspects of coordination and control* (pp. 341–60). Dordect: Nihjoff.

INDEX

Page numbers in *italics* denote a table/diagram